Eighteenth-Century Coffee-House Culture

Volume 2

Eighteenth-Century Coffee-House Culture

Volume 2
The Eighteenth-Century Satire

Edited by
Markman Ellis

Routledge
Taylor & Francis Group

LONDON AND NEW YORK

First published 2006 by Pickering & Chatto (Publishers) Limited

Published 2016 by Routledge
2 Park Square, Milton Park, Abingdon, Oxfordshire OX14 4RN
711 Third Avenue, New York, NY 10017, USA

First issued in paperback 2015

Routledge is an imprint of the Taylor & Francis Group, an informa business

BRITISH LIBRARY CATALOGUING IN PUBLICATION DATA

Eighteenth-century coffee-house culture
    1. Coffeehouses – England – History – 18th century – Sources
2. Coffeehouses – England – History – 17th century – Sources   3. English
literature – 18th century   4. English literature – Early modern, 1500–1700
5. Satire, English   6. England – Social life and customs – 18th century
– Sources   7. England – Social life and customs – 17th century –
Sources   8. England – Intellectual life – 18th century – Sources   9. England
– Intellectual life – 17th century – Sources
    I. Ellis, Markman
820.9'3559'09033

ISBN-13: 978-1-138-66060-1 (pbk)
ISBN-13:978-1-1387-5286-3 (hbk)
ISBN-13: 978-1-85196-829-9 (set)

Typeset by P&C

CONTENTS

INTRODUCTION

At the turn of the eighteenth century, London had grown to be the largest city in Europe, just as Britain was the most prosperous nation. Contemporaries compared London favourably to the glories of ancient Rome, to which it was, they claimed, superior in extent, populousness and wealth. A Huguenot apologist, Mr de Souligné, defended the 'abundance of Diversions' afforded by London, which were 'far better' than those of ancient Rome: 'The Conveniency alone of our *Coffee* and *Chocolate-Houses* goes beyond all the common Diversions they had *at Rome*.'[1] As de Souligné suggests, the signal urban experience of London was the coffee-houses: they were both more common in London than anywhere else, and their convivial sociability best represented the city's unique qualities. After the bloodless revolution of 1688, which secured the Protestant succession, coffee-houses seemed to represent the indigenous spirit of liberty in the English constitution: a living example of the popular discourse of egalitarianism, in which people of differing stations might meet and converse together. In 1698, a French traveller to London remarked that the 'Coffee-Houses, which are very numerous in London, are extremely convenient. You have all manner of news there; you have a good Fire, which you may sit by as long as you please; you have a Dish of Coffee; you meet your Friends for the transaction of Business, and all for a penny, if you don't care to spend more.'[2] Another Huguenot, Guy Miège, observed in 1699 that the drinking of the 'two sober Liquors' coffee and tea, were 'prevalent in *England*' amongst 'Men of Learning and Business'. 'To improve Society, and the life of Recreation' Miège continued, 'the *English* have ... the Conveniency of *Coffee-Houses*, more common here than any where else. In which all Comers intermix together, with mutual freedom; and, at a very easy Rate Men have the Opportunity of meeting together, and getting Acquaintance,

---

1. De Souligné, *Old Rome and London Compared, the first in its full Glory, and the last in its Present State*, 2nd edn (London, J Harding, 1710), p. 155.
2. Henri Misson de Valbourg, trans. by Ozell, *Memoirs and Observations in his Travels over England* (London, D. Browne et al., 1719), pp. 39–40.

with choice of Conversation, besides the Advantage of reading all foreign and domestic News.'[3]

If the coffee-house was depicted in the seventeenth century as the resort of refractory sedition and sectarian faction, in the eighteenth century, the coffee-house was rewritten in a more polite and civilised mode. This was not accidental. Just as the coffee-house had been a central target of Tory satirists in the Restoration, eighteenth-century Whig satirists and wits used the coffee-house as the model for their projects of social reformation. The most celebrated representative of this argument was the journalism of Richard Steele (1672–1729) and Joseph Addison (1672–1719), although their work was preceded by numerous forbears.[4] In their enormously popular essay periodicals *The Tatler* and *The Spectator*, Addison and Steele made the coffee-house both the motor and crucible for the polite refashioning of English society. *The Tatler* identified a series of coffee-houses as the sites from which emanated different kinds of news or thinking. In *The Spectator*, however, the coffee-house plays an important part in the periodical's moral project, both as a site of moral reform and a metaphor for that reform.

'Man is said to be a Sociable Animal' Joseph Addison argued in *The Spectator* No. 9 (Saturday 10 March 1711), for at every opportunity, Addison observed, men take the opportunity of forming themselves 'into those little Nocturnal Assemblies, which are commonly known by the Name of Clubs', joined together in friendship and mutually rewarding discourse.[5] Addison argued that associative friendships, formed in urban society by men of particular interest, supposed a new and wholly original philosophy of urban life that was both counter and superior to the isolated and solitary existence experienced in 'savage' societies. Modern urban life was comprised of civilised and refined social relations with one's fellow citizens, of which the best examples in everyday life were the coffee-house and the club. *The Spectator*, Addison proposed, would use the coffee-house as a model for its convivial moral conversation by urbanising philosophy:

> It was said of Socrates, that he brought Philosophy down from Heaven, to inhabit among Men, and I shall be ambitious to have it said of me, that I have brought Philosophy out of Closets and Libraries, Schools and Colleges, to dwell in Clubs and Assemblies, at Tea-Tables and in Coffee-houses.[6]

---

3.   Guy Miège, *The New State of England, under our Present Monarch K. William III*, 3rd edn (London, R. Clavel, H. Mortlock, and J. Robinson, 1699), part II, pp. 17, 19–20.

4.   Lawrence Klein, 'Coffeehouse Civility, 1660–1714: an aspect of post-courtly culture in England', *Huntingdon Library Quarterly*, 59:1 (1997), pp. 30–51; Brian Cowan, *The Social Life of Coffee: the emergence of the British coffeehouse* (New Haven and London, Yale University Press, 2005), pp. 193–224.

5.   Joseph Addison, *The Spectator*, No. 9, Saturday 10 March 1711, ed. by Donald F. Bond, 5 vols (Oxford, Clarendon Press, 1987), vol. I, p. 39.

6.   Addison, *Spectator*, No. 10, Monday 12 March 1711, Bond, vol. I, p. 44.

In the model of the coffee-house, Addison and Steele argued that a spirit of fellowship or sodality underpinned a harmonious society of mutual trust and reliance. Their philosophical essays themselves exemplified the kind of calm and
congenial rationality they championed. But their own society, and their own
favourite coffee-houses, gave much evidence that both the vehicle and the argument amounted to a form of philosophical idealism. Addison and Steele argued
for the 'improvement' and 'refinement' of human nature, championing a new
paradigm of politeness and civility in literature and society.[7] As Lawrence Klein
has demonstrated, the idea of 'politeness' identified both an elite strata of society
('the better sort', 'the Quality', supposedly practitioners of polite behaviour), but
also delineated a process for achieving proper behaviour.[8] Addison and Steele's
essays both depict and teach the process by which the reader's politeness is refined
and polished. Their essays criticised and satirised all the savage influences in society, including duelling, spitting, rowdiness, wenching, immorality in plays, vulgar language, and immoderate fashions; while other essays wrote in praise of
virtue, honour, good-nature, true worth, and beauty. The Spectatorial revision
of the coffee-house was also played out in genre: early coffee-house satires made
use of low and plebeian forms of vulgar satire (such as the ramble, the mock-
petition or queries, the character). In the Spectatorial mode, these vulgar and
ranting satiric forms are subsumed by the elegant poise of the occasional essay,
whose conversational, sincere, polite, reformist, and mannered style becomes the
characteristic form of the coffee-house.

   In their own lives, Addison and Steele were deeply embedded in the urban
culture of coffee-houses and clubs: these places and associative principles were
in that sense innate to their thinking, even if their coffee-house geography was
focussed on a limited and socially narrow range of high-status institutions in St
James's and the Temple. *The Spectator* proposes that to a gentleman of any consequence in early eighteenth-century London, the coffee-house was the centre
of his social world. The most significant articulation of *The Spectator*'s coffee-
house philosophy was that offered by Steele in essay No. 49 (Thursday, April 26,
1711).[9] There, Steele proposes that

> It is very natural for a Man who is not turned for Mirthful Meetings of Men, or
> Assemblies of the fair Sex, to delight in that sort of Conversation which we find in
> Coffee-houses. Here a Man, of my Temper, is in his Element; for, if he cannot talk,
> he can still be more agreeable to his Company, as well as pleased in himself, in being
> only an Hearer.[10]

   7.   Peter Borsay, 'The Culture of Improvement', in *The Eighteenth Century*, ed. by Paul Langford
(Oxford, Oxford University Press, 2002), p. 189.
   8.   Lawrence E. Klein, *Shaftesbury and the Culture of Politeness: moral discourse and cultural politics
in early eighteenth century England* (Cambridge, Cambridge University Press, 1994), pp. 3–14.
   9.   Steele, *Spectator*, No. 49 (Thursday 26 April 1711), Bond, vol. I, pp. 208–11.
   10. Bond, vol. I, p. 208.

Coffee-house conversation, the essay claims, ought to be sober, controlled and polite. The essay proceeds to demonstrate how this might be achieved, detailing a day in the life of one coffee-house near the Temple, as different kinds of men appear at different times of day. Those championed by Mr Spectator are those 'Men who have Business or good Sense in their Faces' who 'come to the Coffee-house either to transact Affairs or enjoy Conversation.'[11] Such men are content 'to be happy and well pleased in a private Condition', seeking neither advancement in political office nor avarice and greed in commerce, while not neglecting 'the Duties and relations of Life'. These men are the 'worthier Part of Mankind; of these are all good Fathers, generous Brothers, sincere Friends, and faithful Subjects. ... These are the men formed for Society, and those little Communities which we express by the Word *Neighbourhoods*.'[12] In Steele's vision, the coffee-house becomes a 'Place of Rendezvous to all ... thus turned to relish calm and ordinary Life'. Pre-eminent amongst this group is an ideal man Steele calls Eubulus, a man of perfectly tuned virtue in a society ravaged by the corruptions and compromises of luxury and commerce. Eubulus is a rich man, yet he lives modestly; a man of wisdom and influence who holds no political or judicial office; a man who generously lends money at low interest to his friends rather than seeking the highest rate of return on the market. As an object of emulation, Eubulus has simple authority over his coffee-house realm, and governs by commanding internal respect rather than outward regulation — a calculated riposte to the autocratic Stuart political impluse. The example of Eubulus's virtuous behaviour in the coffee-house encourages others to follow his course. The coffee-drinkers venerate Eubulus so that 'when they are in other Company they speak and act after him; are Wise in his Sentences, and are no sooner sat down at their own Tables, but they hope or fear, rejoice or despond as they saw at the Coffee-house. In a word, every Man is *Eubulus* as soon as his Back is turn'd.'[13] Steele proposes that coffee-house politeness is inculcated by virtuous example, a process the sociologist Norbert Elias called self-fashioning, although where Elias argued that 'the compulsion to check one's own behaviour' is motivated by shame and embarrassment, Steele proposes a more positive process of emulation and imitation.[14]

The coffee-house imagined by Steele, presided over by the steady hand of Eubulus, was dominated by calm and rational discussion, 'derived rather from Reason than Imagination', with 'no Impatience or Instability in ... Speech or Action'.[15] But as numerous critics observed, both then and more recently, the

11. Bond, vol. I, pp. 209–10.

12. Bond, vol. I, p. 210.

13. Bond, vol. I, p. 211.

14. Norbert Elias, *The History of Manners*, in *The Civilising Process*, trans. by Edmund Jephcott (1938; Oxford, Blackwell, 1994), p. 66.

15. Bond, vol. I, p. 210.

lived reality of the London coffee-house scene was often more various, cantankerous and violent. In 1710, for example, as Steele was writing, coffee-houses were implicated in the severe riots that broke out in London in support of the Tory clergyman Dr Henry Sacheverell. In the ensuing controversy, coffee-houses were repeatedly represented as the home of trouble-makers and seditionaries, and were commonly blamed for disseminating tracts, rumours and gossip that inflamed the violence and destruction.[16] Throughout the eighteenth century, coffee-houses maintained their enduring connection with news and intelligence. Viewed through the optic of the prevailing Whig ideology, this close connection with news and intelligence made the coffee-house the mouthpiece of public opinion and critical judgement, fulfilling a role somewhat like that of the censor, or the reformer of public morals. In a more hostile light, whether Tory or dissident Whig, the same connection to the news agenda associated the coffee-house with the socially corrosive categories of gossip, slander and scandal, and, more seriously, with socially disruptive ideas of libel and sedition.

Although it is clear that Steele addresses his essay to men only, the exclusive nature of his target for reform is an important aspect of his argument. As he says, he addresses 'a Man who is not turned for Mirthful Meetings of Men, or Assemblies of the fair Sex': that is to say, a man not given to libertine extremes of drink and womanising, nor one who is given to attending heterosexual places of sociability. Habermas argued that the coffee-house proposed 'a kind of social intercourse that, far from presupposing equality of status, disregarded status altogether'.[17] There is much evidence to suggest that contemporaries believed that the coffee-house did allow men of differing ranks to debate issues of importance together; that they did express a kind of egalitarian spirit. Nonetheless, coffee-houses presupposed certain forms of behaviour that were elsewhere associated with the polite culture of the commercial, professional and political elites. The coffee-houses much vaunted egalitarianism is an enabling fiction, local and impermanent, translating hierarchy into new forms.

The most notable instance of the exclusiveness of coffee-house sociability was the ambiguous place within it of women. A series of important articles in recent years have addressed the question whether women were permitted in, or excluded from, coffee-houses and their conversations. Interest in the topic converges on the debate on Habermas's public sphere, allowing scholars to ask what kind of publicness is created by a space which excludes women. Joan Landes, for example, has argued that the effective exclusion of women from the public debates of politics in the early eighteenth century means that 'the bourgeois

---

16. Ian Gilmour, *Riots, Risings and Revolution: governance and violence in eighteenth-century england* (London, Hutchinson, 1992), p. 52.
17. Jürgen Habermas, *The Structural Transformation of the Public Sphere: An Inquiry into a Category of Bourgeois Society*, trans. by Thomas Burger (Cambridge, Polity, 1992), p. 36.

public is essentially, not just contingently, masculinist'.[18] The case of the coffee-houses is thus an important model. As a number of commentators have noted (Bramah, Clery, Pincus and Ellis), there is some evidence that women were seen in coffee-houses.[19] In particular, Steven Pincus rejects 'the claim that women were excluded from the coffee-houses', although his argument, justified by only three ambiguous examples, has been found wanting by others.[20] While it seems women were not explicitly barred from the coffee-house, the social regime of the coffee-house made their presence there uncomfortable and untenable. Women of the middle station who wished to be thought virtuous were not seen in the coffee-house. There was no need to exclude women from the coffee-house because they had never been there: the political and commercial cast of the coffee-house in the seventeenth century established it as a space for men and men only. Only men could and did participate in the public political and commercial culture of the period. There were spaces for heterosexual encounters (parks, pleasure-gardens, play-houses), but these were not places where the business of commerce and politics were seriously entertained.

However, there were plenty of women in coffee-houses who worked there, either as proprietors (coffee-women), or serving staff or managers behind the bar, or as prostitutes. Records suggest that many coffee-houses were owned by women, especially widows. Lillywhite's census of coffee-houses gives evidence of Widow Wells, the proprietor of Mrs Wells Coffee House in Scotland Yard between 1696 and 1712,[21] and of Jenny Man, proprietor of Jenny Man's Coffee House in Charing Cross, in 1712,[22] amongst many others. The presence of serving women in coffee-houses was not unusual at all: they were ubiquitous. Satirists made much of the flirtatious banter between the male clientele and the female staff. Tom Brown commented in 1702 that 'Every Coffee-House is illuminated both without and within doors; without by a fine Glass Lanthorn and within by a Woman so *light* and *splendid,* you may see through her with the help of a Perspective. At the Bar the good man always places a charming Phillis or two, who invite you by their amorous Glances into their smoaky Territories,

18. Joan Landes, *Women and the Public Sphere in the Age of the French Revolution* (Ithaca, NY, Cornell University Press, 1988), p. 7.

19. Edward Bramah, captions in the Bramah Tea and Coffee Museum, Maguire St, London (1996); Emma J. Clery, 'Women, Publicity and the Coffee-House Myth', *Women: a cultural review*, 2:2 (1991), pp. [168]–77; and Steven Pincus, '"Coffee Politicians Does Create": coffeehouses and restoration political culture', *Journal of Modern History*, 27 (1995), pp. 807–34; Ellis, *Coffee-House*, pp. 64–8; Markman Ellis, 'The coffee-women, *The Spectator* and the public sphere in the early-eighteenth century', in *Women and the Public Sphere*, ed. by Elizabeth Eger and Charlotte Grant (Cambridge, Cambridge University Press, 2001).

20. Pincus, '"Coffee Politicians Does Create"', pp. 814, 815. See also Ellis, 'The coffee-women', pp. 31, 47n.; and Cowan, *The Social Life of Coffee*, pp. 246–50.

21. Bryant Lillywhite, *London Coffee-Houses* (London, George Allen & Unwin, 1963), No. 1501, pp. 635–7.

22. Lillywhite, No. 624, p. 625.

to the loss of your Sight'.[23] Male critics complained that the coffee-men 'take Care always to provide such tempting, deluding, ogling, pretty young Hussies to be their Bar-Keepers, as steal away our Hearts, and insensibly betray us to Extravagance'.[24] The Swiss visitor to London, César de Saussure, remarked that many coffee-houses were 'temples of Venus' or brothels: 'You can easily recognise the latter, because they frequently have as sign a woman's arm or hand holding a coffee-pot. There are a great number of these houses in the neighbourhood of Covent Garden; they pass for being chocolate houses, and you are waited on by beautiful, neat, well-dressed, and amiable, but very dangerous nymphs'.[25] Ned Ward's fictional country visitor in *The London Spy* (1698) observed the working life of two prostitutes in the coffee-vaults of the Widow's Coffee-House.[26]

The anomalous position of coffee-women within eighteenth century society is underlined by a series of texts representing an account of their lives. Known collectively as coffee-women biographies (see below pp. 39–88 and 195–220), such texts as *The Life and Character of Moll King* (1747) relate a transgressive narrative of female empowerment. Like criminal biography more generally, and 'whores' biographies' more particularly, the texts' enthusiastic relation of how a lowly born woman is empowered economically and sexually by the work and scandal of the coffee-house is only partially mitigated by the narrator's condemnatory tone of voice.[27] As such texts suggest, there were women in the coffee-house, but only under special circumstances, and not as equals. The egalitarian nature of coffee-house debate only applied to its predominantly male customers. The coffee room was subject to important social divisions and boundaries: one of status, dividing the workers from the customers, and another of gender, excluding all women but the coffee-woman from the coffee-room. Gender and status are not disregarded in the coffee house, but rather, are codified in new forms.

---

23. Tom Brown, 'Amusement VIII', *Amusements Serious and Comical, Calculated for the Meridian of London* (London, 1702), in *The Works of Mr. Thomas Brown. Serious and Comical, in Prose and Verse*, 4 vols (1707; 5th edn, London, Sam Briscoe, 1715), vol. III, pp. 71–2.

24. *The Case between the Proprietors of the News-Papers and the Coffee-Men of London and Westminster* (London, E. Smith 1729), pp. 12–13. See below, pp. 166–7.

25. César de Saussure, *A Foreign View of England in the Reigns of George I and George II*, trans. by Madame Van Muyden (written 1729, 1st edn, London, John Murray, 1902), pp. 164–5.

26. [Edward Ward], *The London-Spy Compleat, in Eighteen Parts*, 2nd edn (London, J. How, 1704), Part II, pp. 25–32. See Cowan, *Social Life of Coffee*, pp. 252–4, for further evidence of prostitutes in coffee-houses.

27. John J. Richetti, *Popular Fiction before Richardson: narrative patterns 1700–1739* (Oxford, Clarendon, 1969), pp. 35–6.

Coffee: a tale (London: printed for H. Curle [sic, for Curll], 1727), [2], xiv, 33pp.; 8°. BL: RB.23.a.5767. ESTCN27164. Extract, pp. 1–33. Hünersdorff.

An extended verse satire directed against the rituals and cultural politics of the Low-Church clergy and the Dissenters. The poem extends to 744 lines and makes use of an unusual verse form of dimeter, consisting of two metrical feet, arranged in four-line stanzas. The form imparts a curious and jaunty rhythm to the verses, which at times jars with the complicated subjects in ecclesiastical politics that the poem addresses. The poem's attitude to the coffee-house is rather old-fashioned, revisiting the seventeenth-century Tory construction of the coffee-house as a site of Low-Church republican sentiment. The poem begins in a light-hearted manner with a comparison between the tavern and the coffee-house, '*nests* of curs'd COFFEE and NEWS!' (p. 9, l. 2). But until the final few pages (p. 32 on), the tale is dominated by an obscure and ill-tempered attack on Nonconformists and Lowchurchmen.

Coffee: a tale was advertised in the *Monthly Catalogue* for July 1727. The poem was anonymous, although internal evidence suggests that the author may have been a school-master. The same writer also published a translation of a Latin ode by Joseph Addison in December 1727, with a fulsome dedication to the newly-crowned George II (*Mr Addison's Fine Ode to Dr Thomas Burnet, on his Sacred Theory of the Earth. Done into English by the Author of a late tale call'd Coffee* (London, T. Warner, 1727)). *Coffee: a tale* was published with an extensive twelve-page preface composed entirely of quotations, mostly from Whig divines. The poem was published by Edmund Curll (d. 1747), a bookseller notorious for publishing contemporary poets without their permission, for selling nostrums for treating venereal diseases, and for printing scandalous texts and pornography. *Coffee: a tale* was included in Curll's made-up miscellany, *The Altar of Love: or, the Whole Art of Kissing*, 3rd edn (London, Colley Cibber, 1731) (in the Houghton Library, Harvard University), which was composed of separately published pamphlets with a new title-page.

COFFEE:

A

TALE.

ভত ভত ভত ভত ভত ভত ভত ভত ভত ভত ভত ভত ভত

Et Dici potuiſſe, & non potuiſſe Refelli.

Οὐαὶ τῷ Ἀνθρώπῳ, δἰ οὗ τὸ Σκάνδαλον ἔρχεται·

ভত ভত ভত ভত ভত ভত ভত ভত ভত ভত ভত ভত ভত

L O N D O N:

Printed for H. CURLE, over againſt *Catherine Street*
in the *Strand.* 1727. Price 1 *s.*

COFFEE:

A

TALE.

 Ccording to *Cuſtom*,
  Which *Verſe-mongers* uſe;
  I call INDIGNATION,
    To ſtand for my *Muſe.*

Amongſt Readers of *Guſto,*
  May this be my *Lot!*
To eſcape like a *Crow,*
  Not worth *Powder* or *Shot.*

B

Yet,

2   *C O F F E E:*

Yet, if *Whifflers* pretend
   To rumple my *Bayes*;
Give 'em *Rope*, I befeech,
   For their *Cavil* is *Praife*.

Some *Bards* of Renown,
   I've obferv'd it *plerúmque*,
Wou'd here foar in grand Strain,
   And fing - - - *Crimen Clerumque!*

But, without farther *Prologue*,
   In Cant *new* or *ftale*;
My *Route* thus difpos'd,
   I proceed to my *Tale*.

At a Chat in the *Veftry*,
   A corpulent *Vicar*
Wou'd prohibit all C o f f e e,
   As *damnable Liquor*:

Where, finding *Opinions*
   Againft him to *run*;
If they'd liften, he'd give 'em
   More *Reafons* than *one*.

                            With

A T A L E.

With *primitive Drams*,
  It bears no *Relation*;
The *Law* fhou'd *fupprefs* it,
  Nor grant *Toleration.*

What Soul ever heard,
  O! ftand ye not Neuter;
Of this *Puritan-Tiff*,
  Before C A L V I N and L U T H E R?

'Tis, methinks, faint defying
  Old-Nick and his *Works*;
To be fond of a *Berry*,
  Which comes from the *Turks.*

To relieve, in a *Morning*,
  Sots over-night drunk;
Is as *finful*, as curing
  Hurts got by a *Punk.*

It quiets the *Spirits*,
  Compofes the *Mind*;
And affwages brave *Heats*,
  Which from *ftrong* Drinks we find:
                    Therefore

4   *C O F F E E:*

Therefore loudly calls on *us*,
   To ufe our beft *Cares*;
Not to lofe Arts, of *fetting*
   The *World by the Ears.*

The Top of it's *Merit*, is
   Clearing the *Head*;
But, at that Rate, you'll ftill
   Have frefh *Herefies* fpread:

I'll charge it on COFFEE,
   For it muft be from *thence*;
Such applauding Crowds flock,
   To hear HENLEY talk Senfe!

How many choice *Taverns*,
   All over the *Nation*;
Have pull'd down their *Bufh*,
   Since this *Drench* came in Fafhion?

'Tis too *plain* to want *Proof*,
   May *Gout* or *Stone* rack us!
If it ben't a *wide Schifm*,
   From the *Temple* of BACCHUS.

                               I'll

A T A L E.   **5**

I'll maintain that the *Nests*,
   Of curs'd C o f f e e and N e w s!
Have done six-times the *Harm*,
   Of the commonest *Stews.*

Some indeed, about P a u l's,
   Are such as become her;
But, a few *Swallows,* alas!
   Fall short of a *Summer* :

Free from *Spies* we just-there
   May *Security* hope,
Whilst we model our *Plans*
   Of a *Protestant*-P o p e

But, None of us All
   Can *elsewhere* propose
To speak *safely ;* tho' under
   Canonical-Rose.

'Tis the *Stage,* where vile *Brokers*
   Their *Stock-jobbers* find ;
Who, of more than poor *Tythes,*
   Bite *bubbled Mankind.*

                               Some

6   *C O F F E E:*

Some *Wand'rers* abroad,
   Was't a Point fit to *dwell on;*
Their long Pilgrimage owe,
   To thefe *Cells* of *Rebellion.*

How they fit, loll, and fhrug,
   Smear *Snufh*, and debate ;
E'en of *Thrones*, and the facred'ft
   Arcanums of *State?*

(Here Some *interrupted*,
   But Others cry'd, *Perge!*)
And their blafphemous *Theme* is,
   Reforming the Clergy!

Extolling the *Virtue*
   And *Senfe* of the *Nation,*
For *Human-Proroguing*
   Divine-Convocation :

Comparing in *Rage*,
   Without Oppofition ;
Our fage *D - - -rs-C - - - ns*,
   To *Spain's* Inquisition ;

                          Where

A T A L E.

Where *Suits* of the People
  Are tumbled and *toſt*,
Till *Temporal Juſtice*
  In *Spiritual's* loſt:

As at *Council o' Trent*,
  That the SAINTS might prevail!
Inſpirations from *Rome*,
  Came by every *Mail*.

All *myſtical Tenets*
  They'd thruſt out o' Doors,
And wou'd ſhow *Pious-Frauds*
  To be *Modeſt-whores*:

Reqüeſting *Church-Wardens*
  To *expunge*, if they *pleaſe*;
From *Windows* and *Walls*,
  The Figure *Iſoſceles*:

To *Mathematics* altho'
  Well-Wiſhers we be,
We ought to forbear
  Audacious *Theometry!*

A proud

8   *COFFEE:*

A *proud* Prieft they play-off,
  As *One* making no Doubt;
So to get *into* Heav'n,
  As the *Devil* got *out*.

Our *Feaftings*, not *Faftings*,
  On the Carpet they bring;
Where our firft *Health's* the Church,
  And then coolly the King:

Even *That* too exprefs'd,
  With *Double-entendre* ;
Innuendo——*Darius*,
  Or elfe *Alexander*.

With one *Toaft* they gagg us,
  Nor leave us a Word;
'Tis the *Mem'ry* immortal,
  Of William the *Third* !

Whofe *glorious* Bequest
  They admire! ever willing
To fhock *Us*, who think
  We're cut-off with a *Shilling* :

                              Whilft,

A T A L E. **9**

Whilft, had we been left,
  For our *Selves* to have carv'd;
Our half-blooded *Breth'ren*,
  E'er Now, might have ftarv'd!

The fpurn-coffee *Vulgar*
  They laugh at, for *Fools*;
Affirming 'em Our attach'd,
  Ale-fwilling *Tools*:

Who can barely pronounce,
  Like *Magpy* or *Daw*;
Come! Here's to all *Truth*,
  That's eftablifh'd by *Law!*

Then *Paffive-Obedience*,
  With - - - Have at ye, *blind Harpers!*
Is thrown in the *Difh*,
  Of *Theological-Sharpers*:

A *Card* kept in *Petto!*
  Which, *Whatever* is bounc'd;
Lies yet only *Drop'd*,
  Not exprefsly *Renounc'd*:
          C

Stupen-

10   *C O F F E E:*

Stupendous *Problem !*
  Since no *Impudence* ever
Forbid *Buckets* at *Fires,*
  Or *Pills* in a *Fever;*

Love's commencing *nigh* Home,
  Self-guard from all *Evils;*
As *Banks* to proud *Waves,*
  And *Refiſtance* to D E V I L S.

Now *Critics* advance,
  And the *Table*'s confounded;
With this *Verſe* not-genuine,
  And *That* wrong-expounded:

For *God's-Word* indeed,
  They Unanimous vote;
But *Ours,* they declare,
  They'd not truſt for a *Groat:*

And are zelouſly griev'd,
  Since the *Matter* ſo ſtands;
That ever the *Other*
  Had paſs'd thro' our *Hands:*

                                    For

A T A L E.   II

For the pureft of *Streams,*
　Which in foul *Channels* flow ;
Seldom fail to collect
　Some *Soil,* as they go.

Our *Embaffy* next
　Is the Subject of *Mirth,*
And our M A S T E R's defcrib'd
　The *Worft-ferv'd* upon Earth.

The *Indeleble-Stamp*
　No fooner is fpoke,
But a *Sanctify'd-Sinner*
　Is made a ftrong *Joke.*

Then another *fmart* M o h o c k,
　Difpos'd to be *arch* on't ;
Diffects ev'ry *Limb,*
　Of a *Spiritual-Merchant:*

Bamboozling fuch *Chaps,*
　As pin *Creed* on thofe *Sleeves* ;
Which metamorphofe G o d's *Houfe,*
　To a *Cavern* of *Thieves.*
                    C 2   Then,

12   *C O F F E E :*

Then, in dolorous *Dumps*,
  We're lug'd-in repenting
The Invention of *Arts* ;
  Efpecially, PRINTING :

Except we cou'd fhield
  Mifdemeanors from *Satire*,
By once-more recov'ring
  Our loft IMPRIMATUR :

Since Lovers of *Juftice*
  Will frankly profefs it,
With *Motto* of - - - *Nemo nos*.
  Impunè lacefſet !

And no *Man-o'-Senfe*
  Can e'er grudge, to perform ;
What, when *trampled-upon*,
  Is the *Right* of a *Worm !*

Thus a prieft-ridden *Pad*
  In *Self-defence* fpoke,
When barbarous *Treatment*
  GOD and *Brute* did provoke.

Then

A T A L E. **13**

Then *Incroachments* are tax'd,
    And such-like *Difafters;*
And our firft *Bifhops* prov'd,
    But *Parochial-Paftors.*

Often *Cafes-o'-Confcience*
    Come under Debate;
About *Swearing* and *Praying*
    For T h o s e, that we *hate:*

Tho' the *Thing*'s not fo new,
    To require fuch a *Fufs;*
On *Delights-of-Mankind,*
    Being odious to *Us!*

A *Prieft,* an *Ox,* and an *Afs,*
    'Mongft *Proverbs,* they find
To be fhun'd; One *all-o'er,*
    One *before,* One *behind.*

With ironical *Leer,*
    At *Pontifical-Copes;*
They then fummon *Emp'rors,*
    To hold *Stirrups* for *Popes:*

                                      Whofe

14   C O F F E E:

Whofe prepoft'rous *Sway*
  To their *Scheme's* a *Sequela*,
Whilft our *Tantamounts*
  Are deem'd *Notes* above *Ela!*

Then they tone a trite *Phrafe*,
  With *North-country* Air;
About *fcanty* Devotion,
  But yet *muckle* Pray'r.

If the Title of *Shepherds*
  We'd *fairly* fuftain;
They candidly bid us,
  Refide on the *Plain:*

And next they difplay,
  For *We* muft endure all;
Our *un-fingle* Hearts
  Declin'd to the *Plural.*

Then the *Mercies* at THORN
  Another derides;
Which *Place*, with a *Pun*,
  Is ftuck faft in *our* Sides.

Jus-

A T A L E. 15

Jus-divinum's evinc'd
  Common Tenure to all ;
As to C R - - N or to M I - R E,
  So to *Cobler's-Stall :*

For, when *Sophs* thro' their *Kingdom*
  Of *Darkneſs* have run ;
Both on *Garden* and *Dunghill,*
  G o d ſhines like the *Sun.*

Then, by *ſpeeching* in Public,
  And rubbing-off *Fears ;*
The *Fronts,* of *Some* of us,
  Are harden'd as *Players :*

In chain of which *Thought,*
  At *Decorations* they ſtrike *;*
And cou'd wiſh *certain* Places
  Leſs *Theatre-like :*

A Man may be *decently* rigg'd,
  Runs the *Mutter ;*
Without coming up,
  To Sir *Fopling-flutter.*

Our

16   *C O F F E E :*

Our fucceeding th'*Apoftles*,
  They own to be *right* ;
But explain it, as *Day*
  Is fucceeded by *Night*.

Then, to twirl a *Globe* round,
  We're infultingly brav'd ;
And to mark the few *Cantons*,
  By *Priefts* un-enflav'd :

On which *Remnants*, thro'-out
  The terraqueous *Ball* ;
Great *G E O R G E* commands *Pity*,
  And barrs ruining *All !*

How many glib *Sermons*
  May we then tear, or burn ;
Long fcrub'd on the *Sleek-ftone*,
  'Gainft a hopelefs *Return ?*

Then, as fquander'd by *Dupes* ;
  They prove *Abbey-Lands*
Now lodg'd, not in *new*,
  But *original* Hands :

And

A T A L E.   17

And endeavour, to make
   Thickeſt *Skulls* underſtand *;*
That *Prieſt-gift* is meant,
   By the Term *Deodand.*

Then, quoting E R A S M U S,
   With *theſe* Words they plague us *;*
Tu Epiſcopus es!
   Ne Satrapam agas.

Then they bid us, not *flatter*
   G R E A T - M E N *;* to out-do
The *Fineſſe* of C O L B E R T,
   Or *Monſieur* R I C H E L I E U.

Then B E R M U D A'S ſaluted,
   Thrice-fortunate *Iſle !*
For a *Bleſſing,* which there
   Will *diffuſe* in a While.

Then, what *Buſtles* we've made !
   They cite *Hiſt'ries* to ſpeak it *;*
In all *Times* before, whilſt,
   And ſince T H O M A S - *a* - B E C K E T.

D

Then,

18   *C O F F E E:*

Then, as-tho' *Heav'n* and *Earth*
  Where two *different* Things,
They fift our dear *Maxim*;
  No B – – – – P S, no K – – G S!

In *Tally* to which,
  A round *Kitchen-Belief*
Might this *Paradox* ftart ,
  No PUDDING, no BEEF!

Whereas in good *Sooth*,
  Which we *French-Cooks* wou'd fmother ;
The *Laft* might be Living
  In *Clover*, fans t'*Other*.

Then they *offer*, pretending
  Long *Beadrolls* of Evil;
Great *Laud* to the LORD,
  Little LAUD to the *Devil!*

Producing one pleafant
  Punctillio aim'd-at,
To d'off before *Priefts*
  A JACK-GENTLEMAN'S *Hat!*

                                    Whilft

A T A L E. 19

Whilſt to *Miniſtry* 'twou'd
  Be no *blotting* of Fame,
If *more* of that *Function*
  From ſuch *Origin* came.

Then, as to the *Wall*,
  If *Material* We make it ;
The *Layman* ſhou'd give,
  But the Priest ſhou'd n't take it :

Howe'er, the *bright* Many
  Diſtinguiſh no *Fault* here ;
But bow juſt to *Us*,
  As We bow to the Altar :

That *Judaical-Word*
  To diſuſe, they're unable ;
And, tho' *Un-circumcis'd*,
  Can't think of a Table :

Which, conniv'd-at by *Us*,
  This *Convenience* may bring ;
To retain an old *Name*,
  May recover the *Thing :*
                D 2   As

20   *C O F F E E:*

As a LANE, ſtill ſo call'd,
 May in time prove the *Via* ;
To guide us *ſafe* back,
 To our AVE-MARIA !

Then WILKINS and WOLLASTON
 Are *Sainted* it-ſeems,
For ſupplying the *World*
 With their *Natural-Schemes* ;

As kind *Succedaneums.*
 Againſt the *ſad* Day,
When *Prieſtcraft* ſhall fright
 REVELATION away.

Phyſicians, of all Men,
 Are *moſtly* ſevere ;
Who our dry *Meta-Phyſics*
 Inceſſantly jeer :

And, with *fatal* Advantage,
 Have well-nigh undone us ;
By turning, as *Scholars,*
 Our own *Batt'ries* upon us.

This

A T A L E.

This made the *wife* Antients,
   Keep *Things* in the dark;
Nor train-up a *Leudman*,
   To read like a *Clerk*:

Whereas in our *Schools*,
   O! Common-fenfe, *Vale*;
We teach 'em - - - Who's *Animal*,
   Ah! *Rationale.*

Some *fcarlet-dye* Crimes
   Are laft touch'd, without *Jefting*;
Abhorr'd for their *Mifchief!*
   As Nuptials-clandestine :

Wherein Alma-Mater
   Forbids us to *act*;
But yet, with *great* Goodnefs,
   Approves of the *Fact*:

And, when *fuch* a Caufe
   By *warp'd* Counfel's harangu'd;
Againft *Grain* fufpends *Him*,
   Who deferves to be *Hang'd!*

                  So,

22   *COFFEE*:

So, whilft *Murd'rers* depend
   On *'Scapes* without Failure ;
Th' *Executive-Pow'r*
   Refts in Hands of a Jaylor.

The *Delinquent*'s attended,
   By th' *Tribe* far and near ;
As *twenty* Pigs fqueek,
   Pluck but *One* by the Ear :

Tho' fome *reas'nabler* Beafts
   Might *well* here be preferr'd ;
For the *Deer*, that's *condemn'd*,
   They extrude from the *Herd* :

But our Canonoclast
   Has this *Merit*, o'-Pox !
To be *Tenderly* touch'd
   Becaufe *Orthodox* :

The Senfe of which *Gibbrifh*
   We can't *more* exhibit,
Than by Jerry-White's *Sneer*,
   That it *fhifts* with the Gibbet.

                             Then

A T A L E. **23**

Then Reprifals to *Parents,*
    For *Children* fo loft;
Are long *P - - - rs-Bills,*
    And *four Fifths* of the Coft:

To deter carnal Arm,
    Styl'd in Technic *profane;*
From aiming at *Scopes,*
    Where the Shot's fo in *Vain!*

Poftponing here *Perjury,*
    Forgery, Rafure,
Non-adherence, and latent
    Skreens; till more Leifure:

Vide . . The *traytor'd* * Cafe,
    Of M - - - r P - - - n;
Contrá . . The reverend
    Joiner, Rabbi B - - - n.

To *quafh* a juft Caufe,
    By *o'er-awing* the P - - - r;

---

* Which, if *Leave* can be obtain'd from the injur'd *Gentle-man,* may fometime be publifh'd for the *Common-Weal;* with a *due* Explanation of the prefent *Blanks* and *Allufions.*

Is

24 *COFFEE:*

Is *poys'ning* a Patient,
   By *Hand* of the Doctor !

Deserting a *Cl - - nt,*
   Enhans'd by *Evasion;*
Is the *Prank* of a JUDAS,
   A vile *Abdication !*

W H O here thinks himself *wrong'd,*
   May have *Honour* rebuilt
On fair *Public-Defence ;*
   Or else, *Silence* is *Guilt :*

Which the *Law* has discreetly
   Put past a Dispute,
By hearing the *Pleader,*
   Whilst it tortures the *Mute.*

Nor can *Justification*
   In flat *Charge* arise,
From * *Advertisements* cram'd
   With most insolent *Lyes !*

* See *Mist's* Weekly-Journal, the Post-Boy, &c. in or about
Nov. 1726.

Since,

A T A L E. 25

Since, if *Things* by apt *Names*
    Diftinctly we'd call ;
A *Falfehood*'s ftill worfe,
    Than no *Speaking* at-all.

One PERSON here *Faultlefs*
    To think I'd incline ;
But, if he purge not *Himfelf*,
    'Tis no Bufinefs of *mine*.

Of all MASQUERADES,
    'Twere the *honefteft* Task ;
To rebuke *Marriage-Bans*,
    Atchiev'd in a MASK :

For indeed, to the *Prophet*
    The clofer we keep ;
'Tis fullfilling - - - a *Wolf*
    In the *Garb* of a *Sheep* !

Then, to propagate *Faith*,
    We *fantaftickly* roam ;
To *Infidels* foreign,
    From fuch *Mifcreants* at-home !

E   Still

26   *C O F F E E:*

Still on the *Deserving,*
  Tho' *Few,* of our *Coat* ;
They make it their *Boast,*
  That they *perfectly* doat :

Sincerely concern'd,
  That the *Steps* of the *Best*
Sink e'en to *Contempt,*
  In the *Eyes* of the *rest* :

With express *Non-obstante,*
  Reserving *those* FEW ;
As Objects of *Honour,*
  Where *Honour* is due !

So the *Fry* in the *Sea*
  Are beholden to Them,
Who for *Turbuts* or *Mullets*
  Profess an Esteem :

However, some *Modesty*
  This Part discovers ;
For it proves 'em to be,
  No *general* Lovers.

In

A T A L E. 27

In vain, with *Greek-Fathers*,
  We cumber our Shelves;
If ATHEISTS go-on thus,
  To think for *Themselves :*

You may urge what Ye pleafe,
  But I ftick to my *Notion* ;
Our *Ruin* impends,
  From this peftilent *Potion !*

BEN JOHNSON, of old,
  Lov'd Us and *Canary* ;
But WIT, once our *Bawd*,
  Now's a *Jilt* quite contrary :

E'en the MUSE, fipping COFFEE,
  Is dwindled to *Jeft* ;
And her *modern* HEROIC is,
  Lafhing a *Prieft :*

Tho' the WORLD has long known
  Such *Attacks* to be loft,
For they might full-as-well
  Ufe a *Scourge* to a *Poft.*
          E 2

By

28　*C O F F E E:*

By Monition let *Learners*
　To Ethics be brought,
We *Teachers* may furely
　Difdain to be *Taught!*

But, why do I let my *Self*
　Thus be perplex'd;
By *Digreffions* from Coffee,
　Which ftrictly's my *Text?*

It banifhes *Sleep*,
　And fo ruffles the *Scheme*;
Of lulling *Lay-Drones*,
　In an indolent *Dream:*

Tho' our *darling* Diana
　This *Solace* may take;
That her *thorow-bred* Babes
　Snoar hard, whilft *Awake.*

Let your Wives, he next faid,
　Speak *What* it deferves;
For drying your *Fluids*,
　And laxing your *Nerves:*

For

A T A L E. 29

For damping *their* Sex,
   Form'd o'-purpofe to *Pleafe*;
And for feeding fuch *Vapors*,
   As *Words* can't appeafe :

By which they loofe *Beauty*,
   And all *winning* Matters ;
And then tear the *Fames*,
   Of their *Neighbours*, to fhatters.

One far-fetch'd *Conceit*
   Made him *frantickly* ftorm,
'Twas - - - nine *Difhes* in ten
   Are fwallow'd Lukewarm.

Some wou'd mix it with *Tea*,
   But that *Project* mifs'd ;
For he palpably fmelt
   Comprehension in *Twift*.

To dafh it with *Brandy*,
   Wou'd comfort the *Sternum* ;
But *That* was, he faid,
   Jugulare Falernum.

                                 Bread-

30 *C O F F E E*:

Bread-and-butter, with COFFEE,
   Hit *Somebody's* Tooth;
'Twas n't *Man's-meat*, he fwore,
   And a *Plea* only fmooth.

After forty *Demurrs*,
   On that CLAN appendent;
To tire-out a *Plaintiff*,
   Or vex a *Defendent* :

With fulfom *Apologies*,
   Meant for Applaufe;
From *partial* By-ftanders,
   Alarm'd at the CAUSE :

'Twas *determin'd* at-length,
   Leaft it might be difgrac'd;
That its *Venom* was quell'd,
   Provided 'twas *Lac'd*.

Then a WAGG in the Room,
   Full of *Quibble* and *Scoff*;
Rejoic'd, to fee COFFEE
   So *fweetly* brought-off !

                                The

A T A L E.

The VICAR knock'd-under,
　Tho' *inwardly* mad;
And look'd, as if *Juſtice*
　Was n't *there* to be had:

ASTRÆA, he mumbled,
　Was fled to the *Skies*;
And had left a vaſt *Gulfe*,
　'Twixt *her* Heels and *their* Eyes:

Tho' all the *While* conſcious,
　Nor is he be-ly'd;
Had that LADY been preſent,
　She'd *Not* took his Side:

Or meddled with *Men*,
　Who have made ſuch a *Stir*;
From *Time* out-o'-mind,
　To *excommunicate* HER!

But my STORY's too long,
　And I *tedioufly* fail;
Not confid'ring, *Short-Life*
　Is compar'd to a *Tale*:

So,

32 *C O F F E E:*

So, with *Licence-poëtic*
  To *Whate'er* before is ;
Admit *one* Word more,
  In tutamen Authoris :

Whose Name, tho' *Concealment*
  Much *rather's* desir'd ,
Will be *easily* learnt,
  If by Culprits requir'd. ———— :

What's ask'd of those *Wights*,
  Who *provok'd* this *Behaviour* ;
Is, in *Phrase* suiting *Them*,
  A clear *Stage* and no *Favour.*

For my *serious* Design,
  If I'm *right* understood ;
To shame *Those* into Virtue,
  Who *ought* to be Good :

For touching the Gangrene,
  A little too *bold* ;
And applying more *Med'cine*,
  Than Stomach may hold :

                                        For

A T A L E. 33

For legal *Remonſtrance,*
   If Law's built on Sense;
And for asking no *Pardon,*
   Where *no* true *Offenſe:*

For *un-ſtoical* Feeling,
   At each *Finger's-end;*
Not *amiſs* for One's-Self,
   And much *leſs* for a Friend:

Shou'd my Bones be dug up,
   And from Holy-Dirt hurl'd;
This *Exegi-Monumentum*
   I leave to the World:

'Twill *out-laſt,* peradventure,
   Corinthian-Braſs;
Tho' perhaps *not* the *Metal,*
   That's *bronz'd* on a Face!

Making-free with a*Word,*
   Of Poeta Divinus;
I onely fear——Si *propiùs ſtes,*
   Te capiet Minus.

F I N I S.

The Velvet Coffee-woman: or, the Life, Gallantries and Amours of the late famous Mrs Anne Rochford, etc. (Westminster, printed for Simon Green, 1728), [2], 46pp.; 8°. BL: 12331.c.39. ESTCT100189. Hünersdorff.

A substantial coffee-woman's biography, satirically describing the life of Anne Rochford, including the notorious occasion when she was presented to the king, George I, wearing a velvet dress, in the guise of a woman of substance. Anne Rochford was raised in Lambeth, the daughter of a waterman called Francis Woase. After some years in service in the City, when she was about twenty years of age, she took the name Rochford and, by some complicated financial engineering, completed the building and renovation of four houses in Stangate, Lambeth. After 'some Vicissitudes of Female Affairs' (p. 75) – never explained – she began a new life as a courtesan and coffee-woman in a coffee-house in the Royal Mews, Charing Cross, at some time before 1713.

The coffee-woman's biography is a sub-variety of the genre of the whore's biography, itself a sub-genre of the criminal biography (see Bradford Mudge, *The Whore's Story: Women, Pornography, and the British Novel, 1684–1830* (Oxford, Oxford University Press, 2000)). All these genres have frequent recourse to a form of mock-heroic irony, in which low and vulgar events are narrated with pomp and grandeur. *The Velvet Coffee-woman* begins with an ironic funeral oration, delivered by a female writer anxious that her pen will be inadequate to the extent of Rochford's amatory victories, and detailing a catalogue of amorous women, hetaerae, courtesans and prostitutes. Almost all of this oration is taken directly from Captain Charles Walker's *Authentick Memoirs of the Life, Intrigues and Adventures of the Celebrated Sally Salisbury* (London, 1723).

Rochford's Coffee-house (Lillywhite 1086) first comes to notice in 1713. An advertisement for a lost Portugal dog in Richard Steele's periodical *The Englishman*, No. 31 (Saturday 12 December 1713) refers to 'Madam Rochford's Chocolate House by Charing Cross'. Macky lists 'Mrs Rochford's Coffee-house' amongst those frequented by a high-status Court clientele in 1714 (John Macky, *A Journey Through England* (London, J. Roberts for T. Caldecott, 1714), p. 112).

In 1716, in response to an attack on courtesan politics in Addison's periodical *The Freeholder* (No. 23, Friday 9 March 1716 (ed. by James Leheny (Oxford, Clarendon Press, 1979), pp. 135–8), Nanny Rochford (or someone purporting to be her) wrote a ten-page satirical reply, vindicating the Whig allegiances of the prostitutes, and self-deprecatingly claiming to be a mere 'Bar-Slave' herself (*Nanny Roc—d's Letter to a member of the B—f Stake Club* (London, J. Roberts, 1716), p. 8).

The Velvet Coffee-woman claims to be 'printed for Simon Green within the Verge of the Court', perhaps a legal evasion to avoid prosecution for obscene libel. An advertisement on the final page, for Edmund Curll's *Altar of Love*, and various notices of his lubricious publications in the text, suggest that this notorious publisher was responsible. The listing for the *Velvet Coffee-woman* among the 'Miscellaneous Pamphlets' in the *Monthly Catalogue*, III (October 1727), p. 113) states that it was to be 'Printed for H. Curll in the Strand. Price 1s'. In the *Catalogus Bibliothecae Harlianae*, 4 vols (London, Thomas Osborne, 1744), vol. IV, p. 821), it is catalogued under 'Ludicrous, Entertaining, Satirical, & Witty' books. Anne Rochford maintained a close allegiance to jokes about politics and textiles throughout the century, as is shown in *Polly Peachum's Jests. In which are comprised most of the Witty Apothegms, diverting Tales and Smart Repartees* (London, J. Roberts, 1728): 'A Gentleman ask'd *Nanny Rochford*, why the Whigs, in their Mourning for Queen *Anne*, all wore Silk Stockings: because, said she, the Tories *were Worsted*' (p. 30).

THE
Velvet *Coffee-Woman:*
OR, THE
L I F E,
GALLANTRIES and AMOURS

Of the late Famous

Mrs. *Anne Rochford.*

Particularly,

I. The Hiftory of Her going by *that Name.*

II. The Adventures of her noted *Irifh-Lover* MAC DERMOT.

III. An Account of that unparalelled Impoftor Count BRANDENBURGH.

IV. A *Funeral Oration* to her MEMORY, and all *Ladies of Induftry,* as well among the *Grecians* and *Romans,* as thofe of our own Nation.

The many Others *that are with* Her *Shown,*
Prove that no Merit's equal *to Her* Own.

WESTMINSTER:

Printed for SIMON GREEN, within the Verge of the Court.   1728.

(Price One Shilling.)

(1)

A

Funeral Oration, &c.

NEVER was *Poet* fo much tor-
tured about the Choice of a
Patron, as I have been for proper Materials on this mournful Occafion. For
though in the *Female Clafs* of Life, I
could have faftened upon Numbers,
which bear fome Refemblance to the
general Behaviour, and Actions of the
Deceafed ; and though many of our
Own Sex, would have gloried in the
leaft of her Amorous Adventures: Yet
in fo vaft a Collection, I could not
find One equal to the *Singularity* of
her Character.

B   A *Beau*

2   *A* Funeral *Oration,* &c.

A *Beau* of the firſt, or ſecond Rank, would have made but inſipid Orators; a *Coquet* would have proved a miſchievous One ; a *Jilt,* a negligent One; a *kept Miſtreſs,* a weak One ; or a *common Runner* of the *Town,* a ridiculous One.

I had once determined to requeſt the Favour of ſome One of her numerous Military-Prolocutors to have recorded her Fame, a *perfeϐt Hero,* that ſhould like another QUIXOT defend her *Reputation* right, or wrong; but upon ſecond Thoughts, I concluded the Task too hazardous for any BESSUS * of this Age ; that he ſoon would have been obliged to carry his Arm in a Scarf, and her Honour left to ſhift for

* *The General, who Aſſaſſinated* DARIUS, *King of* Perſia.

it

A Funeral *Oration*, &c. 3

it felf; and fo I difmiffed that Project.

Then I was hot upon begging the
Affiftance of fome *powerful Man* to
fing her Praife, famed for Wit and
Love, but I forefaw what Envy it
would create to the Perfon, placed, in
a manner, at the *Head* of her *Affections*
by executing fuch a Theme : Befides,
I was fearful of giving her Relatives a
very fenfible Difguft, in making her
feem the *Propriety* of *one Man*, when
we all knew her *ordained* for the Comfort and Refrefhment of *Multitudes*.

At laft, for the avoiding Offence,
and gaining a ftrong Party, I had almoft refolved to devolve this laudable
Task upon the *Oratory*. But then I
confidered what endlefs Quarrels might
rife amongft fo many Competitors,
about the foolifh Punctilio of who was

B 2   deareft

4   *A* Funeral *Oration,* &c.

deareſt to her when Alive, and who had poſſeſſed her ofteneſt, ſo that I ſoon went off from theſe Intentions.

From this Inſufficiency in the *Men,* to preſerve ſuch great Merit, I caſt my Eyes toward the *Female World,* to find a Help-meet there; but I perceived my ſelf running into equal Improprieties on that Side alſo.

Were I to compare her to ſome *Leading* BELLE of a Modern *Aſſemblée,* with what Indignation would ſhe hear her Name mentioned with that of ſuch a *proclaimed Wanton,* whilſt ſhe keeps up an unſuſpected Gallantry with Thouſands.

Were I to have had Recourſe to a PRUDE, what a tacit Reflection would it be upon her ſtolen Joys with her Coachman ; and how ſtrangely would

A Funeral *Oration,* &c. 5

would fuch a Compliment have difor-
dered her Stoical Face, and precife Behaviour.

I had once a *pretty Penitent* in my
Eye, who has paffed thro' many de-
lightful Stages of Life, whofe Wit could
have juftified moft of the gay Exceffes
of our Heroine ; but I hear, fhe is employing all thofe fine Talents in polifh-
ing that little Stock of Reputation,
which is left her, and fo, lefs capable
of giving a Glofs to the Defunct : So
that,

You fee, my Beloved, I am under
an invincible Neceffity of making her
the PATRONESS of her own *Fine
Actions:* And to be plain, who is there
in all the Fair Circle of Female Practitioners that has Spirit enough to defend
each Article of her Converfation ? What
Woman befides her felf had the Wit to

extenuate

6   *A* Funeral *Oration*, &c.

extenuate the moſt Criminal Parts, or Art to add a Luſtre to the beautiful Extravagancies of human Life.

No, none alas ! ſhe was the ſole Perſon, beſt able to protect her ſelf. When Naked and Defenceleſs, how Lovely did ſhe appear? How great in this *State* of *Independency* ?

But though it was not eaſy to find a proper Advocate amongſt the Race of *Men*, yet the whole Warlike-Corps were ever at her Devotion, and the ſeeming Diſdain of her *own Sex*, proceeded not ſo much from an Unwillingneſs to Patronize her Actions, as an Incapacity of Copying ſo bright an Example.

There was a certain Propriety in her Character, which was not communicable to any Woman in *Her Way*, and even

A Funeral *Oration,* &c.   7

even the neareſt Imitation would become prepoſterous in another Hand.
Her polite Deviations from Virtue, and
graceful Wantonneſs, are what Alarm-
ed her whole Sex, and from deſpairing
to Imitate, they fell to Railing.

Having ſuch ſuperior Advantages,
think not that I will run any mean
Parallels between Her and the *modern
Ladies* of Her *Profeſſion,* or that I will
Honour them even with a D A S H.

No, Her Sphere of Elevation was
much higher, and ſhe moved with an
Elegance peculiar to Her ſelf.

I am half diſtracted when I hear a
diſſolute Creature, formed only for *falling Backwards,* and ſuch inſipid Dalli-
ances, as *Matrimony* affords; compare
thoſe *barren Pleaſures,* to the Picquan-
cy, and Heightenings which ſhe gave

to

8   *A* Funeral *Oration*, &c.

to that *fupreme Joy* of SENSE: Or
a *Termagant* born only for Noife and
Clamour, juftify herfelf by thofe gay
Rhapfodies, and infpired Rants, with
which fhe engaged Her Lovers.

As fhe ftood without a *Rival* in *Great
Britain* amongft the Profeffors of *Love's
Myfteries*, fo it is difficult to match
Her amongft the *Ancients*. The *Gre-
cian* Ladies of Pleafure were delicious
in their Way ; they had fine Particu-
larities, but were not fo univerfally
Attractive as the Deceafed.

PHRYNE, of *Bæotia*, was a *celebrated Toaft* in her Day ; fhe had a pout-
ing Lip, and a melting Eye, which
gained her more Admirers, than the
fiercer Beauties of her Time : She was
moft remarkable for the *Elafticity* of
her *Parts*, and a certain *Spring* in her
Motion, which endangered the *Rider* :

But

A Funeral *Oration*, &c.   9

But fomewhat mercenary in Abatement
of her other amiable Qualities.

LAMIA of *Athens*, though engaging beyond Meafure, at firft Sight, yet
was high-feafoned with the *Jilt* ; fhe
had a peculiar Knack of firing the Imagination with an Opennefs of Behaviour ; would fhow her pretty Foot, and
well-turned Leg, and then Drop the
Curtain on a fudden, and retire, to the
unfpeakable Torment of her Lover; a
Fault, the Enemies of our departed
Sifter could never reproach her with,
fince fhe was generally fo Compaffion-
ate as to go thro' the *whole Exercife.*

LAIS of *Corinth* was a Lady of
High Mettle, Generous and Entertaining ; though her Demands ran high,
when a wealthy Magiftrate was to make
a *Love-Purchafe* ; yet, to her Honour
be it recorded, fhe never let a younger

C   Brother

10 *A* Funeral *Oration,* &c.

Brother pine to Death for want of a *Favour* ; but what gives fome Alloy to her Chara&er, is, that fhe was much *Commoner,* than ever our *Nancy* permitted *her Self* to be.   But,

THAIS is the Girl, which comes up nearest to a R——*d's* Standard ; fhe had fomething *Strong* in her *Diverfions,* loved to affociate chiefly with Rakes, and affe&ed *Mafculine Pleafures* : She would make a Party at a *drinking Match,* and Loved a *midnight Revel* at her Soul. And how often has the Defun& quitted the *fine Gentleman,* and the *Colonel* to drink half a dozen Bottles of *Burgundy* with an *Illuftrious-Debauchée* ; with an Eye perhaps to the Example of A R I A D N E, who quitted her Lover T H E S E U S, for the tumultuous Converfation of B A C C H U S.

Amongft the *Roman Ladies* of her Calling, to pafs over the C E L I A S, the

A Funeral *Oration*, &c. 11

the MANILIAS, the JULIAS, and Thoufands more of that Stamp, famed for little elfe than *ftrong Guftoes* of *Plea-fure*. I cannot find even the *kept Mif-treffes* of the *Roman Wits*, reach up near to our *Nancy*'s Perfection.

The LYCORIS of GALLUS was a *lufcious Bed-fellow*, but then, fhe ufed, by Way of Provocative, to read the *wanton Verfes* of her PARA-MOUR in the Day-time ; without which Helps, Mrs. R——d was, *Tout-jours Preft*, always ready.

CORINNA, the Miftrefs of OVID, Loved a *Game* at *Romps* in her *Cloaths*, and was fo *infatiable* in her *Play*, that there was no holding out the *Game* with her : This Miftake our Sifter judicioufly avoided, by permit-ting all her *Lovers* to *rife* with an *Ap-petite*.

C 2 The

12 *A* Funeral *Oration,* &c.

The beloved LELAGE of HO-
RACE appears to me in no more
agreeable Light, than that of a pretty,
laughing, talkative Hoyden.　And,

The LESBIA of CATULLUS
was everlastingly Slabbering, and Sucking his Lips.　But,

In all this Fine *Groûpe* of *Obliging
Ladies,* none, singly, could ever furnish out that Variety of Delight which
was to be met with in her *Person:* In
her the happy Man enjoyed the different Graces of all Climates.　In her
were collected the scattered Beauties of
her whole Sex. ˌ In short, She was the
PINE-APPLE of *Great Britain,*
which includes the several Flavours of
all the delicious Fruits in the World.

Those Hypocrites who pretend to
dif-esteem her upon the Account of
her

A Funeral *Oration,* &c. 13

her *Profession*, neither confider the *Antiquity* of it; the *Ufefulnefs* of her *Labours* to the *Publick*; or the *Honours* conferred upon her Loving *Sifterhood* by the greateft, and wifeft *Law-givers, Princes,* and *States* in all Ages.   For the *Antiquity*—from *Venus,*

> Parent of *Gods* and *Men,*
> Began the Sportive-Dance.

For the *Ufefulnefs* of it—It will be readily granted.   The *Ladies* of her *Univerfal Charatter* are of wondrous Service to thofe who cannot comply with the Infolence, Clamour, Infatiablenefs, Lazinefs, Extravagance, or Virtuous Naftinefs of a *Wife.*

It muft be allowed, that fuch *Gay Volunteers* as our *Nancy,* gave a *young Fellow* an handfom Profpect of the Town, led him through all the inchanting Mazes, and even furfeited him

with

14 *A* Funeral *Oration,* &c.

with Delight ; fo that by the time he was come out of her Hand, he was grown very Tame, and prepared for the dull Solemnity of *Marriage*. It cannot be likewife denied, but that Recreations of that Delicacy are much more excufable, than the fmalleft Exceffes of any other Kind.

That this *familiar Intercourfe* keeps *Mankind* in the *proper Channel* of *Nature*.

That more Diftempers are prevented by fuch *kind Alliances*, than gained ; and *critical Fevers* of the *Blood* mitigated, if not cured, by thefe *feafonable Interpofitions*.

From fuch a kind *Medicine* as dear *Nanny*, was always capable of *difpenfing*, the pious Father St. AUSTIN, whom Mother CHURCH with fo

much

A Funeral *Oration, &c.*   15

.much Juftice Reveres, found great *Re-lief* in his *Neceffities* : He had a *Pair* of clever *Wenches* for his Share : By *One* he had a *Love Child*, whom he called ADEODATUS, that is, the *Gift of God* : She teized him, and followed him, till fhe grew *Vexatious*, and the *Holy Father* then threw her off with a good deal of Gallantry : The *Other* he ufed to recreate himfelf with, after he had been folemnly Contracted to his intended Spoufe who was in her *Nonage*, and kept her till his Wife was ripe for *Confummation*.

But that *Ladies* of this *Charačteriflick* are of more important Service to the CHURCH, and the PUBLICK, than moft of the *liberal Arts*, is evident from Experience *.

---

* For farther Concernment, perufe diligently, *Two Practical Treatifes*, viz. 1. *A Modeft Defence of Pub-lick Stews.* 2. Its Counterpart, *A Modeft Defence of Chaftity.* Sold at the *Red-Lyon* in *Brentford*.

At

16 *A* Funeral *Oration*, &c.

At *Rome* every pleafurable Female pays a J U L I O *per* Week to the C H U R C H ; *a Curate*, whofe Income amounts to no more than thirty Crowns *per Annum*, having an Affignment out of the Fees of three Curtezans in the *Publick Stews*, picks up a comfortable Subfiftence, and to diftinguifh fuch *pious Church-Women*, as our departed Sifter, Pope S I X T U S erected a noble *Brothel-Houfe*, with Partitions, for the more commodious Reception of Strangers.

Neither have they been lefs ferviceable to their *Country* than to the C H U R C H, as appears by the great *Succours* they have afforded to the Common-wealth of *Venice* out of their *Bodily Induftry*.

Here I cannot omit the great Genius of *One*, and the extenfive Charity of the *Other*.

R H O-

A Funeral *Oration,* &c. 17

RHODOPE, at her own Expence, and out of the *modeſt* Fees of her *private Office,* built one of the ſtatelieſt *Pyramids* of *Egypt.* And FLORA generouſly left the *Roman-People* her Heirs.

Their *Duty* to *Parents* likewiſe muſt not be paſſed over in Silence. The *Babylonian* Virgins uſed to grant Favours for the Support of their aged *Fathers.*

Neither muſt the *Induſtry* of the *Cyprian Girls* want a due Encomium : For they publickly *proſtituted* themſelves to every Stranger, to make a *Fortune* equal to their *Ambition* before they ſettled in *Matrimony.*

But here we muſt not forget the Honours, even the ſacred Honours,

D   conferred

18 *A* Funeral *Oration*, &c.

conferred on this *Profeſſion* by Antiquity.

The *Corinthian-Dames*, being the
moſt elegant Miſtreſſes of *Greece*, had
it always in Charge, from the *State*,
to intercede with VENUS in any
Caſe of Importance; and when *Xerxes*
invaded the *Peloponeſus*, they had the
Privilege of compiling *a publick Form of
Prayer* for the Safety of their *Country*.
SOLON, the *Athenian* Law-giver
being ſenſible of the Strength of their
Party, built a *Temple* to VENUS,
out of the Amorous Perquiſites of her
Tribe, which was devoutly Copied
here, in that worthy Collection made
ſome Years ſince, for a CHAPEL
of *Eaſe* in *Ruſſel Court*, *Covent-Garden*,
out of the *pious Gains* of the THEATRE,
and for which the *preſent* Manager will
be remembered to *late* Poſterity.

Thus

A Funeral *Oration,* &c.   19

Thus, my Beloved, you fee, thefe *Amorofa's* have the whole Current of *Antiquity* on their fide, and we may affure our felves, the *Party* will be ever as victorious in *Great Britain,* tho' we are too Phlegmatick to pay fuch folemn Honours to this ufeful Confederacy, as the Antients.

But what the Laws of our Country forbids us to act in *Publick,* reft fatisfied, we make more than a Recompence for in *Private.*

What *Catholick* has ever offered up more Extafies at the Shrine of his *Tutelar Saint,* than has been paid to the fimple Brade of our *R—d's* Slipper, a difcoloured Top-Knot, or perhaps two Spans of unravelling Gartering.

D 2   Yet

20 *A* Funeral *Oration,* &c.

Yet amidſt the *good Offices,* ſhe was
continually doing to Mankind, I often
intreated her not to indulge the Vanity
of thinking herſelf exempt from the
invidious Whiſpers of a thoughtleſs
Multitude : No, there were a Set of
Goſſips of both Sexes, who were endeavouring to fix a Blemiſh on her
Bright Character, inſinuating, that the
moſt blooming Part of her Life was
ſpent amongſt the *Royal Japanners* ;
which, at preſent, for our Comfort is
no deſpicable *Corporation* ; whilſt others
equally detracting, failed not to leſſen
the Dignity of her Education, in that
famous *College* of the celebrated Mrs.
Weybourn.   But her good Senſe was
always preſent with her, to pity their
Ignorance, and place ſuch popular
Miſtakes to a Narrowneſs of Genius :
For what Seminary is there, even at
Chelſea or *Hackney,* which can boaſt of
half

A Funeral *Oration*, &c.   21

half thofe Improvements, in Five Years, as that School wherein fhe had been Educated, can furnifh out in three Months? There, the young Practition-ers are led into a promifcuous Con-verfation from the Day of their Ad-mittance. There, is foon learned an eafy and graceful Behaviour, and a Pre-fence of Mind, which never leaves them in an Extremity. In that Academy there can no Danger accrue to the fair Nymphs, from broken Vows, and neglected Charms : There, the Lover has nothing in View, but a Run of Joy without Tiezing, Fears, or Cautions; and for the Satisfaction of all *jealous Pa-rents*, there never was a Fortune ftole out of that *pious Nurfery* fince its firft Erection.

Times and Cuftoms alter ; but had poor *Weybourn* been fo fortunate as to have lived in that elegant Period of Time,

22 *A* Funeral *Oration,* &c.

Time, when *Greece* carried away the Prize of Wit, and Prowefs, from all the World, both *She*, and *You* would have been the immediate Care of the Publick.

The famous ASPASIA, was much of Mrs. *Weybourn*'s Complexion, and Vertue, and fo tender was *Athens* of the Safety, and commodious Subfiftence of that *Lady* and her *Virtuous Nurfery*, that PERICLES, the famous General, began the *Peloponefian* War in Revenge of the Injuries offered to *Her*, and the young Ladies of Pleafure under her Care, by the People of *Megara.*

Thefe Honours paid by *Antiquity* to the Profeffors of *Love's Myfteries*, cannot fail of giving us an high Opinion of their good Senfe, and likewife an Opportunity of bewailing the ftrange

Degeneracy

A Funeral *Oration*, &c. 23

Degeneracy of the Men of the prefent Age, who concern themfelves no farther in fo good a *Caufe*, than when the *Fair* are contributing to their Pleafures: But I prefume, my Brethren, ye will ftill perfevere in this *Virtuous Courfe*, in hopes of feeing fome Amendment in the Times.

But now to conclude, and take my Leave on this folemn Occafion, I think our Sifter had this peculiar Advantage over the reft of her Sex, by feeing the *worft* of her *Actions* publifhed in her *Life-time*, as can be witneffed by her laft Lover, an Antiquated, Ecclefiaftical *Amorofo*, whofe Fortune was totally Shipwrecked by *South-Sea-Tempefts*, and his Veffel, not only Stranded, but funk, in the *Gully-Hole* of the *Meufe*.

And

24 *A* Funeral *Oration*, &c.

And now fince, as SHAKESPEARE fays, that, *with all her Imperfections on her Head, fhe is called to her Account;* CHARITY obliges us to wifh, that her *Reckoning* may be made Eafy.

F I N I S.

(25)

SOME

ACCOUNT

O F

Mrs *ROCHFORD*.

DEATH having now poſſeſſed himſelf of our Female Triumvi-ate, (*Sally Salisbury*, the *Royal Sovereign*, and Mrs. *Rochford*,) it is but requiſite the ſame Honours ſhould be paid to the Memory of the laſt, as have been offered up to the *Manes* of her two departed Siſters. I am foreſtalled in at-tempting to ſay any Thing of her refined Qualifications, both of Mind and Body, thoſe Topicks being fully exhauſted by our learned Orator. She is with one * VOICE proclaimed, to have been the Na-tural Daughter of a *Waterman* of that Name, and as ſhe loved a Pun at her Heart, I have choſen to Uſher in her Vir-gin Appellation in this Way. As an In-

---

* Her Father's Name was *Woſſe*, vulgarly called *Voice*.

E   ſtance

26 *Some* ACCOUNT *of*

ftance of which, I have often heard a Gentleman relate this Story of Her.   That being very nicely Hungry, he came into her
Houfe one Evening, and defired her to
rehearfe the particular Accommodations of
her Larder, the laft Article of which was
Woodcock, here he fhook his Head, and
faid, it was the only Thing that would
humour his Appetite, but his Pocket would
not reach it ; fhe asked him, why ? ah
Nanny ! fays he, you know *Woodcocks*
have *damnable long Bills*, fhe was fo taken with the Jeft, that burfting into a
hearty Laugh, fhe fet her Cook to work,
and dreffed him a Brace *gratis*.

Suitable to the Storms of Life and Love,
which fhe bravely weathered, was the
Place of her Nativity, a Sea-Port Town,
having the Honour of her Birth.

But now to be ferious ; Her Father was
one *Francis Woafe*, Waterman to the late
Earl of *Torrington*, and formerly at Sea
with him, and Coxfwain of his Boat ;
Woafe was a genteel Man, and his Education had been above the Level of a common Sailor, which made that noble Earl
take a particular Fancy to him, and often
employ him in his Love-Adventures, of
which in a fhort Time he became fo perfect a Mafter (being himfelf, as to his Perfon, by Nature, framed to pleafe the fair
Sex, his Stature fomewhat inclining to
Tall, and every other Part proportionable)
that

Mrs. Rochford's *Life.* 27

that when in Purfuit of Game he had sprung a *Pheafant* or *Partridge* for his Lord, he likewife took Care to fecure a *Snipe* or *Woodcock* for himfelf; and whilft his Mafter was in Raptures above Stairs, *Woafe* was as well pleafed below. 'Twas fome fuch Adventure as this that firft brought him acquainted with Mrs. *Rochford's* Mother. For one Time coming from Sea with the Earl, and Landing at *Deal*, he went in Queft of frefh Provifion to a Farm Houfe near that Town, at which Place fhe then lived ; he taking a liking to her, made her feveral Vifits, as tenders of his Affection for her, and having *(according to the ufual Method of betraying the innocent)* promifed her Marriage, he fo far gained the Afcendant over her, that fhe granted him the laft Favour, and which in the End (to her) proved a very fatal One. Some few Years after the Birth of this Love-Child, the Subject of thefe Memoirs, his Lordfhip leaving off the Sea, and retiring to his Seat at *Weybridge,Woafe,* with the Fruits of his Labour, came from *Deal,* and fettled at, or near *Stangate,* in the Parifh of *Lambeth*, and ply'd there as a Waterman : There is a Report of her being employed, when a Girl, at the *Mitre* Alehoufe near thofe Stairs, to fetch in Pots, as they Phrafe it ; which Report is entirely falfe, and what gave Birth to it I

take

28 *Some* ACCOUNT *of*

take to be this. Her Father was a good
Cuſtomer to that Houſe, and he being frequently there, and loving his Girl well,
ſhe was often with him, and as Children
are active, and fond of running up and
down, ſhe might perhaps go along with
the Servant of the Houſe when ſhe went
out with Drink, or to fetch in Pots, and
this is certainly the Ground of that Report.   However, all who knew *Woaſe* at
that time, knew him to be a very proud-
ſpirited Man, and one who would never
have ſuffered his Daughter to do any
Thing ſo mean, eſpecially ſo near him
But,

Woaſe had not been long at *Stangate*,
before he committed Matrimony, the News
of which ſoon reach'd *Deal*, and thence
the Ears of *Nanny's* Mother, who thereupon was taken very Ill ; which Illneſs, in
a ſhort time, terminated in her Death.

Many are the Reports concerning the
State of Mrs. *Anne's* Affairs under the Age
of Twenty, and indeed the chief part of
them are not to be relied on ; however, 'tis
certain, that part of the time ſhe was Nur-
ſery Maid at a Merchant's in the City of
London, and during her Stay there, ſhe
always appeared and behaved with great
Decency, often coming to the *Old Swan*
Stairs (with the Children ſhe had under
her Care) to enquire of the Watermen
concerning

Mrs. Rochford's *Life.* 29

concerning the Welfare of her Mother-in-Law. How long she remained in this Service is unknown, and the Enquiry unnecessary ; when she launched into the World as a Mistress for her self, she took the Denomination of ROCHFORD, either from some contracted Amour, or reading the Memoirs of the *Comte de* ROCHEFORT, though some Reports run, that she was married to a Gentleman of that Name, the Spelling being various ; but as to this Incident of her Life,

Utrum harum mavis accipe.

However, the above-mentioned Book was one of her favourite Authors, and well thumb'd about the middle of it, on Account of a very merry Adventure of this *French* Nobleman, which for the Reader's Diversion, I shall so far digress, as to insert it in this place.

" The Count *de Rochefort* one Day be-
" ing at Court, where the Apartments of
" the Maids of Honour are always o-
" pen to the Gallery, he went and fell in-
" to a Chat with the good old Lady their
" *Governante*, she was (says he) one of
" my old Acquaintance ; and walking up
" and down with her, I saw lying upon
" the *Toilet* several Combs, and a Powder
" Box,

30 *Some* ACCOUNT *of*

" Box, and all the neceffary Impliments
" of the Dreffing-Box; and amongft the
" reft there ftood a fmall Pot of *Pomatum,*
" fo I muft needs take fome to rub upon
" my Hands, becaufe they were a little
" rough; I found it quite of another Co-
" lour than the ordinary fort, which made
" me fancy that it might be good for the
" Lips too, and fo without any Confide-
" ration, applied fome to mine, they be-
" ing a little chop'd; but I foon paid for
" my Curiofity, for immediately my Lips
" were all on Fire, my Mouth was con-
" tracted, my Gums fhrivelled up, and
" when I went about to fpeak, I made
" Madam the *Governante* laugh at that
" rate, that I might eafily fee I had very
" finely expofed my felf; and which was
" worft of all, I was not able to bring
" out one Word diftinctly; and running
" directly to the Looking-Glafs to take a
" View of my Face, I was fo damnably
" afhamed of the Figure I made, that I
" run away to hide my felf; but juft as I
" was going out I met the Duke *de*
" *Roquelaire,* who was coming to make
" his Court to one of the Ladies, and be-
" ing fcared to fee me in that Condition,
" he asked me, what the *Devil ailed me?*
" I told him very fimply my Misfortune,
" but inftead of pitying, he fell a Laugh-
" ing at me, and faid I was but right-
                                    " ly

Mrs. Rochford's *Life.* 31

" ly ferved ; that at my Age, I ought to
" know, that there are feveral forts of
" *Pomatums* ; that the fort I had meddled
" with was not either for the Hands, or
" the Hair, but was defigned for another
" fort of Ufe ; after he had had his fill of
" this rallying, he left me, and went to
" the Apartments of the Queen-Mother,
" where he made his Court at the Ex-
" pence of my Misfortune. Immediately
" all the Town came to fee me, and find-
" ing that I had really furnifhed them
" with fufficient Matter for their Mirth,
" I would have been one of the firft to
" have laughed at the Jeft, if I could but
" have opened my Mouth. This Adven-
" ture was the Entertainment of the whole
" Court, at leaft, a Week ; they were fo
" taken with it, that they fent an Account
" of it to *Nantz,* where the King was,
" who, as ferious as he is, could not
" forbear fmiling at it ; for my part, I
" had as much Inclination to Laugh as
" any Body ; when I thought of this Ac-
" cident, though I wafhed my Mouth
" often with frefh Water, and fometimes
" with warm Wine, yet nothing but time
" would bring me to rights again. This
" little Difgrace, however, hindred me
" from appearing again in Publick for a
" confiderable Time *.

* See MEMOIRS of the Count *De Rochéforte,* printed 1705.
pag. 208, 209.

But

32 *Some* ACCOUNT *of*

But to return to our Heroine, Mr. *Woafe*
did not long furvive her Mother, and in a
reafonable time his Widow became match'd
again, with another of the rowing Fraternity, the Badge of whofe Honour was,
his being a Waterman to the *Sons of the
Clergy*. This floating Son of the *Church*
had the Misfortune to die Iffue-lefs, and
his Widow the good Fortune to be left
poffeffed of two Houfes at *Stangate* afore-
faid, the Income of which for fome time
afforded her a comfortable Subfiftence;
but at length, whether through the want
of Repairs, which the old Woman neglected upon the Leafe being near expired,
or through her Inability to do it, I know
not ; however, the Houfes were very
much decayed, upon which *Nanny* (who
always behaved with a dutiful Refpect to
her doubly-widow'd Mother-in-Law) living then in good Credit, made a Bargain with Mrs. *Wefton*, for (that was her
laft Name) that upon her furrendering
the Title to Her, fhe would renew the
Leafe, and likewife give her fome other
Satisfaction ; the which was agreed to,
and the Articles performed by her Weekly allowing her Mother-in-Law a fufficient Maintenance during her Life : After
Nanny had thus purchafed the Houfes, fhe
Repaired them, and Built two others adjoining to them, but fo uncertain are the
                                    Viciffitudes

Mrs. Rochford's *Life.* 33

Viciffitudes of Female-Affairs, that fhe who was then at her Meridian, in a fhort time was brought to her Wain as the Sequel will fhow. But,

It muft not be looked upon as the *leaft* memorable Incident of Mrs. *Rochford's* Life, that, of her being introduced at Court in *Velvet,* (accompanied by her two other Sifters of the *Calling* both for *Coffee* and *Intrigue*) tho' it will be always regarded as an act of the *greateft* Imprudence in the Conduct of that noble Peer, who played the *Mafter* of the *Ceremonies* upon this Occafion ; infomuch, that he was feverely lafhed by another noble Lord in a fatyrical Ballad, intituled, *Strange News from St.* James's : Or, The three Coffee-Women *turned* Courtiers.---This Piece of Humour was adapted to the fame Tune as Mr. *Congreve's* Song —— *Ye Commons and Peers,* &c. viz.

I.

For an *Apple* of *Gold,*

To a *Shepherd* of old,

Three *Goddeffes* deign'd to come down ;

But now *Drabs* as many,

Jenny, Fenwick, and *Nanny,*

Demand a *Gold Key* of the *Crown.*

F

2. In

34 *Some* ACCOUNT *of*

2.

In *Velvet* ſo fine,
The Court-Dames to out-ſhine,
The Gipſies forſooth were equipt,
Introduc'd by a Star †
Though fitter by far,
To be Carted to *Bridewell* and Whip'd, *&c. &c.*

This Ballad being in the Hands of moſt curious Collectors of *State-Poems*, I ſhall not burden the Reader with the Recital of any more of it in this place, but only obſerve, that the chief Point of the Satire lies in the Pretenſions each *Coffee-Lady* aſſumed at this Interview —— *Jenny Man*, pleaded her *Intereſt* with the *Officers*. Mrs. *Fenwick* her *Influence* over the *High-land-Clans* in *Scotland*. But it was our Heroine only, who enforced the *Cauſe of Love.*

Excuſe Me cry'd *Nan*,
And at length ſhe began,
If I plead not ſo well by *this Light* ;
But let mine be the Prize,
And a Word to the Wiſe,
You're welcome to *Rochford* each Night.

---

† Alluding to the Star of the Duke of———— who introduced Them.

Her

Mrs. Rochford's *Life.* 35

Her two Sisters of the *Coffee-Pot* and
C---y-Burrough, went unrewarded as they
came, but Mrs. *Rochford* for her *Love*,
and her *Loyalty*, so far shared the Royal
Favour, as to obtain Leave to build a
House in the *Meuse*. Upon this Success,
she soon flourished both in Wealth and
Fame, left off retailing *Coffee*, *Tea*, and
Chocolate, soon changing those Female Con-
comitants into the sprightly *Juice* of the
Grape, *Arrack Punch*, and *L'Eau de Barbadé*. But in a little time after she had
opened this polite *Caberet*, both for eating
and drinking, she unluckily fell a Victim
to that noted *Irish*-man *Mac Dermot*, of
whom we shall here give some Account.
Mac, hearing that she stood so high in the
Esteem of a certain Colonel, as to have a
Side-board of Plate presented her marked
with his own Arms, his Mouth began to
water as much after the Dishes, as the
Food they contained, and nothing would
serve *Mac*, but truly he wanted to play
the *Sosia* with the Colonel, and to be
cloathed likewise in Regimentals. Besides,
the bold Attacks made by *Mac* upon Mrs.
Rochford, there were several Incidents in
his Behaviour, which must have occasioned a Blush upon any Check but *a True-
born Irishman*'s. In short, *Mac*'s Adventures not only became the Talk of the
whole Town, but furnished out a very

F 2   notable

36 *Some* Account *of*

notable poetical Entertainment for the Ladies, (intituled, *Mac Dermot : Or, The
Irifh-Fortune Hunter,* a Mock-Héroic Poem,
in fix Cantoes.) This Piece was printed
for a Bookfeller in the *Strand, Tota notus
in Urbe,* with a compleat Collection of
whofe natural Rarities Mrs. *Rochford*'s
Library was replete, from the *Cafes* of *Impo-
tency* to the *Treatife* of *Flogging,* and from
Eunuchifm Difplayed to the *Myfteries of
Human Generation* fully revealed ; not o-
mitting either the *Love-Poems* of *Bonefo-
nius,* or the *Altar* of *Love* it felf. There
being daily as great refort to his Shop by
the fair Sex, for Inftructions in the Science
of Love, as there is to the Chambers of
Temple-Barrifters the Night before a Term
begins. The Reader, I hope, will pardon
us for this ufeful Digreffion, and give us
leave to return to the Qualifications of
Mac. Notwithftanding the boaft of his
high Defcent from the *Kings* of *Munfter,* I
am affured by a *Noroy* lately arrived from
Dublin, that, the Male-Line of the *Mo-
narchs* of *Munfter* have been Extinct upwards of four hundred Years in the Perfon of *Teague O-'Donald,* who died without Iffue ; and even upon the ftricteft Survey of the Archives, and Records of that
antient Kingdom, it does not appear to
him that any of the Daughters of that Illuftrious Houfe had ever been married to
the

Mrs. Rochford's *Life.* 37

the *Dermots,* who were of obscure Extraction, and whose Bearings were no where to be found in any of the Volumes of *Munstrian-Heraldry.* Now, tho' *Mac's* Pretensions to a high Birth were all proved *fabulous,* yet by the innate Assurance peculiar to his Countrymen, he had totally jostled the Colonel out of *Nanny's* Affection, and she declared that his Qualifications were *real.* And thus, upon first seeing Him in the *Park,* did she fall into the most extatick Raptures.

Hail lovely *Irishman,* if right I guess,
Thy Features, Air, and Shape that Land confess;
They all proclaim Thee of *Hibernian* Race;
Thy Back how strong! how brazen is thy Face!
My Name is *Rochford,* from all Parts repair,
To my fam'd Roof the discontented Fair;
Rich City Wives, and some not far from Court,
Who loath their Husbands, and who love the sport;
Brides match'd with Impotence, that want an Heir,
And Nymphs that fear to let their Joys take Air;
Numbers of these I succour ev'ry Day,
Who keep their able Stallions well in pay;
If then Thou dar'st be my adopted Son,
And in that Croud of happy Youths make one,
Hie to the *Meuse,* before the Clock strikes Eight,
Find out this Night, my hospitable Gate;
There, if thou answer'st Expectation well,
(As by some sure Prognosticks I foretel)
The Powers of Love, with Fortune shall combine,
To make my Side-board and my Person thine.

The

38 *Some* ACCOUNT *of*

The Refolutions *Mac* came to, and many of his Adventures, before Mrs. *Rochford* engroffed him, may be found in the Poem called, *The Irifh-Fortune Hunter*.

The Colonel finding her Heart wholly eftranged from him, fell off, both from his Annual Allowance, and the Prefents he was wont to make her. So that in a fhort time *Mac* not only poffeffed, but fpent all fhe had; obliging her to Mortgage her Houfes, as well as continuing daily to empty her Purfe, infomuch that as they were one Day going by Water, fhe plainly told him, that *fhe could no longer fupport his Extravagancies*, and the Debate was carried fo far, that very angry Words paffed between them. But now all thefe Storms are over, fhe being, as it is hoped, at reft; and our *Mac* returned to his *Fortune-Hunting Society*, in order to get Intelligence for fpringing frefh Game.

Before I clofe thefe Memoirs, I fhall infert fome Account of another moft notorious foreign Impoftor.

There needs but very little Introduction to make the Reader fenfible, that the Perfon, with part of whofe Adventures I am about informing the Publick, is no other than the *Braggadocio* who was lately fo well known in and about the COURT of St. *James's*, by the Title of Count *Brandenburg*. Monfieur *Conftantine de Renneville,*

Mrs. Rochford's *Life.* 39

neville, to whom I am indebted for my Intelligence of what relates to this notorious Impoftor, has, it feems, to his Sorrow, all imaginable Reafon to be thoroughly acquainted both with his *good* and *bad* Qualities ; though, as to the former, the only Syllable I find him fay in his Commendation, is, that he underftands *Latin* well, and talks it with wonderful Fluency.

They were Fellow-Prifoners in the *Baftile* for feveral Years, and for fome Months Chamber-Fellows ; before which time, their only Communication was by Stealth in the Night, through a Hole in the Chimney, from an upper Floor, where this Seraphick Difciple of St. *Francis* was, to that beneath, which was the Refidence of our Hiftorian, who then knew the Capuchin-Count for no other Man than a *German* Prince, who, for many important Reafons, carefully concealed his Name.

In the third Chamber of our Tower, fays this Author, was Father *Florentius Van Brandenburg* of *Namur*, a *Capuchin* Friar, to whom I fhall no longer give the Title of Prince, having been informed, that his Moft Serene Highnefs was neither better nor worfe than a Monk of that Order, and that all the fumptuous Equipages and magnificent Train of which he had fo often boafted to us, terminated in a Coul, a Rope, and a Staff : Thus I difcovered it.

One

40   *Some* ACCOUNT *of*

One Day, as I intreated Monfieur *De Joncas* (the King's Lieutenant in the *Baftile*) to remove me from the wretched Company in which I underwent fo cruel a Martyrdom; the three mad Fools I was with, fuffering me not to take a Moment's Reft, neither by Day nor by Night, I earneftly conjured him to put me with the Prince. He was at Lofs to guefs whom I meant, as being not able to imagine who this Prince fhould be; when *Rue*, the Turn-Key, told him, it was the *Capuchin*, who had the ridiculous Vanity to make him-felf pafs for a Prince. Monfieur *De Joncas*, laughing very heartily at this Piece of monkifh Rhodomantade, protefted, that I was ftill lefs unhappy where I then was, adding, that this *Capuchin* was, without Exception, the moft troublefome Prifoner in the whole *Baftile*, and that I could not poffibly bear with him a fingle Week. Notwithftanding all he faid was moft ef-fentially true, neverthelefs I afterwards did not fail bearing with this reverend Paftor, tho' fore againft my Inclinations, for up-wards of twenty-two Months, that we were fhut up together, all which Time I underwent the moft infupportable Rigours of a Prifon. Monfieur *Janiçon de Mont-devis*, a polite young Gentleman, was all the while a Witnefs and a Co-partner of my Sufferings.

As

Mrs. Rochford's *Life.* 41

As for the poor Devil, the Curate of *Léry* *, he ran ſtark mad, to which the officious Care of our moſt Reverend *Capuchin* did not a little contribute. When they were Chamber-Fellows, that good Prieſt, out of all Patience to find, that this beatified Father, far from going about to comfort him under his Afflictions, and not ſatisfied with devouring up all, or the greateſt Part of his Wine and Commons, did nothing but perpetually teaze, provoke and perplex him, he one Day, without any Reſpect to the venerable Frock, flew upon him, got him down, and trampled him under his Feet, and with both his Hands violently eradicated above three Quarters of that reverend Beard, which ever after he carefully preſerved, as a Relick of extraordinary Virtue. He ſhewed it to that Scoundrel *Pigeon,* when he was placed with him and *Cotereau,* in the uppermoſt Room of the Tower: But before he took it out of its Shrine, where he kept it depoſited, he inſiſted that *Pigeon* ſhould down upon his Marrow-Bones, in Order to kiſs it with the profoundeſt Reſpect. The good Prieſt, ſome Time after, falling out with *Pigeon,* whom he belaboured moſt outrageouſly for not kiſ-

---

* A moſt profligate Prieſt, of an infamous Character. He was in *England* in King *William*'s Time, where he turned *Proteſtant,* but ſoon re-turned *Papiſt.*

G   ſing

42 *Some* Account *of*

fing the feraphick Beard, as he directed, with fufficient Signs of Veneration, was dragged away to a Dungeon, together with poor *Cotereau* for Company, whofe only Offence was his remaining an inactive Spectator of the Drubs which the vigorous Curate had fo munificently beftowed upon that reverend Elder.---But to return to our *Capuchin*.

After this abrupt Rencounter with the furious Prieft (who expofed to all that came near him thofe rubicund frizzled Locks, as a glorious Trophy of his triumphant Atchievement) the next Companion given him was Mr. *Schrader*, of whom I fhall infert a fhort Account, for the better underftanding this Narrative, fince with him our Monk had two remarkable Scuffles, one in the *Baftile*, where the Scene proved bloody, and the other of a more Comick Nature, at *Hampton-Court*, and that in the Prefence of her prefent Majefty, when Princefs of *Wales*, and feveral of the prime Nobility; nay, his late Majefty himfelf had a Share in fome Part of the Comedy.

This Mr. *Schrader*, who called himfelf the Baron *De Peck*, is a Subject to his *Britanick* Majefty, being a Native of *Hamelin*, near *Hanover*. His Name is *John Chriftian Schrader de Peck*. Being a Captain of Dragoons in the Emperor's Service,

Mrs. Rochford's *Life.* 43

Service, in the Camp before *Landau*, commanded by the King of the *Romans*, in 1702, he had the Misfortune to kill an Officer of his own Regiment, in a Quarrel that arose in his Tent where he was entertaining several Friends. His younger Brother, a Lieutenant in the same Regiment, and their Cosin Mr. *Wiperman*, Cornet in Captain *Schrader*'s Troop, were his Seconds, and consequently they were all obliged to make off the Ground. They got away safe to *Thionville*, whither they were soon followed by the Captain's Wife (a beautiful young Gentlewoman about seventeen) with two Lackies and a Chamber-Maid; tho' I have heard this last Article disputed, and that neither the Lady was a Wife, nor had she any Attendants.

Be it so or not, the Gentlemen and Lady made the best of their Way to *Paris*, where the Captain had several powerful Friends, which he had made during the Time that he served, in that Capacity, in *Surlaube*'s Regiment. The Day of his Arrival there, he wrote to the Marquiss *De Rocilly*, one of his Patrons, gave him the Particulars of his Adventures, and prayed him to procure some Employment for himself, his Brother, and his Kinsman. He had an Answer from that Nobleman the very next Morning, af-

G 2   suring

44 *Some* ACCOUNT *of*

furing him, that he had delivered his Petition to Monfieur *Chamillart*, protefting
he would ufe his whole Intereft in his
Service, and doubted not of meeting
with Succefs.   Notwithftanding all which,
a very few Days after, fome Exempts,
followed by a Troop of *Satellites*, early
in the Morning, feized them all, at their
Lodgings in the Suburb St. *Germain*, and
conducted them to the *Baftile*, from whence
the Captain (of whom alone we fhall here
have Occafion to treat) could never obtain
a Releafe, till the Conclufion of the late
Peace between *France* and the Emperor.

But before I proceed, I think it requi-
fite to infert what my Author farther
fays concerning this Gentleman, as to his
Qualities and Character.——I never faw
him, fays he, till I met with him at *London*, where, not long fince, by Inquiry,
he found me out, tho' we had frequently
communicated at the *Baftile*, by Way
of *talking with a Stick*, as I ufed to term
a certain Method of converfing, of my
own Invention, and which enabled us to
make ourfelves intelligible to each other
from one Extremity of a Tower to the
other.   This was by ftriking hard and
pretty quick, as many Strokes againft the
Wall, as anfwered the Rank each Letter
we wanted to compofe a Word, held in
the Alphabet, and to make a fhort Paufe
between

Mrs. Rochford's Life. 45

between the Words; for an *A* one Stroke, for a *B* two, and so on. This was tedious, but we found it amusing. Mr. *Schrader*, during the whole Time of his Imprisonment, was continually changing and removing from one Tower to another; his mercurial Vivacity, and volatile Disposition not suffering him to remain long in any Apartment, in all which he was very frequently at Loggerheads with his Comrades, not excepting even our *Capuchin*, whose Chamber-Fellow he once was, as has been already observed. Of this Quarrel I could recite the Particulars, but it is not worth while. Besides, his unpassive, turbulent Spirit, joined to the ill Humour of the Officers of the *Bastile*, especially towards *Foreigners*, occasioned his being, at several Times, put into every Dungeon of that Prison.

But enough of this profligate Priest in Masquerade, those who desire to know more of him may have Recourse to the History of the *Bastile*, the many Treats he and others run on Tick for, at Mrs. *Rochford's*, the Expences of her *Irishman*, together with her own high Way of Living, frequenting the *Bath*, and other publick Places, reduced her Circumstances to that low Ebb, as to Mortgage her Houses on both Sides the Water. I am told, she made a Will, but did not live to sign it, being

46 *Some* ACCOUNT *of,* &c.

being taken off fuddenly by a Mortifi-
cation in her Bowels, in the Forty-fifth
Year of her Age ; this may create fome
Difficulties among her Relations in di-
viding the Effects fhe left; however, her
Body was decently interr'd in the mid-
dle Ifle of *Lambeth* Church, on the 29th
Day of *Auguft* 1727.

F I N I S.

Juft Publifh'd, Adorn'd with fine Cuts,

THE ALTAR of LOVE. Being a New Collection of
Poems and other Mifcellanies. By the moft eminent Hands.
This Collection of Poems, &c. is wholly turned for the Improvement of both Sexes. And the chafteft Ear will be equally
entertained, and forewarn'd by a Recital of the alluring Wiles
of the fair Sex, at the fame Time that the difhonourable Attacks of Mankind are expofed, in order to preferve the Ladies
Reputation. For, from the Court to the Cottage, the Affair
of Intriguing-Gallantry is fully traced thro' its moft intricate
Labyrinths. The Tales from Boccace to Chaucer are moder-
niz'd in a fmooth and eafy Manner by Mr. Markland, of Peter-
Houfe, and Mr. Davis's Poems are very lively. The Ode to
Love, in Spenfer's Style, is an elegant Piece. And the Tranflations from Secundus and Cardinal Barbarini are extremely
nice ; and I think our Prudes, Coquettes, Belles and Beaus are
finely delineated in the Ridotto a Satire. And the Progrefs of
Deformity. An Allufion to Lord Lanfdown's Progrefs of Beauty, is a well drawn Contraft. Mr. Bond's Poem on Bucking-
ham-Houfe in St. James's Park, the late Duke ufed to fay,
Would laft much longer than the Building. The Rape of the
Smock, and the Welch Wedding, are Pieces of uncommon Humour. To conclude, It is the beft modern Collection I have
met with; and not to mention the large Share Mr. Pope has
therein, Mr. Addifon's Speech at Oxford 1693, in Defence of
the New Philofophy, is worth more than the Price of the
whole Volume, which is but Six Shillings.

Coffee-man, *The Case of the Coffee-men of London and Westminter [sic]. Or, an Account of the Impositions and Abuses, put upon Them and the whole Town, by the present set of News-writers. With the Scheme of the Coffee-men for setting up News-Papers of their own; and some account of their Proceedings thereupon. By a coffee-man* (London, printed by and for G. Smith, and sold by J. Marshal [sic], [1728]), 40pp.; 8°. BL: 12316.i.32. ESTCT128525.

A substantial octavo prose account of the initial stages of the controversy between the coffee-men and the newspaper publishers that erupted in 1728, defending the coffee-men's position. Tensions between the newspaper proprietors and the coffee-men were long-running, with the former claiming that men came to coffee-houses only to read newspapers for free, while the latter claimed that the cost of subscriptions to numerous papers was ruinous. A news-writer complained in 1721 that 'the coffee-house men have met in form, and agreed to receive no new papers. The confederates in excuse pretend expence, that papers given at first, are not always given, and that some coffee-men are at £150 per ann charge or more for papers of all kinds' (*The Projector*, 17 February 1721, quoted in Jeremy Black, *English Press in the 18th Century* (Philadelphia, University of Pennsylvania, 1987), p. 20). By 1728 the coffee-men were conspiring to seize control of a slice of the newspaper business. On 6 November 1728, a circular letter from eleven coffee-men was disseminated to the proprietors of the coffee-houses of London, asking them to attend a public meeting to address the impositions of the 'news-writers'. The letter proposed that the coffee-men should establish their own morning and evening newspapers, to be published by subscription, and made available to the coffee-houses without further charge. On 18 November 1728, an advertisement was published in the *Daily-Post* further advertising the proposal, and giving notice that the subscription would close on 25 November. On 30 November a meeting of the subscribers was held at Tom's

Coffee-house in Wood-Street, declaring their intention to go forward with the plan. An advertisement was printed for each subscribing coffee-house announcing the plan to publish two half-sheet papers comprising foreign and domestic news. To gather domestic news for their newspapers, the coffee-men proposed to collect 'intelligence' from the coffee-houses themselves twice-daily, using an ingenious system of anonymisation and untraceability to ensure the quality of their intelligence. This pamphlet was probably published in December 1728. The opening eighteen pages outline the coffee-men's complaints against the news-writers: that their news is old and unreliable; that it is collected from the coffee-houses of the town by disreputable hacks; that the newspapers are a ruinous expense for the coffee-men; and that the news-writers profit both from the sale of the newspaper and the sale of advertising space.

The author of the pamphlet is not known, although they claim allegiance with the group of coffee-men listed on p. 115. Internal evidence suggests *The Case of the Coffee-men* was published in December 1728, although the pamphlet is undated (and in the BL copy the title-page is dated in manuscript pencil 1729). It was published by the printer Godfrey Smith of Princess Street, Spitalfields, and sold by John and Joseph Marshall at the Bible in Newgate Street. The pamphlet attracted an immediate reply from the news-writers, for which see below, pp. 131–51. One copy of the coffee-men's newspaper for 28 April 1729, entitled the *Coffee-house Morning Post*, is listed in R. S. Crane and F. B. Kaye, *A Census of British Newspapers and Periodicals 1620–1800* (London, The Holland Press, 1927), no. 1129b (untraced). In addition, there is a four-page critical prose analysis of the first six numbers (*Observations on the first six of the morning and evening papers, publish'd by the Subscribing coffee-men of London and Westminster* (London, 1729) in the BL: Cup.651.e(138), ESTCT13115). Further copies of *The Case of the Coffee-men* are held in Bodleian Library, Oxford University; Houghton Library, Harvard University; University of Texas Library, Austin.

THE
CASE

OF THE
COFFEE-MEN

O F

LONDON and WESTMINTER.

O R, A N

ACCOUNT

OF THE

IMPOSITIONS and ABUSES,

put upon Them and the whole Town,
by the prefent Set of

NEWS-WRITERS.

WITH THE

SCHEME of The COFFEE-MEN,
for fetting up *News-Papers* of their own;

And fome ACCOUNT of their PROCEEDINGS
thereupon.

By a COFFEE-MAN.

LONDON:
Printed by and for G. SMITH, in *Princefs-ftreet*,
Spittlefields: And Sold by J. MARSHAL, at
the *Bible* in *Newgate-ftreet.*

T H E

C A S E

O F   T H E

COFFEE-MEN, &c.

 *Ecessity is the Mother of In-vention*; and a Common Grievance the Parent of a Common Good. Men rarely think to Purpose till they are forc'd to it, by the Load of some present Oppression, or the Terror of some present Danger; but generally lay hold of any Excuse to put off so troublesome a Business, till the Weight of One, or the Dread of the other, leaves them Nothing else to do. Hence it

comes

[4]

comes to pafs, that there are few Inventions, or Regulations, of any great or general Ufe, which do not owe their Being and
Inftitution to fome great or general Grievance; which firft led Men to think of
them, and without which they had never
come into their Heads.

It was juft and natural, for Example,
Twenty Years ago, for the Coffee-Men of
London and *Weftminfter* to confider their
Houfes as the Staples of News, and Themfelves as the fitteft Perfons in the World to
furnifh the Town with that Commodity.
Yet none of them have thought fo far till
juft now, that the Common Abufe in that
Article, is become a Common Complaint;
and the Impofitions they fuffer in it are no
longer to be born. Neceffity has taught
them to think right, and think home; and
led them to the Knowledge of their true
and natural Intereft; which is, to furnifh
the Town with News themfelves, from the
Stores of Intelligence in their own Hands,
of which they have been the blind Pof-
feffors to this Day. They are, accordingly,
preparing to fet up Publick Papers of their
own: And I am very much miftaken, if
the Scheme they have concerted for this
Purpofe, does not foon fhew it felf in one
of

[5]

of the moſt uſeful and entertaining Inſtitutions that have appear'd in this Age.

Nothing was ever more flagrant than the Impoſitions and Abuſes put upon them and the whole Town by the preſent Set of News-Writers; who might have maintain'd their Ground and Credit without Interruption, if they had not carried Matters too far. For the World is contented enough to be deluded and impos'd on, provided the Trick is not too glaring, and People do not ſuffer too much by it. But 'tis the Fate and Folly of all who practiſe and impoſe on the World with Succeſs, that they never know when they are well; but by a wanton Abuſe of the Publick Indulgence, provoke People to fly in their Faces, rip up their Machines, and on the Foundation of Common Evils to promote and eſtabliſh the Common Good.

The Methods made uſe of by the preſent Set of News-Writers, to get Intelligence, and fill up their Papers, expoſe both them and their Productions to the utmoſt Contempt.

Firſt: Persons are employed (One or Two for each Paper) at ſo much a Week, to haunt Coffee-Houſes, and thruſt themſelves into Companies where they are not known,

[6]

known; or plant themfelves at a convenient Diftance, to overhear what is faid, in
order to pick up Matter for the Papers.
By this Means Gentlemen are often betrayed and embarrafs'd in the Management
of their private Interefts and Concerns. And
by this Means too, the greateft Falfhoods
and the idleft Fictions are often publifh'd
for Matters of Fact. For thefe Sons of
Mercury are often diftinguifh'd by Perfons
of Difcernment; and when they are fo,
fome rouzing Falfhood is utter'd in their
Hearing for a Truth; which the next Day
comes out, upon *Credible Information*, to
the great Wonder and Edification of the
whole Town.

THE Market-Crofs of *Sherborn* in *Ox-
fordfhire* has fallen down twice after this
Manner in my Memory: And The *Conde
de las Torres*, at the Siege of *Gibraltar*, loft
his Boot-Heel by a Canon-Shot the fame
Way. The Minifters have been indifpos'd,
and died of Apoplexies, at the Time they
were in perfect Health: And Grants have
been made, and Honours conferr'd, which
were never intended or fought for. Coblers
and Bed-rid Old Women have inherited
great Eftates; and Earthquakes and Inun-
                                        dations

[7]

dations done incredible Damage in Places where they never happen'd.

THE fame Perfons are employed to fcrape Acquaintance with the Footmen and other Servants of the Nobility and Gentry; and to learn from thofe knowing and ingenious Perfons the Motions and Defigns of their Lords and Mafters, with fuch Occurrences as come to the Knowledge of thofe curious and inquifitive Gentlemen. By this Means Family-Secrets are often betrayed, and Matters facred to Privacy and the Firefide, made the Talk of the World.

THE fame Perfons hang and loiter about the Publick Offices, like Houfe-breakers, waiting for an Interview with fome little Clerk, or a Conference with a Door-keeper, in order to come at a little News, or an Account of Tranfactions; for which the Fee is a Shilling, or a Pint of Wine. By this Means Gentlemen in Employment are frequently betrayed in Matters of Secrecy and Importance, the Publick Service hinder'd, and excellent Defigns o'erthrown, or thwarted, by getting Air too foon; or fuffer in the Senfe of the People by Mifreprefentation; not to mention the Lies and Abfurdities, which Clerks and Doorkeepers often report for the fake of the pitiful

[8]

tiful Reward. The Lords of the Admiralty are well aware of this; and seem to
have searched the Matter to the Bottom;
since I am inform'd, there are Orders at
the Admiralty-Office, that *the Fellow with
the Black Wig* be never allow'd to come
within the House; and that the Clerks and
Door-keepers beware of him; and never
speak of any Thing transacting in that Office for the Publick Service, for fear of
that Mortal, and his Fellows.

THE same Persons call in at Ale-houses
where they are acquainted; and there from
Carmen, Porters and Common Fellows,
pick up Matter for the Publick Attention.
There is, indeed, no Harm in this, with
respect to Method; but here, likewise, they
are often *taken in :* For all Men have the
same Spirit and Inclination to divert themselves with these Fellows, when they find
them out. Accordingly, a famous Dealer in
Politicks and old Shoes, near *Bartlet*'s Buildings, often puts in for a Word to the Publick; and makes his Brags over his Beer, that
He has the Honour to entertain the Best
Lords of the Land with his Notions. " Why,
" says he, there is *Jo---s* now, the Trunk-
" maker that was. He says, the Hammer
" craz'd his Brain. He is one of your Col-
                                        " lectors

[9]

" lectors of News. The Fellow now and
" then comes to me for a Story. I tell
" him what I think fit: And the next Day
" 'tis all in Print, as plain as the Nofe on
" your Face, and carried all over among
" Lords and Gentlemen.

BUT when it happens, that thefe wretched Scouts, after running a whole Day a-
bout Town, or neglecting Bufinefs to play
at *Cribbage* in an Ale-Houfe, are not provided with Intelligence fufficient to recommend their Zeal and Diligence to their
Mafters, they fall to work with Invention,
and *Give*, *Grant* and *Confer*, of their own
Heads; raife Armies in *Perfia*, and Hurri-
canes in the *Weft-Indies*; make Treaties,
and diffolve Alliances; concert Marriages,
and inflict Diftempers; *hang* for Love, and
drown for Defpair; tell of Deaths, Robberies and Revolutions, and turn the World
up-fide down; and thus getting rid of the
Bufinefs of the Day, go to Sleep with great
Satisfaction, till the rifing Sun calls them
again to the fame fhining Employments.

ANOTHER Method practis'd by the prefent
Set of News-Writers, to make up Deficien-
cies, and impofe on the Publick, is to draw
up imaginary Accounts and Articles from a-
broad; Letters from the *Hague* and Advices

B   from

[10]

from *Paris*; with ftrange Wonders from *Germany* and the *Black Sea*, and new Difcoveries of Antiquities in *Italy*. This is always the Game when the Wind holds long in the Weft: And happy is he who has the moft fruitful Invention.

A third Method taken by thefe dexterous Sons of *Mercury*, to fupply themfelves with Matter, is to fteal from One another. They copy every Tale that is publifh'd to their Hands, good and bad, without Diftinction; and the moft bare-fac'd Lie, as well as the moft pitiful Trifle, once publifhed, has the Sanction of them all. But every Body knows this fo well, that 'tis needlefs to dwell on it.

ANOTHER Artifice, often practifed by the prefent Set of News-Writers, efpecially in a Dearth of News, or in very rainy Weather, is to rummage old Chronicles, Hiftories of Antiquity, and other Pieces recording Accidents and remarkable Occurrences of Times long fince gone, for old forgotten Stories; which they publifh as Relations of Matters juft happen'd, only changing the Scenes. Accordingly, old *Stow* has been often plundered by thefe Enemies to Truth and Chronology; and Lies of *Geoffery* of *Monmouth* frequently impofed

[11]

impofed on the Town for modern Facts.
Mr. *Eachard* has been robbed of many a
notable Paragraph; and the fame Form of
Words made the Record of more Dreams
than his own. 'Tis not long ago, that *Luther*'s *Table-Talk* was pillag'd by thefe Bar-
barians; and his Tale of the *Drowned Afs*
and the *Law-Suit* acted over again in *De-
vonſhire*. The late Account, in the *Poſt-
Boy*, of a Gentleman who was robbed by
two Foot-pads, as he was going to *Highgate*; and afterwards found his Money and
Watch in the Pockets of the Coat, which
one of the Rogues had exchanged with him
for his own, is related by Sir *Richard Steele*
as the Blunder of an *Iriſh Pad* in *Chelſea*-
Fields, and well known, under that Shape,
to all the Story-Tellers within the *Bills*.

THERE is a Sort of People about Town,
called *Death-Hunters*; who are employed
by the Companies of *Upholders*, to enquire
up and down, and give them Notice, when
Death knocks at the Doors of the Nobility
and Gentry, or of other eminent and wealthy Perfons, who can afford to go to their
Graves genteely, and be interr'd *à la Mode*;
to the End they may apply in Time to
contract for embalming, furniſhing black
Cloaks and diſmal Faces, and other Enſigns

of

[12]

of modern Sorrow for the Dead: And each Company has a Set of thefe People. Thefe *Death-Hunters* are met by the Collectors of News in certain Parts of the Town; and for a Treat and a little Money tell them what they hear: And by this Means the Publick is informed of the Progrefs of Death and Diftemper among People of Condition. But how often is the Publick impofed on in this Article! And the Reafon is a very good One: For there is Somthing fo fhocking in Fellows running about Town, like *Jack-alls*, to find out who is Meat for the *Undertakers*, as juftly raifes every ones Indignation; and ftirs up all that know 'em to cramp and difcourage the Practice by all the Inventions and idle Stories they can throw in their Way.

Such are the Arts and Methods practifed by the prefent Set of News-Writers, to get Intelligence and fill up their Papers: And fuch are the Impofitions and Abufes they put upon the Publick: Always excepting the Publifhers by *Authority*. By their Means the wife and excellent Defigns of honeft and able Minifters, are frequently betrayed and mifreprefented; and idle and groundlefs Jealoufies fpread and fomented among the People. By their Means the Trade

and

[13]

and Credit of the Kingdom are often at a Stand. By their Means the Secrets of Families, and the private Interefts and Concerns of particular Perfons, are often betray'd and blown about the World. By them the Publick is miflead and diftraƈted, and People fent from One End of the Town to the other, and fometimes to the fartheft Parts of the Kingdom, upon Fools Errands. By them the Channels of *Hiftory* are corrupted and poifon'd with numberlefs Lies and Abfurdities; and all the laudable Ends and Defigns of Publick Intelligence defeated.

WE will now confider the Tricks and Hardfhips thefe Sons of *Mercury* put upon the Coffee-Men.

FIRST. They thruft fuch a Number of Papers upon 'em, the Week round, that the Charge of them is more than the Trade and Profits of one half of the Coffee-Men will allow. This, perhaps, will be faid to be no Hardfhip, fince the Coffee-Men are at their Liberty, to *take in*, or *turn out*, as they think proper. But this is little lefs than a Miftake: For when a News-Paper is firft fet up, if it be good for any Thing, the Coffee-Men are, in a Manner, obliged to take it in: And a Paper once received into a Coffee-Houfe, is not eafily thruft out again.

[14]

again. The Proprietors of a New Paper bestow extraordinary Care and Expence to stock it with useful and authentick Matter, and provide it with every Accomplishment and Advantage they can come at; to the End it may out-shine and out-do the old-Standers, and get a good Name and a sure Footing in the World. These Advantages recommend it to People, who still hope to find a good and faithful Paper at last; and they insist on its being taken in at the Coffee-Houses they use. Accordingly *in* it goes (for they must not be denied) and is received with great Respect and Distinction, as a Thing that will set us all right in the Business of Intelligence, and thrust the other Papers out of Doors. But (here is the Trick) no sooner do the Proprietors of a new Paper see it safe in all or most of the Coffee-Houses about Town, and *well settled* in the World, than they strip it of every Advantage, which costs them any Thing; and leave it to stand upon the sole Credit of its Name, as naked and bare of Truth and Novelty as the Rest. They no longer consult the Favour of the Publick, or the Interest of Truth, but their own Gains only; knowing, that a Paper once received into a Coffee-House is not easily dismiss'd: And that a *Coup de Maitre,*

[15]

tre, once in three Months, will fupport its Credit when it begins to reel, and keep it up againft the World. And 'tis plainly a difficult and a hazardous Thing for a Cof-fee-Man to leave off a Paper he has once taken in: For his Cuftomers feeing it once in his Houfe, always expect to fee it again (that is, fome or other of 'em) be it good or bad; for as every *Wit* has his *Match*, fo every *Fool* has his *Fellow*; and every Paper in a Coffee-Houfe has its Set of *Par-tizans*, to whofe Humours and Underftand-ings it is better fuited than the Reft: And if a Coffee-Man turns a foolifh rafcally Pa-per out of Doors, 'tis ten to one but fome or other of his Cuftomers follow it, and he fees no more of them. The Number of Papers now publifhed is therefore a Hard-fhip upon the Coffee-Men; fince they coft moft of 'em *Ten*, many *Fifteen*, and fome *Twenty* Pounds a Year, and upwards. But now the Myfteries of News-Writing are laid open, and the Impofitions and Abufes prac-tifed by the People in that *Craft* are fo mani-feft, 'tis not to be doubted but Gentlemen will readily concur to fupport and encourage an Undertaking to reform the State of Publick Intelligence, and clear it of all Impofitions and Abufes; and that none hereafter will
be

[16]

be fuch Humourifts, or fuch Slaves to *Party*, as to encourage any particular Paper, which has no apparent Merit to recommend it.

THE Coffee-Men, however, don't pretend to direct Gentlemen in the Choice of Publick Papers; but refer it wholly to their Judgments, whether the Papers now exifting fhall *live* or *die*, after their own are in Being : Nor will they offer to throw out any Paper 'till it has been univerfally rejected.

ANOTHER Complaint the Coffee-Men have againft the Managers of the prefent News-Papers, is that they are made Tools and Properties of in the Bufinefs of *Advertifing*. They ftipulate for *News*; not for *Advertifements :* Yet the Papers are ordinarily more than half full of them. The *Daily Poft*, for Example, is often e-quipped with Thirty ; which yield *Three Pounds Fifteen Shillings* that Day to the Proprietors, for the leaft : And fometimes that Paper has more. Well may they divide Twelve Hundred Pounds a Year and upwards : They are paid on both Hands; paid by the *Advertifers* for taking in *Advertifements*; and paid by the Coffee-Men for delivering them out : Which (to make
                                             ufe

[17]

ufe of a homely Comparifon) is to have a good Dinner every Day, and be paid for Eating it. *Here's Luck, My Lads!* Never was there fo fortunate a Bufinefs.

But will People be pleafed to confider who they are that really ferve the Purpofes of the *Advertifers* : Who they are that circulate an Advertifement and direct it to its proper Ends. Is any Thing due on this Account to the Genius or Dexterity of the Proprietor of a Paper? Or is it owing to the Care or Ingenuity of a Printer, that an Advertifement paffes thro' Twenty Thoufand Hands in a Day? The Anfwers here run both in the Negative : And the Matter can only be affirmed of the Coffee-Men. The *Coffee-Men* are the Perfons who do the Bufinefs of the *Advertifers.* The *Coffee-Men* are They who *circulate* Advertifements, and direct them to their proper Ends. The *Coffee-Men* pafs them from Hand to Hand, and make them known to the whole Town. And, if the Coffee-Houfes were to be fhut up, I would ask what would become of *Advertifements?* Whether they would not be driven to their old Habitations, the City-Gates, The Corners of Streets, Tavern-Doors and Piffing-Pofts? And what they would be worth in fuch Situations? The

C   *Coffee-*

[18]

Coffee-Men, therefore, are the only Perſons who deſerve to reap the Profits of 'em. And the Matter is ſo juſt and ſo plain, that 'tis not to be doubted but Gentlemen would readily encourage and ſupport a Deſign of the Coffee-Men to ſet up Papers of their own, were it only to do Themſelves Juſtice in this ſingle Article. But if, by the due Execution of the Undertaking before them, the Coffee-Men will not only be put in Poſſeſſion of the Buſineſs of *Publiſhing* Advertiſements, as belonging properly to them; but will likewiſe be eaſed of the heavy Charge of the preſent Papers: And if, by the ſame Means, the Town will be deliver'd from the Impoſitions and Abuſes before recited, and Publick Intelligence be brought to the higheſt Perfection (and by the due Execution of their Scheme all theſe Things will be brought to paſs) what Support, what Encouragement, may they not hope for from all Ranks and Degrees of Men.

The Scheme is ſhewn in the following Circular Lerter, which was ſent to the Coffee-Men of *London* and *Weſtminſter* the Beginning of laſt Month.

Gentle-

[19]

S I R,

November 6th, 1728.

'THE Affemblies and Meetings of your
' Brethern, the COFFEE-MEN of the
' Cities of *London* and *Weftminfter*, to concert
' Meafures for Reftraining the Impofitions
' and Abufes, put upon them and the Town
' in general, by the prefent Set of News-
' Writers; and for Reforming the State of
' Publick Intelligence in the Two Cities, by
' fetting up Publick Papers of their own,
' are Things that are too well known to be
' News to any one within the Bills of Mor-
' tality. But as the particular Steps that
' have been taken towards the Accomplifh-
' ment of thefe Defigns, are not fo general-
' ly known; and it may be a Satisfaction to
' your felf, as well as a natural Introduction
' to the Bufinefs of this Letter, to give fome
' Account of them, we fhall trace this Mat-
' ter from its Beginning.

' THE News-Papers of thefe Cities being
' grown, within a few Years, fo numerous
' and chargeable, as to be an intolerable
' Burthen to many COFFE-MEN; and moft
' of the faid Papers having little of Novel-
' ty, or any other Merit, to recommend
' them, being only Copies or Extracts from
' one another; and the Matters contained

in

[20]

‘ in them being often Fictions and imperti-
‘ nent Relations, whereby the Patience and
‘ Underftandings of Gentlemen are abufed,
‘ and the proper Ufe and Defign of fuch
‘ Papers defeated; the Flagrancy of fuch
‘ Abufes on the Town, and the Weight of
‘ fuch Impofitions on the COFFE-MEN, put
‘ fome among them upon Confidering how
‘ thofe Grievances might be redrefs’d : And
‘ to that End they invited the COFFE-MEN
‘ of the two Cities to a General Meeting;
‘ and propofing the Matter to a numerous
‘ Affembly of them, the faid Affembly was
‘ pleafed to appoint us, the under mentio-
‘ ned, to confult, for the Common Benefit,
‘ the propereft Means for Reftraining the
‘ faid Impofitions and Abufes, and for Re-
‘ trieving the ill State of Publick Intelli-
‘ gence; with Power to become Managers
‘ for the Execution of any Scheme that
‘ fhould be thought proper for thofe Ends.

‘ Accordingly We, the Under-mentioned,
‘ fo appointed, have had feveral Meetings
‘ to confult on proper Remedies againft the
‘ faid Evils and Abufes; and had once come
‘ to feveral Refolutions, which we caufed
‘ to be printed and difperfed into the Hands
‘ of a great Number of the COFFE-MEN of
‘ thefe Cities, under the Title of Propofals.
But

[21]

' But feeing good Reafons, upon fuller Con-
' fideration and Enquiry, to depart from fe-
' veral of the faid Refolutions, and to
' change the Face of the Scheme then con-
' certed and agreed on, We now offer to
' your felf, and the Reft of our Brethren,
' another Plan, as the final Refult of our
' Deliberations. It PROPOSED then,

' I. That Two Papers, of Half a
' Sheet each, be publifhed on eve-
' ry working Day; One in the
' Morning, the other in the Eve-
' ning, with Portions of Foreign
' and Domeftick News.

' II. That this Undertaking be car-
' ried on by Subfcription : And
' that the Subfcribers be the Cof-
' fee-Men of the Two Cities only.

' III. That the Subfcription be One
' Guinea.

' IV. That the Price of a fingle Pa-
' per be Three Half-pence.

' V. That the Profits arifing from
' this Undertaking, be equally divided,

[22]

' vided, from Time to Time, a-
' mong the Subfcribers.

' VI. That every Subfcriber keep
' a Book; wherein he fhall enter
' the Minutes of all fuch Matters
' and Occurrences, as come to his
' Knowledge, and are proper to
' be communicated to the Publick;
' and fix up an Advertifement in
' his Houfe, giving Notice to Gen-
' tlemen frequenting it of this Un-
' dertaking; and defiring them to
' acquaint him with fuch Events
' and Tranfactions, as they fhall
' judge worthy of Publick Notice.

' VII, That Perfons be appointed
' to collect twice a Day all the
' Intelligence fo gather'd at each
' Coffee-Houfe concerned; and to
' carry it to the Compiler, to be
' digefted and related in a proper
' Manner.

' VIII.

[23]

' VIII. That every Coffee-Man con-
' cerned, taking in an Advertife-
' ment, to be publifhed in the faid
' Papers, fhall be allowed Six-
' pence for the fame.

' Such are the Meafures We have concert-
' ed for the Common Relief and Benefit of
' the COFFEE-MEN of thefe Cities; and for
' Reforming the State of Publick Intelli-
' gence: And fuch are the PROPOSALS we
' recommend to your Acceptance: So rea-
' fonable, we conceive, and advantageous, as
' readily to induce you to embrace and fup-
' port them.
' The COFFEE-HOUSES being the Grand
' Magazines of Intelligence, the COFFEE-
' MEN, by the due Execution of this Defign,
' will be better able to furnifh the Town
' with News-Papers, than any other Per-
' fons whatever.   And 'tis not to be doubt-
' ed but Gentlemen will readily concur to
' affift in it; fince by every one's communi-
' cating, in the Manner propofed, what
' fhall come to his Knowledge as Matter of
' News, every one will have Accounts of
' all remarkable Events and Occurrences at
' Home, with a Multitude of Advices from
' abroad,

[24]

' abroad, that are ordinarily buried in Pri-
' vate Letters; and more Materials will be
' furnished out for History and Observati-
' on, than were ever known in any Nation:
' And Publick Intelligence, upon such a
' Foundation, will be brought to the high-
' eft Perfection; and the Benefits accruing
' from it fecured to the COFFEE-MEN; to
' whom, of moft Right, they belong.
 ' IT would be a tedious Thing to be par-
' ticular on the Advantages that will arife
' to every Perfon concerned, from the due
' Execution of this Defign. A little Re-
' flection will lead you to many of them.
' We fhall only take this Opportunity to
' mention One, as the foremoft of 'em all;
' and that is, we find, upon feveral Efti-
' mates of Expences and Profits, that if thefe
' projected Papers meet but with the fame
' Encouragement that is given to one or
' two of the Daily Papers now publifh'd
' in *London*, there will be fuch a Dividend
' in one Year, for more than 300 Subfcrib-
' ers, as will reimburfe them the Charge of
' thefe Papers, with a confiderable Over-
' plus into the Bargain.
 ' IF, therefore, you are willing to be-
' come a SUBSCRIBER, you are defired to
' pay in the Subfcription-Money to any one
of

[25]

‘ of us, in Twelve Days after the Date of
‘ this Letter; otherwife you will be ex-
‘ cluded the Benefit of this Undertaking.
‘ We are,
‘   *S I R,*
‘   *Your moſt humble Servants,*
‘ JAMES ASHLEY. *Kent's* Coffee-houfe, *Chancery-Lane.*
‘ STEPHEN WIGGAN. *Baker's* Coffee-houfe, *Change-Alley.*
‘ WILLIAM BRAITHWAITE.*Robin's*Coffee-houfe,*Old-Jury*
‘ THOMAS JOHNSON. *Elford's* Coffee-houfe, *George-Yard.*
‘ CHARLES MOLINS. *Anderton's* Coffee-houfe, *Fleet-ſtreet.*
‘ THOMAS WILLS. *Tom's* Coffee-houfe, *Wood-ſtreet.*
‘ LAWR. PAGE. *Will's* Coffee-houfe,*Lincolns-Inn Back-Gate*
‘ GEORGE ABINGTON.*Abington's* Coffee-houfe, *Holborn.*
‘ JOHN MORRIS. *Garraway's* Coffee-houfe, *Change-Alley.*
‘ WILLIAM FEILDER. *John's* Coffee-houfe, *Sheer-Lane.*
‘ THOMAS JEMSON. *Lloyd's* Coffee-houfe, *Lombard-ſtreet.*

THE foregoing circular Letter not being
deliver'd in Time to many noted Coffee-
Men in feveral Parts of the Town, the
Managers thought fit to enlarge the Time,
therein mentioned, for taking in Subfcrip-
tions, by the following Advertifement in
the *Daily-Poſt.*

Lloyd's *Coffee-Houfe,* Monday, *Nov.* 18. 1728.
‘ THE printed Circular Letter of the
‘ 6th Inftant, from feveral Coffee-
‘ Men in *London* and *Weſtminſter,* to their
‘ Brethren, the Coffee-Men of the faid Ci-
‘ ties, containing PROPOSALS for fetting up
                    D   ‘ News-

[26]

' News - Papers by Subscriptions among
' themselves, in order to remove the Im-
' positions and Abuses put upon them, and
' the Town in General, by the present Tribe
' of News-Writers, not having been deli-
' ver'd to many of the said Coffee-Men in
' due Time, thro' the Negligence of a Per-
' son employ'd to do it; and the Time li-
' mited in the said Circular Letter for tak-
' ing in such Subscriptions, expiring this
' Day, 'tis thought proper to enlarge the said
' Time to *Monday*, the 25th Instant; to the
' End such as have received the said Circu-
' lar Letter out of Time, may have Leisure
' to consider of the said Proposals, and none
' hereafter have Cause to complain they
' were excluded the Benefit of this Under-
' taking for Want of timely Notice to come
' in.

   ' SUBSCRIPTIONS will therefore be taken
' in at *Lloyd*'s Coffee-house, *Lombard-street*;
' *Baker*'s Coffee-house, *Change-Alley*; *Kent*'s
' Coffee-house, *Chancery-Lane*; and *John*'s
' Coffee-house, *Temple-Bar*, till *Monday* the
' 25th Instant; when the said Subscriptions
' will be finally closed, and Notice given
' immediately after, for a General Meeting
' of all the Subscribers, in order to come to
' a final Settlement of this Undertaking.

Ac-

[27]

ACCORDING to the Tenor of this Advertisement, on *Monday*, the 25th of *November*, the Subscriptions were closed ; and, a Day or two after, Notice was given for a General Meeting of the *Managers* and *Subscribers* at *Tom*'s Coffee-house in *Wood-street*, on *Saturday, Nov.* 30th, at Three in the Afternoon. All Parties being accordingly met, Mr. FIELDER, on the Part of the *Managers*, declared the Purpose of this General Meeting in the following Speech. I beg Mr. *Fielder*'s Pardon, that, without his Leave, I mention his Name to the Publick on this Occasion.

Gentlemen,

‘ THE SUBSCRIPTIONS for Carrying on
‘ the Undertaking of the COFFEE-
‘ MEN, to furnish the Town with News-
‘ Papers, being closed, the *Managers* for the
‘ Direction of this Undertaking have called
‘ you together, according to the Notice
‘ given in their last publick Advertisement,
‘ to make you acquainted with several
‘ Things, necessary for you to know, and
‘ to recommend to your Care the Performance of certain Offices, necessary to be
‘ done, in order to secure the Success of
‘ this Undertaking, and to settle it on a
D 2   ‘ good

[28]

' good and lasting Foundation.   For the
' whole Care and Conduct of it neither
' does nor can lie in the *Managers*, as
' you have, undoubtedly, perceiv'd by the
' PROPOSALS published in their
' Circular Letter ; but several necessary and
' indispensible Duties lie upon every *Sub-*
' *scriber*, without the careful, constant and
' universal Discharge of which, this Under-
' taking will inevitably fail.

' THE Foundation of the Whole is laid
' in the Concurrence and Assistance of Gen-
' tlemen frequenting the Coffee-Houses ;
' who, 'tis not doubted, will give all the
' Support and Encouragement, which can
' be expected from them, to a Design so well
' formed for the general Use and Enter-
' tainment.   It is not doubted but we shall
' have more useful, more entertaining, and
' more authentick Intelligence, as well *Fo-*
' *reign* as *Domestick*, than is, or ever has
' been published in this or any other Nation.
' We find, that GENTLEMEN already have
' conceived so favourably of this Design,
' that we have no Room to doubt of their
' Assistance, or our own Success, if e-
' very one concerned does but carefully
' and constantly perform the Part which
' lies

[29]

' lies on Him. And the Part, the principal
' Part, which lies on every one embarked
' in this Undertaking, is, to guard againſt
' falſe Intelligence ; to watch againſt Im-
' poſitions and Abuſes by Falſhoods and
' groundleſs Stories, with which we ſhall in-
' fallibly be attack'd by two ſorts of People:
'   First, The vain and frothy Part of the
' Town, who are little ſenſible to any Plea-
' ſure but what ariſes from Irregularity; and
' take a Delight in defeating and overtur-
' ning moſt Deſigns that are grave and uſe-
' ful, it is juſtly apprehended, will attempt,
' as they have Opportunity, to render this
' Deſign abortive, by Falſhoods and Foo-
' leries of their own inventing. Every Man
' will be ſenſible of this, who looks into
' the World: And we ſee every Day Mat-
' ters of Weight and general Uſe, and often
' the greateſt and moſt important Deſigns,
' turn'd into Burleſque and Ridicule, and
' render'd of little or no Service, by the un-
' generous, unmanly Conduct of Perſons of
' this Turn.
'   In the next Place, the Authors and Ma-
' nagers of the News-Papers, now on Foot,
' their Friends and Dependants, will do all
' they can to overthrow this Deſign by the
                                ' ſame

[30]

' fame Methods; and ftudy to get what
' Falfhoods they can, into the Books, to
' be left with every Subfcriber for the Re-
' ception of Intelligence.

'   THESE are our principal Enemies; and
' after this Manner 'tis apprehended we fhall
' be attack'd. We ought therefore to be upon
' our Guard: And the moft effectual Way to
' difappoint them, we conceive, will be,
' for no Subfcriber to allow the Ufe of his
' Books but to fuch as he knows to be Per-
' fons of Integrity and good Meaning, and
' upon whofe Credit he can fafely depend.
' There refort to moft Coffee-Houfes Per-
' fons of all Characters conftantly; and be
' the Coffee-Man what he may, he knows
' the Characters of Perfons conftantly ufing
' his Houfe.   He knows, and puts a Diffe-
' rence between the Gentlemen who are
' *grave, generous*, and *undefigning*, and Per-
' fons who are *ludicrous, wanton*, and *Lov-*
' *ers* of *Mifchief*.   It is, therefore, recom-
' mended to you by the Managers, to be very
' careful to whom you permit the Ufe of the
' Books; and to allow them to none but fuch
' as you know, and whom you know to be no
' way concern'd in the Papers now publifh'd,
' and on whofe Credit you can fafely de-
                                        ' pend.

[31]

' pend. For, if through Neglect in this Mat-
' ter, we are betray'd into any confiderable
' Errors by falfe Intelligence, we fhall be
' branded our felves for the very Evils we
' complain of in others, and the Undertak-
' ing will beexpofed to Contempt and Ruin.
   ' It is neceffary to lay before you a *Re-*
' *folution*, taken by the Managers, in the
' Courfe of their Confultations, upon the
' Method of Receiving and Collecting In-
' telligence. 'Tis this,

Lloyd's Coffee-houfe, Nov. 18. 1728.

Refolved,

' THAT in Regard Gentlemen, who
'   may be ready to communicate any
' ufeful Intelligence by the Canals of the
' feveral Coffee-Houfes concern'd, will not
' care, perhaps, to do it by Pen, Ink and
' Paper; becaufe their Hand-Writings may
' thereby become known, and they may
' juftly apprehend ill Ufes would be made of
' that Knowledge by ill-defigning Perfons;
' and in Regard the Ufe of Pen, Ink and
' Paper, for this Purpofe, will occafion
' Wafte and Expence, and be liable to ma-
' ny Difficulties and Confufions; Two
' fmall *Slate* or *Ivory* Books, with *Slate* or
' *Brafs* Pencils, fhall be provided at the Ex-
' pence

[32]

' pence of the Managers, for the feveral
' Coffee-Houfes concern'd; and on the
' Backs of the two Books fhall be marked,
' or written, in large Characters, the Name
' of the Coffee-Houfe to which they be-
' long: And one of them being left in the
' Morning at fuch Coffee-Houfe, for the
' Minutes of fuch Intelligence as fhall hap-
' pen to come in there, fhall be call'd
' for by the *Collector* in the Afternoon, who
' fhall then leave the other: And the *Com-*
' *piler*, digefting and relating the faid Mi-
' nutes for the Prefs, fhall fet down in the
' Margin of his Paper, againft each Para-
' graph, the Name of the Houfe from
' whence it comes, which he has on the
' Back of each Book, as before. And when
' he has done with each Book, the Minutes
' fhall be rubbed clean out, that it may be
' ready for the *Collector* at his next Re-
' turn, to be delivered at the proper Cof-
' fee-Houfe again. By this Means, Wafte,
' Expence and Confufion will be avoided ;
' and if there fhall happen to be Occafion
' to enquire afterwards into the Origin of
' any Article of News, it will be readily
' traced by the Notes in the Margin of the
' Compiler's Paper.

Gentle-

[33]

Gentlemen,

‘ It is likewife recommended to you to
‘ ufe all due Care and Application, by other
‘ proper Means and Opportunities, to obtain
‘ ufeful and authentick Intelligence for the
‘ Support and Credit of this Undertaking.
  ‘ These are the Things which lie upon
‘ you, and equally upon every Perfon in the
‘ *Management*, to be obferv'd and perform-
‘ ed ; and when I have given you a fumma-
‘ ry View of the Profits and Advantages,
‘ with which fuch your Care and Exactnefs
‘ will be attended, it is not to be doubted
‘ but, for your own fakes, you will do all
‘ that is required of you for the Reputation
‘ and Eftablifhment of this Undertaking.
  ‘ The Profits, by way of Dividend, to all
‘ the Subfcribers, will, if we fucceed, be
‘ very confiderable ; and nothing can hin-
‘ der our Succefs but the Negligencies and
‘ Overfights againft which I have been
‘ warning you. We intimated in our Circu-
‘ lar Letter to you, that if our projected
‘ Papers did but amount to the ordinary Sale
‘ of one or two of the Daily Papers, now
‘ publifh'd in this City, there would be fuch a
‘ Dividend, in one Year, for more than 300
‘ Subfcribers, as would reimburfe them the

E   ‘ Charge

[34]

' Charge of thefe Papers, with a confider-
' able Overplus into the Bargain. But as we
' can inform you, that the Number of
' Subfcribers is much fhort of 300, and yet
' enough to enable us to carry on the Un-
' dertaking in all its Parts and Branches,
' provided every one is careful and active
' in it, fo you may be affured, that on the
' fame Foundation, there will be a far more
' confiderable Sum to be divided: I may
' reckon it, at the leaft, Twenty Guineas a
' Man. But if, as there is the greateft
' Room to believe, upon the Care and Ac-
' tivity of every one concerned, our Papers
' obtain fuch Credit, Reputation and Uni-
' verfality, as to thruft the Papers now
' publifh'd, out of Doors, we leave you to
' imagine what a Dividend they will yield;
' and to judge whether it is not well worth
' all the Attention and Affiduity you can
' beftow upon this Undertaking.

   ' ANOTHER Advantage, which will arife
' to every Perfon concern'd; and, indeed, to
' all the COFFEE-MEN, who fhall take in
' our Papers, is the greater Frequency of
' Company at their Houfes; for a Frefh
' News-Paper being publifh'd every Morn-
' ning and Evening, the Week and the
' Year round, every Morning and Evening
                                    ' will

[35]

' will Company refort to the Coffee-Houfes
' to fee the News. This is pretty evident
' from the Cuftom of GENTLEMEN upon
' Poft-Nights; who refort in greater Num-
' bers, and more frequently, to the Coffee-
' Houfes on thofe Nights than on any other:
' And the Reafon is, becaufe the *Evening-*
' *Papers*,now on Foot, are publifh'd on thofe
' Nights only.

Gentlemen,
  ' THE Managers are not forgetful, that
' this Undertaking wants a legal Settlement.
' They know, that Inftruments in Law are
' neceffary to fecure and afcertain every
' one's Property. But they do not think it
' advifeable to go this Way to Work in the
' Beginning and Infancy of this Defign.
' How reafonable, fure and promifing foe-
' ver it be, they confider it may mifcarry;
' and, therefore, judge it more advifeable to
' refer the getting proper Securities and E-
' ftablifhments in Law, till they fee more
' clearly how it is like to fucceed: And
' they queftion not but they have your
' Concurrence in this Matter. But they
' affure you, that as foon as any Succefs
' fhall make it neceffary, or advifeable,
' they will take Care to eftablifh the Un-
            E 2   dertaking

[36]

' dertaking on a legal Foundation ; and
' to procure fuch Securities for every one's
' Property and Share in it, as fhall be to the
' Satisfaction of all concern'd.

Then was read the following Advertifement, to be fixed up in the Houfe of every
Coffee-Man concern'd.

To the Gentlemen *frequenting This Houfe,
The Humble Reprefentation and Requeft
of The Coffee-Men of* London *and* Weftminfter.

Gentlemen,

' THE Town in general, and the Cof-
' fee-Men in particular, being highly
' aggrieved by the Authors and Managers
' of the *Britifh* News-Papers; who (excep-
' ting the Publifhers by *Authority*) forfaking
' all Regards to Truth and Decency, and
' being only intent on their own Gains,
' thruft numberlefs Falfhoods and Fooleries
' on the Town, and intolerable Burthens on
' the Coffee-Men, every Day ; thereby mif-
' leading and diftracting the Publick ; op-
' preffing and difabling the Coffee-Men;
' and defeating all the laudable Ends and
' Defigns of Publick Intelligence ; The
' Coffee-Men of ***London*** and *Weftminfter*,
                                        ' feeing

[37]

' feeing no Probability of any Remedy for
' thofe Evils from any other Quarter, have
' refolved to attempt one themfelves, by
' taking the Management of Publick Intel-
' ligence into their own Hands; and accord-
' ingly have concerted certain Meafures,
' by the due Execution whereof, a fpeedy
' and effectual Stop will be put to the faid
' Evils on every Hand; and Publick Intel-
' ligence be brought to the higheft Perfect-
' ion on the beft and fureft Foundation.
' But the Meafures they have concerted for
' thofe Ends, being grounded on the Con-
' currence and Affiftance of the GENTLE-
' MEN frequenting their Houfes, and im-
' practicable without them, it is their hum-
' ble Requeft to fuch GENTLEMEN in gen-
' eral, that for the Eafe of the Coffee-Men,
' and the Common Emolument, they
' would be pleafed to favour them with
' their Concurrence and Affiftance; which
' will be done by their Communicating,
' from Time to Time, to the Mafters of
' the Houfes they ufe, or inferting in Books,
' kept for that Purpofe at the Bars of the
' faid Houfes, the Minutes of all fuch Mat-
' ters and Occurrences as fhall come to
' their Knowledge, and they fhall judge
' worthy of Publick Notice.

' On

[38]

' On this General Foundation, and the
' Publick Advices from abroad, they propose
' to publish Two Papers, of Half a Sheet
' each, on every working Day; one in the
' Morning, the other in the Evening, with
' Portions of Foreign and Domestick News;
' and to that End have appointed Persons to
' collect twice a Day all the Intelligence so
' gather'd at each Coffee-House; and to
' carry it to able and experienc'd Compi-
' lers, to be fitted in a proper Manner for
' the Press.

    ' The Publick Advantages, which will
' be promoted and established by the due
' Execution of these Measures, will, doubt-
' less, induce every GENTLEMAN to lend a
' generous Hand to assist in it.   For by this
' Means all the remarkable Events and Oc-
' currences, throughout the Kingdom, will
' be speedily and universally known; since
' there is not an Accident happens in or a-
' bout Town, which some or other of the
' GENTLEMEN, using the Coffee-Houses,
' have not Opportunities of knowing; nor
' a Town or Village in the Kingdom, from
' whence some or other of the said GEN-
' TLEMEN have not Advices of every Event
' and Occurrence, The Town being the
' RENDEZ-VOUS of Gentlemen from all
                     ' Parts

[39]

‘ Parts of GREAT BRITAIN, and the Cen-
‘ ter of DOMESTICK INTELLIGENCE. And
‘ FOREIGN INTELLIGENCE will likewise,
‘ by this Means, be vaſtly augmented and
‘ improved; ſince there is not a Nation or
‘ Country round about us, nor any Part of
‘ the Trading World, from whence the
‘ Merchants, or other Gentlemen reſiding
‘ in Town, have not often very material
‘ Advices, touching Political Tranſaĉtions
‘ and remarkable Occurrences; which, for
‘ Want of ſuch a Canal, are rarely com-
‘ municated to the Publick; but, by this
‘ Means, will be publiſhed with the great-
‘ eſt Facility. And the Satisfaĉtions and
‘ Advantages, which will be procured to
‘ Perſons of all Ranks and Conditions, and
‘ the Services which, in many Caſes, will
‘ be done the State and Civil Government,
‘ by Intelligence ſo ſpeedy univerſal and au-
‘ thentick, are as obvious as they are nu-
‘ merous and conſiderable.

‘ You will, therefore, be pleaſed to fa-
‘ vour them with your Concurrence and
‘ Aſſiſtance in the Carrying on ſo uſeful an
‘ Undertaking, by communicating, from
‘ Time to Time, to the Keeper of this
‘ Houſe, or inſerting in a Book kept for
‘ that Purpoſe at the Bar, the Minutes of
‘ ſuch

[40]

' such Events and Transactions as shall come to your
' Knowledge, and you shall judge fit to be publickly
' known.

THE foregoing Advertisement being read, and the
Subcribers made acquainted with every other Preparation
and Disposition made by the Managers for Carrying
on this Undertaking; They were desired to declare their
Sentiments of the Proceedings of the Managers; and all
of them declaring they were extremely satisfied, and very
ready to perform what was enjoin'd them in the Great
Point of Receiving Intelligence , the Meeting broke up to
the Satisfaction of every one present.

WHAT remains is only to acquaint the Reader, that the
Managers have every Thing, requisite to the Undertaking
before them, in such Readiness, that they wait only the
Arrival of the *Foreign Papers* they have contracted for in
order to go to Work: So that the Town may expect to see
the Fruit of their Labours every Day.

F   I   N   I   S.

*The case between the proprietors of news-papers, and the
subscribing coffee-men, fairly stated. Being remarks on
their case lately publish'd. Wherein The False Pretences,
Wild Project, and Groundless Complaints of that Insolent
Set of Men are duly Examined, properly Exposed, and
thoroughly Confuted; And their Calumny of Abuses
and Impositions justly Retorted. With a Proposal for
Remedying the flagrant, scandalous and growing
Impositions of the Coffee-Men upon the Publick* (London,
printed for E. Smith; A. Dodd; and N. Blandford, 1729),
19, [1]pp.; 8°. BL: 1093.d.61. ESTCT133054.

A prose reply to *The Case of the Coffee-men* (see above, pp. 89–130), which is
here described as 'a stupid Pamphlet'. This pamphlet defends the point of view of
the newspaper proprietors in their contest with the coffee-men for the newspaper business. It proceeds with a point by point refutation of the key arguments
advanced in the coffee-men's pamphlet. It argues that, as men come to the coffee-house for news and conversation rather than coffee, the coffee-men rely on
the news-writers, even though they make their profit from the drinks they sell.
As the pamphleteer comments, '*Papers* mutually beget *Company*, and Company
Papers' (p. 141, l. 40). The news-writer also pours scorn on the coffee-men's plan
to publish their own papers, especially their plan to collect news from the coffee-house. The pamphlet attacks the low origins of most coffee-men, objects that
the number of newspapers in London is not excessive, and complains that as the
price of coffee has risen from one pence to two pence while the tax on coffee has
declined, it is the coffee-men who are profiteering. Furthermore, the newspaper
proprietors complain that in the coffee-house, numerous readers make use of
one copy of a paper, harming their legitimate sales. Finally (pp. 149–51) the
writer advances his own set of proposals, that the newspaper proprietors should
make common cause, and open six coffee-houses near to those of the subscribing

coffee-men, selling coffee at a reduced price and advertising on a sign that 'All the papers taken in here'. Nothing became of the plan, presumably because of the failure of the coffee-men's newspapers.

The text is anonymous and unattributed. The style of writing bears some resemblance to that of Daniel Defoe. The pamphlet was published by a triumvirate of booksellers comprising E[lizabeth?] Smith at the Royal Exchange (who published several tracts attributed to Defoe); Anne Dodd at the Peacock without Temple Bar; and Nicholas Blandford at Charing Cross. Blandford and Dodd were also publishers of newspapers.

THE

CASE

Between the

PROPRIETORS *of* NEWS-PAPERS,

AND THE

Subscribing Coffee-Men,

FAIRLY STATED.

Being REMARKS on their CASE
Lately Publish'd.

WHEREIN

The False Pretences, Wild Project, and Groundless Complaints of that Insolent Set of Men,
are duly Examined, properly Exposed, and
thoroughly Confuted; And their Calumny
of Abuses and Impositions justly Retorted.

With a PROPOSAL for Remedying the flagrant,
scandalous, and growing Impositions of the
Coffee-Men upon the Publick.

Ne Sutor ultra Crepidam.

LONDON,

Printed for E. SMITH, at the *Royal Exchange*;
A. DODD, without *Temple-Bar*; and N. BLAND-
FORD, at *Charing-Cross*. 1729. [Price 4*d.*]

[3]

The CASE between the *Proprietors of News-Papers* and the *Subscribing Coffee-Men,* fairly Stated.

IT is not eafy to decide, whether the prefent wild Attempt of fome of the Keepers of Coffee-Houfes, to prefcribe to the Entertainment of the Town, in the Way of Publick Intelligence, has more in it of Folly or of Arrogance ; and tho' the Perfons and the Projeɛt deferve to be treated with the greateft Contempt, and it may perhaps be thought fufficient Punifhment for them to be permitted to purfue their chimerical Scheme, till they are convinced of the Vanity and Folly of it, by their own Expence ; yet fome few defpicable Folks among them, who want better Bufinefs, having publifh'd, as from a Coffee-Man, a ftupid Pamphlet, (which all the Confederacy have fince avow'd) intituled, *The Cafe of the Coffee-Men of* London *and* Weftminfter, *&c.* for which, as an early Specimen of their Intèntion to prevent Impofitions, they tax their Readers Six-pence, it may not be amifs to beftow a little Confideration on what they alledge in Vindication of their Arrogance, and the rather, becaufe they have long impofed on the Indulgence and Credulity of fome Gentlemen with their pretended Hardfhips from the Publick Papers, to which, however, they principally owe their Subfiftence.

They begin their Cafe with the grand Grievance of moft of thefe Subfcribing Gentry, by telling us, that *Neceffity is the Mother of Invention :* But however true this may be, and however it may intitle the poor Men to the Commiferation

A 2 of

[4]

of Mankind, yet, furely, no-body would have imagin'd, that fuch a Set of Creatures as thefe Men generally are, fhould plead their Neceffities for turning Authors and Directors of the Entertainment of the Town ; and lefs ftill, that they fhould quarrel with the very Means by which only they can hope to fupply thofe Neceffities, and whereby they actually fubfift.

It was *juft and natural*, fay they, *for the Coffee-Men to confider their Houfes as the Staples of News.* It was juft and natural, indeed, for them to think their Houfes Places of Publick Refort, where Gentlemen often meet to read the Publick Papers, and from the Topicks furnifh'd by them, defcant on what they read, and fall into Converfation upon thefe Occafions, which made them confider the News-Papers as an agreeable Amufement, and Entertainment for a vacant Hour, and, in Confideration thereof, call for a Difh or a Dram, which they know they pay for far above the intrinfick Value ; and many Gentlemen, who frequently meet there to go to drink better and more generous Liquor, often lay down Money at the Bar, without drinking any thing, as a Gratuity for the Entertainment they have received from the Publick Papers there taken in. And indeed, were not the News-Papers of the Day, the principal Inducement, and that thofe Houfes are proper Places of Appointment, what Gentleman of a hundred is there, who does not drink at his own Houfe or Chambers, far better Liquor than thefe People furnifh? Wherefore, if it was juft and natural for the Coffee-Men to confider their Houfes as the *Staples of News*, it muft be acknowledg'd, that the Proprietors of Papers are the true and proper *Merchants* of that *Staple* ; and what follows muft be exceedingly ridiculous, That it was *therefore* juft and natural for the Coffee-Men to confider *Themfelves as the fitteft Perfons in the World to furnifh the Town with that Commodity.* I'll fubmit it to the Gentlemen who frequent Coffee-Houfes, what fort of Vehicles the Keepers of moft of them muft make, for conveying Publick Intelligence to the World, and how capable they think they are, generally fpeaking, of any other Poft than of the mean fervile Offices proper to their Bufinefs, and taking a Meffage from one Gentleman to direct another to fome more eligible Place of Entertainment.

They proceed, that *Neceffity* (poor Men! I fhould pity their Neceffities with all my Heart, if they would be modeft, and move in their proper Sphere!) *has taught them*

[5]

them to think home, and led them to the Knowledge of their true and natural Interest ; which, it feems, fome wife Heads among them have lately difcover'd to be no lefs than *to furnifh the Town with News themfelves* ; and that, as they fay, *from the Stores of Intelligence in their own Hands, of which they have been the blind Poffeffors to this Day!* — Blind Poffeffors indeed ! and as lame Managers they will make, no doubt !— But let us examine what they mean by *the Stores of Intelligence in their own Hands :* Why it muft be, that thefe arrogant Fellows think it not enough to make every Gentleman pay Two-pence for what they ufed to fell for a Penny, (of which more anon) and is not the intrinfick Value of a Half-penny, but they think themfelves intitled to the *Converfation* and *Difcourfe* held in their Houfes, and, with equal Decency and Prudence, each is to fet up a Board to inform Gentlemen, that he, the very indi-vidual Coffee-Man before them, looks upon himfelf as a juft, natural, and proper Vehicle of Publick Intelligence, and that whatever they fhall think fit to talk of *among themfelves*, he will take great Care to furnifh them with *next Day*, for their *Entertainment*, at *Second Hand*, after it has pafs'd the thick Clouds of his dull Apprehenfion, and the Refining Fire of his Compiler's Digeftion.

But furely, if thefe wife Projectors were capable of judg-ing of the juft and natural Confequences of this chimerical Propofal, they would have greater Reafon to apprehend, that all Gentlemen of good Senfe and Solidity will rather avoid than encourage thefe *Boarded Houfes*, which avowedly fet out at the *Expence* and *Trouble* of their Cuftomers, and, 'tis more than probable, on the Foot of *betraying private Converfation*. For what elfe can thefe inconfiftent Creatures mean by the Stores of Intelligence *in their Hands*, than that all the *private Converfation* of their *Benefactors* lie at their *Mercy* and *Difcretion* ? They can be the *actual Pof-feffors* of no other Stores, but what they muft be furnifh'd with by *their own* or *Servants* hanging at Gentlemens El-bows, to *hearken* to their Difcourfes ; for as for any other, they are fo far from fuppofing any fuch to be in *their Hands*, that their *Brother Board* is to fupplicate for 'em, that every Gentleman will be pleas'd to *commence Author* for *their* Advantage, and furnifh 'em with fuch Stores of Intelligence that they *have not*, and fo club to his own Entertainment ! —A very pretty Scheme truly !— A Scheme, which, in my Opinion, they'll get no-body into, but thofe very *vain* and *frothy* Gentlemen, as they are pleas'd modeftly to

censure

[6]

cenfure one confiderable Clafs of their Cuftomers, the Young and Gay Part of the World, whom their wife and pragmatical *Sheer-Lane Chairman* faucily recommends (*p. 29.*) to his Brethren to exclude, together with their Intelligence, from the mighty Favour of their *Slates* or *Books*.

It is further obfervable, that, according to this Propofal of theirs, if any Gentleman was to indulge them with an Article, he would lie at the Coffee-Man's Mercy, in Cafe of Inquiry whence it came, whether he would think it his Intereft to conceal his Author, or take it upon himfelf and Partners; for 'tis provided, that the Compiler fhall write againft *every Paragraph*, whofe Coffee-Houfe it came from, that it may be *traced* to its *Fountain* (*p. 32.*); and according as the Article may be, this may fubject Gentlemen to Broils and Troubles, which may poffibly be attended with very bad Confequences; and all for no other End, than to ferve, as it may happen, a very worthlefs ignorant Coffee-Man, who in the common Part of his Bufinefs is *too well* paid, and from whom neither Honour or Integrity is fo much as expected, excepting in the abject Way of his Livelihood.

As to what they alledge of the mean Methods ufed by fome of the Collectors of Home News, to get Intelligence, it may be true in Part; but then, thofe Fellows are eafily known, and avoided, and have often been rewarded with a hearty Baftinado, which they richly deferve, when they take too great Liberties with Peoples Reputations, and abufe the Publick by falfe Reprefentations: But are thefe merry Remarkers to be told, that this does not at all affect with Blame the Proprietors of the Papers, who are ftill more impofed on than the Publick, becaufe they give a *Salary* for *better Advices*, and are often brought into odd Scrapes and Dilemmas by the Indifcretion of fuch Perfons? But thefe Projectors may know, for their Comfort, that when thefe Collectors have been reprimanded by their Employers for their falfe Intelligence, they have declared, that they were impofed on by fuch or fuch a Mafter of a Coffee-Houfe which they frequent, whofe Plea of *Ignorance* the next Day has been their only Excufe to fcreen them from the Wrath of the very Collectors, they make fo free with as a Body: And by this, the Fraternity will be able to guefs, how far they will be obliged to the Difcretion of fome of their own Body, in furnifhing Materials; and, of Confequence, the Publick, how far it may be entertain'd by

the

[7]

the Attempts of thefe fage Reformers. But to refume; Even this *mean* Method, as they call it, of procuring Intelligence, with all its Inconveniences, is more tolerable to Gentlemen, than to have always at their Elbow an ignorant and impertinent Coffee-Man, or a faucy liftning Waiter, againft whom no Gentleman, that ufes fuch a *News-furnifhing* Houfe, has any Defence; but muft be at the Difcretion of fuch a Reprefenter, for what Ufe may be made of his *private Difcourfe*: For 'tis to be obferved, that this Method of procuring Intelligence, is the *only* one they have in their *Hands*: They even difclaim all others, propofing *Themfelves* to fupply the Place of the *Eves-droppers* they arraign. —— Indeed, if a Gentleman will be fo kind, at the Requeft of thefe Impertinents, to turn Author, for the Pleafure of feeing himfelf *in Print* next Day, he may poffibly, if the Compiler pleafe, (who, after all, has Liberty, under Pretence of digefting, &c. to give it what Turn he thinks proper) ftand a little better Chance than that which the dull Comprehenfion of an illiterate Coffee-Man will fubject him to. Upon the whole, thefe People, who blame fo freely the Collectors they intend to *fupplant*, know nothing of the Arduoufnefs of the Tafk they have undertaken, and feem ftill lefs aware of their own Incapacity for purfuing it; and we may appeal to the ridiculous Specimens they have already given us, how well they make good their Pretenfions, and fteer clear of the *Giving, Granting*, and *Conferring, Hanging, Marrying*, and *Drowning* Articles, with which they make themfelves fo merry in others.

I come now to take Notice of the pretended Hardfhips of the great Number of Publick Papers upon the *Coffee-Houfes*; for at laft, all the Noife of their Impofitions on the Publick, terminates upon this inconfiderable Body of Men only, who, with an Arrogance peculiar to them, conclude themfelves *the Publick*, as all the Redrefs they propofe to the fuppofed injured Publick, ends in a Calculation exclufively and avowedly defigned for their own particular Advantage. And here I fhall fhew my Reader,

First, *What fort of Perfons the Generality of Coffee-Men are; and how little Confideration they merit from the Publick.*

Secondly, *I fhall undertake to prove, That the Number of News-Papers at prefent, is fo far from being a Prejudice, that it is a Benefit to the Coffee-Houfes in General.*

Thirdly,

[8]

Thirdly, *That this Project of some of the Coffee-Men, instead of lessening the pretended Hardships, will saddle the Generality with a still greater Expence than before.* And,

Fourthly, *That the Coffee-Men themselves are guilty of such gross and scandalous Impositions upon the Publick, as exceed, beyond all Comparison, the Hardships they complain of, supposing them, which they are not, real.*

And if I make out these Particulars to Satisfaction, I believe this servile Set of Subscribers will appear in the Light they deserve, and meet with the Contempt which they have so justly brought upon themselves by their Arrogance.

The first of these Articles, to wit, *what sort of People the Generality of Coffee-House Keepers are, and how little they merit from the Publick,* might appear a little invidious, if the insufferable Insolence of these Projectors had not call'd for this Vengeance upon themselves.

And here it will be found, That if we except a very few Widows and single Women, and a very few Men, render'd, by Years, incapable of a more Manly Employment, and a few Hereditary (as one may say) Coffee Houses, that are kept by the Descendants of such Persons, as we have excepted, and have the best Title to pursue their Parents Calling ; the Bulk of these clamorous Regulators are the very *servilest* and most *contemptible* of that Part of Mankind which pretends to subsist by Trade.

Many of them are cast-off Valets, discarded Footmen, &c. who marrying their Fellow-Servants, turn into this Way of Business, purely because they can do nothing else ; and have no other Pretensions to it at all.

Others, and indeed a more regular Sort of 'em, are bred up to it ; But from what? — Why, from the Children of destitute People, who at first are taken perhaps at Eighteen-Pence, Two Shillings, or Half a Crown a Week, for the meanest Purposes, and who otherwise must have been, very probably, Japanners, and Vagabonds, till, by a supple and tractable Behaviour, they are promoted to the Dignity of Waiters, and in Process of Time, scraping together a little Money by Vails, and the Bounty of their Master's Customers, and joining themselves to a Helpmate of the same Quality, who likewise by Pains and Care has saved a little Matter in Service, by the kind Assistance of a believing Distiller, and benevolent Druggist, set up for themselves, and become rightful and regular, tho' it seems, till now, *blind* Possessors of Stores of Intelligence, &c.   A

[9]

A third Sort are broken Tradefmen, undone fome by Negligence, fome by Misfortune, who having contracted an idle and loitering Habit of Life, make fhift, by Remnants of Compofition-Money, &c. to pop themfelves, or Wives, or Daughters behind the Bar of a Coffee-Houfe, and fo become a worthy Part of this formidable Society : And from this motley Confederacy, a few of each Sort club together, as we fee, and determine, at laft, to turn Regulators, Authors, and Collectors, Eves-droppers, News-Staplers, Committee-Men, Orators, and what not?

Of fuch as thefe, excepting fome worthy honeft Perfons, as above, are compofed the Generality of the Coffee-Men about Town, and 'tis to fuch as thefe, (for the better Sort have difclaim'd the Project, and laugh at the Scheme and Schemifts) that the Town is to owe the great Reformations of Intelligence which are now pretended to ; and 'tis for the fake of *fuch as thefe*, that the Publick are prefs'd to come into, and encourage this wild Project.

I come now, in the *fecond Place*, to prove, *That the Number of News-Papers at prefent is fo far from being a Prejudice, that 'tis even a Benefit to the Coffee-Houfes, in general.*

All the confiderable Coffee-Houfes find this to be fo true, that we need only appeal to them for the Proof of this Affertion ; where, inftead of thinking there are too many Papers on Foot, they find their Account in taking in, conftantly, fome two, fome three, fome four of a Sort of the Leading Papers, every Day, befides Duplicates of moft of the others, and are fo far from repining at the Expence, that they think it a Happinefs to have Cuftomers enough to call for 'em, defpifing the little mean Manner of the Generality, who impofe on their Readers Patience, with the *perpetual* Refponfe, that fuch and fuch a Paper call'd for, *is in Hand*. And they find their Account accordingly ; for the Number of their Cuftomers, and thofe of the beft Sort, is fo far from being an Objection to Gentlemen to go thither, that (knowing every one may be accommodated with the Papers of the Day) they chufe to diftinguifh a Houfe, where every Gentleman, befide, is likely to meet fome Friend or other. And thus the *Papers* mutually beget *Company*, and *Company Papers* ; and the Mafters of thefe Houfes wifely confider *one* as the *Occafion* of the *other*.

Several of 'em have declared, that they cannot poffibly do with lefs ; and others of 'em have affured me, (for I

have

[10]

have taken fome Pains, upon the arrogant Pretenfions of this Set of People, to prefcribe to us our Entertainments, to inquire into the Matter) that they are always glad of the *Rife* and *Succefs* even of a *New* Paper, finding an Increafe of Bufinefs on that Occafion, which over-compenfates the trifling Expence of it. And the Reafon's plain, for if they fell but 2 or 3 Difhes of Liquor extraordinarily, they are fure of gaining by taking it in ; and one Perfon going away, becaufe they don't, is the Price of the Paper loft to them; fo *great* is the *Gain* by what they fell, and fo *groundlefs* the *Clamour* that thefe genuine Sons of Stupidity make on this Occafion.

It muft be confefs'd, That the meaner Coffee-Houfes, poffibly may find the Number of Papers fome Hardfhip upon them: But this very Hardfhip, is but the *Effect*; the *Caufe* is certainly the Poverty of their Spirit, which makes them decline taking in all, or moft of the Papers. The main Inducement to Gentlemen to ufe their Houfes, is undoubtedly, to read the Papers of the Day, and there is no Paper publifh'd, but often affords fomething curious that another has not : And where will they go to gratify their Curiofities, but to thofe Houfes which conftantly take in all the Papers?— I believe if thefe *fubfcribing Gentry*, to whofe Trade the Number of Papers, may really, as they manage it, be an Over-Match, inftead of purfuing their prefent wild Scheme, would turn their propofed *Board out* of the Houfe, rather than put it up *within*, and fix it to their *Sign*, with this plain Infcription, inftead of the nonfenfical tedious Jargon they intend,

ALL THE PAPERS TAKEN IN HERE;

it would turn much more to their Account than That is likely to do.

This, befides, is what they *ought* to do : They *owe* it to their Cuftomers. It was the Pretence for raifing to Two-pence, what is not the intrinfick Value of a Halfpenny, efpecially as thefe Folks generally coddle and ftew their Teas, &c And in one Difh at that Price, they pay for the Paper in Queftion.

But let us afk thefe impertinent Complainants of the Hardfhips from Papers, if moft of 'em do actually take in *all* the Papers ? How often have I heard an arrogant Mortal behind the Bar, with as much Lordlinefs as if the Fate of Papers was in his Breath, anfwer to a Gentleman that has inquired for a particular Paper, *We don't take it in*?—

And

*

[11]

And I have generally obferved that Anfwer fatisfy for the Time, but the Gentleman perhaps has never given Occafion for the Repetition of it; but, if the Paper be of any Credit, taking that for a Mark of an *obfcure Houfe*, he goes next to one, where he is likely to have his Curiofity gratified : —— And yet this very Coffee-Man, who lofes his Cuftomers for want of taking in the Papers, is the moft clamorous upon the Hardfhip of their Number, when, at the fame time, he never takes half of 'em in! —— What follows will fully confirm, even in their own Senfe, the Truth of what I have here obferved : For,

In *p*. 15. of their Cafe, they obferve, in Terms inimitably infolent, that when once they have taken a Paper in, their *conftant Benefactors expect* to fee it continued; And fo, fay they, *if a Coffee-Man turns a foolifh rafcally Paper out of Doors, 'tis ten to one, but fome or other of his Cuftomers follow it, and HE SEES NO MORE OF THEM.* This makes it plain, by their own Confeffion, that 'tis their Intereft to take in the Papers. —— But here is the Hardfhip, that *conftant* Cuftomers *expect* to be obliged! What an intolerable thing this is, that a Coffee-Man (a *foolifh rafcally* one too, as he muft be that can treat his Benefactors thus) cannot make free with a *foolifh rafcally Paper*, of the Merits whereof, to be fure, he is a *much better* Judge than his *Cuftomers* ; for, as they modeftly obferve, by way of Compliment to the Perfons who *feed* 'em, Every *Wit* has his *Match*, and every *Fool* his *Fellow !* — Was ever any thing fo impudent ! — But, pray, don't *conftant* Cuftomers pay, every Day in the Week, over and over, for the Requeft they make ? Is it not richly worth while to humour them by keeping in a Paper, which a *Cuftomer* is *foolifh* enough to like, tho' the *fagacious* Coffee-Man fees it has nothing in it ; and that 'tis *want* of *Underftanding* only, that makes his Cuftomers defire to fee it ? — No Wonder they treat their *Elder Brethren* the prefent Set of *Home Collectors*, whom they defign to *fupplant*, in the Manner they have done, when the Perfons by whofe *Bounty* they *live*, are thus *abufed* and *vilified* by them ! The Town may expect from this Specimen the Treatment it would meet with, were it to fuffer thefe rude infolent Creatures to be the *Vehicles* of their *Morning* and *Evening Entertainment*.

They further urge, That the News-Papers coft moft of 'em 10, many 15, and fome 20 *l*. a Year.— But does the principal Branch of their Trade, to which their very *Being*, as Coffee-Men, is owing, coft them no more ? — We all

B   know,

[12]

know, as well as they, what even the *beſt* of their Liquors, and Ingredients coſt them, when they buy the *beſt*, which is *very rarely* the Caſe, eſpecially ¡of the *inferior Part* of them, *theſe* 10 *l. a Year Men*, who are the *greateſt Complainants*. We know how many *Two-penny* Drams a *Quart* of *Spirits* will make, and how many *Two-penny Diſhes* an Ounce even of *un-coddled Tea*, or *Coffee*: And I think they muſt be well off, if what occaſions the Conſumption of *ſuch Quantities* of all theſe, ſtands 'em in no more *per Annum*.

3dly, A manifeſt Proof of the Third Article, (viz. *That theſe Projectors are augmenting, inſtead of leſſening, the Evils they complain of, by their preſent Scheme)* naturally reſults from what has been ſaid : They themſelves acknowledge, and make it Matter of Grievance, that it is not eaſy to throw a Paper out that has once been receiv'd, becauſe every *Fool* has its *Fellow*; and P. 16. they declare, that they will **not** offer to throw out any Paper till it has been *univerſally rejected*: If this be the Caſe, What do theſe *Gothamites* do? Becauſe there are already too many Papers, they will add 12 more per Week to the Number.—— For they may depend upon it, that were they all to join in a Body, (which there is no Likelihood of, becauſe ſome of them, and thoſe the moſt conſiderable, look upon the Scheme with Contempt) the Proprietors of the Publick Papers, even ſuch as may make no extraordinary Hand of it, are too tenacious of their Property to give it up, becauſe the Coffee-Houſes refuſe to take it in : —— If there were no Coffee-Houſes, or if the Papers were not to be taken in by them at all, do theſe *Wiſeacres* think there would be an End of the Papers? —— When *they* laid them down, would not Gentlemen that now go to the Coffee-Houſe take 'em in themſelves, and read them over a Diſh of *better Liquor* than they are generally furniſh'd with by *them*? Indeed it will be objected, that in that Caſe, Gentlemen would not take in all the Papers; no, neither do ſome of theſe Complainants; but they would ſome take in one, and ſome another, as they could *match* their *Wits*, as our well-manner'd Friends intimate, and when any Paper made a Noiſe by its Contents, they would in all Probability purchaſe that too; and all this would be ſo far from falling ſhort of the preſent Con-ſumption, that it would very probably exceed it.

The chief, and in a Manner only Benefit that Coffee-Houſes are of to a Publick Paper, is at its *firſt ſetting out*, where they are indeed neceſſary to make it known ; though their ſordid Intereſt makes them take quite a contrary Me-thod, for fear of increaſing their *Expence*, tho' at the ſame time it would probably increaſe their *Trade*: 'Tis well known, that the Coffee-Men generally ſet themſelves ſo re-ſolutely againſt New Papers, that a Paper muſt by Dint of

Merit,

[13]

Merit, or Dint of Impudence, (which my honeſt Friends, who have diſcover'd that every *Fool* has his *Match*, know is the ſame thing) make its own Way, and be call'd for repeatedly, before it can be admitted the Privilege of their Tables. It has been a diſputed Point, whether the Proprietors of an *Eſtabliſh'd Paper* do not receive more Hurt by Coffee-Houſes than Good; and I think the Matter will not bear a Queſtion, for the Number of *Readers* is no Profit to them, but the Number of *Buyers* only; and many a Paper would be bought by Gentlemen, if they could not ſo readily ſatisfy their Curioſities at the Coffee-Houſe, in which Caſe the *Proprietor* of the Paper receives manifeſt Detriment, and the Coffee-Man *only* reaps the Benefit: So that theſe *wiſe Men* may obſerve, from this natural and juſt manner of Reaſoning, what a Blow they may poſſibly give *themſelves* by their *cunning Projeckt*, in endeavouring to turn Things out of their natural Channel. 'Tis true, every now and then, a New Paper ſtarts up, which may add to their Expence; but then, like a Ghoſt, it vaniſhes, very frequently, as ſoon almoſt as it appears: And the once ſanguine, but then penitent, Proprietors ſit down (as I believe our ſage Brethren ſoon will) convinced of the Vanity of their Attempt, each a few Pieces lighter than when they begun: And this the Coffee-Men themſelves have had ſome Experience of, to their Advantage, while the jolly ſprightly *Beginners* of New Papers at *firſt ſetting out*, have ſought to purchaſe by a *Profuſion* of the *Spirits* of *Brandy*, and their own *Spirits*, the Coffee-Man's Countenance; which mean Method has given theſe very Men the *Air* of *Conſequence* that they aſſume on the preſent Occaſion. Another thing to be conſider'd is, that for every New Paper that ſucceeds, the Coffee-Houſe Charge upon ſome of the Old ones is diminiſh'd; for 'tis certain, the Number of Buyers does not much increaſe, but as one makes its Way, another declines, or goes off the Stage; and thus as they puſh one another out, the Number of Papers is not likely to be much increaſed, at leaſt to any Degree equal to the *Braying* of theſe *ſenſible Animals.* I might give Inſtances of this with regard to the paſt and preſent State of ſeveral News-Papers, that have had ſtrange Revolutions in my Remembrance; but as I have no Concern in any of 'em, I am not tempted to ſay any thing in the Praiſe of any one, that may be at the Expence of ſome other. If it be objeckted, That there are, however, a greater Number of them now than ever; I anſwer, 'Tis true, and a greater Number than the Coffee-Houſes in general encourage, (and ſo They ought not to complain of Expence, that don't contribute to it;) and a greater Number than the Proprietors of ſome of 'em have perhaps Reaſon to wiſh: But then is this a Grievance to Coffee-Houſes, who are paid for this very Conſideration, above 100 *per Cent.* for almoſt

B 2   every

[14]

every thing they fell; and this without *any other* vifible **Merit** in Nature? I fhall clofe this Article with obferving, **that** as 'tis probable the Non-Subfcribers will take in their **Brethrens** Paper, if it be only to contribute to the *Diverfion* of their *Cuftomers*, and becaufe they will want *nothing* that their Brethren have, at the fame time that they will bear away the Bell in many that our Politick Dablers have not, (which is another Point worthy the Reflection of thefe fagacious Projectors) fo of Confequence it will, as I propofed to make appear in this Article, *augment*, inftead of *diminifh*, the Evil complain'd of, as to the *Generality* of the Coffee-Houfes, and even to *all*, if the *Schemifts* adhere to their Promife, *to throw no Papers out of their Houfes, till they are univerfally rejected*.

I come now to the *Fourth Particular* propofed, *viz.* *That the Coffee-Men themfelves are guilty of the moft fcandalous Abufes of the Publick, the Enormity of which is infinitely greater than the Hardfhips they complain of, from the Papers, upon themfelves, even fuppofing* (the contrary of which we have abundantly demonftrated) *that their Allegations on that Head were true.*

There was a Time, within the Remembrance of moft Men of any Standing in Bufinefs, that this Important Set of People made a tolerable Subfiftence by felling their Coffee and Tea at One Penny *per* Difh, and their other Liquors in Proportion; and then the Bufinefs was principally in the Hands of the Wives of Men who purfued their own feparate Bufinefs, and who were put into this Way as a comfortable *Reverfionary Profpect*, in Cafe of their Husbands Death, to prevent a deftitute Widowhood : But afterwards, the Price of Coffee, upon a Scarcity, being raifed, they took that Opportunity to raife the Price of their Liquor one half, and fold it for Three half-pence a Difh; and then as foon as the Men began to find the Sweets of the Profit, they left off their more careful Employments to purfue this, as it gave them a lazier and lefs fatiguing Opportunity of Subfiftence;—Juft in the fame Manner, to make a Comparifon not *very much* below the Mark, as the Trade of *Japanning* was at firft carried on by *Boys* and *Children* only; but when the multiplied *Halfpence* began to produce tolerable Opportunities for fubfifting thefe poor Wretches, we faw at the End of every Street, a Parcel of *bulking Rafcals* and *Men grown*, fupplanting the *poor Children*, and with their *Stools* and their *Blacking*, perpetually folliciting your *Honour's Favour*, when they ought rather to have been beating Hemp, for the future Ufe and due Reward of themfelves and Brother Vagabonds.

Thus the Coffee-Men went on, and got Money, at Three half-pence a Difh; but as they always lay in wait to make a *Property* of their Cuftomers, fo, when the Tax on News-Papers commenced, which obliged the Proprietors to raife

[15]

raife their Price from One Penny to Three Half-pence, (which was but merely the *Stamp-Duty* Advance, tho' vaft Numbers of their Sale were ftruck off by it) thefe modeft People, one and all, agreed to raife their Price to *Two pence per* Difh, tho' the *extraordinary Price* of Coffee, *&c.* had lately been reduc'd, which was their Pretence of raifing to Three Half-pence, and one would have thought, might have been a Motive for them to have kept it at that Standard. —— However, fo indulgent were their Cuftomers to them, that not confidering what a vaft Augmentation a Halfpenny *per* Difh would make to their Profits, or if they did confider, no doubt, expecting that no reafonable Expence fhould be thought much of by thofe People for their Entertainment, they readily came into it, and fo eftablifh'd upon themfelves this *extraordinary Tax*, for the Benefit of a moft undeferving Set of Men. —— Here then one would have thought they might have refted, enjoying but too much the Liberty of rejecting what Papers they thought fit, and having it in their Power to prefcribe as they judg'd proper, to the Tafte of their Benefactors; efpecially when their Chocolate was indulg'd them at Threepence. But fo far were they from being fatisfy'd with their exorbitant *Gains* by their *Coffee, Teas,* and other Liquors, that laft Year, upon a Scarcity of Cocoa, which enhanc'd the Value of that Commodity, they rais'd the Price of that Liquor to Four-pence, and fome of them even agreed lately among themfelves to keep it there, but could not prevail upon the reft to countenance them in it, and fo were oblig'd, to their great Regret, to reduce it again to Three-pence, tho' almoft all of them have thought fit to leffen their Difhes, which makes it tantamount to Four-pence ftill.

Thefe Wife Men have further laid themfelves open in P. 17. of their Cafe, where they are pleading a Right alfo to *Advertifements*: They calculate, that by *their Means* a Paper paffes through no lefs than Twenty thoufand Hands in a Day; every one of thefe fpends, at leaft, Two-pence for his Share; and if we take in thofe that drink *more* than *one* Difh, and alfo the *Evening* as well as *Morning*, and *other Parts* of the Day, this Twenty thoufand may be reckon'd at Thirty thoufand Two-pences, at a moderate Computation, befides the *Gill* and *Fine Ales*, which fome Houfes have a greater Call for than *Hot Liquors*; and befides the great Quantities of *Punch* (*Arrack, Rum,* and *Brandy*) which in fome Houfes, is more than equivalent to all the reft of their Trade put together, and in all which they reap an exorbitant Profit: Befide which, thofe Coffee-houfes that open of a Sunday, and Sunday Evening, have an Opportunity
of

[16]

of a *Seventh Day* to the Week, on which no Papers come out, and confequently produces them a clear Gain, without any extraordinary Charge at all. Exclufive of all thefe Articles, I fay, here are Thirty thoufand Two-pences collected, out of which, Twenty thoufand may modeftly be averr'd to be *clear Gains* reap'd by them from the Pains and Rifque of the Proprietors of Papers, every one of which goes through, as they fay. Twenty thoufand Hands in a Day in Coffee-houfes, which confequently diminifhes the Sale, and while it contributes to fuch great Gains to the Coffee-men, affords no more than a poor Half-penny, exclufive of Advertifements, (which thefe Wretches alfo lay a Claim to) for defraying the Charges of Paper and Print; for every Paper fells but for Three half-pence, and *one Half-penny* goes to the Crown for *Stamps*, and *another* is the Profit of the *Mercury* and *Hawker*; and as for the Number of Advertifements which they take Notice of in the *Daily Poft*, that Paper has often eight or ten Partners to fill up the large Size, which that, as alfo the *Daily Journal* affords to the Publick, in 3 large Columns, at the common Price, and which, by the Duty, are a Charge, and no Benefit at all to the Paper. So that the *Benefit* or *Luck*, as thefe Mongrels call it, is not fo large as they ignorantly imagine; and as they'll foon find by their own Experience.

From this curfory State of the Matter, would any body believe, that thefe are the fame Peopie that clamour againft the great Branch by which they live, the *Charge* of the News-Papers? And lefs ftill, that thefe *Ingrates* fhould take it into their Heads to *turn upon* and *circumvent* their *Benefactors*, the Proprietors of News-Papers, who, at their own great *Rifque*, and fome of 'em at *Expence*, furnifh them with the very Entertainment that brings them the Means of fuch comfortable and ample Subfiftance: And whofe Combination in this Cafe is as *unnatural* as a *Rebellion* of the *Belly* or *Members* againft the *Head*? ——— Indeed, the Extravagance of thefe Creatures is the lefs to be wondred at, when their Scheme is thoroughly confider'd; by which they propofe to make a *further Property* of their *Cuftomers*, and even of the *Converfation* held in their Houfes; and accordingly form a *Demand* upon them to furnifh them with *Materials* for their *new Defign*: So that they evidently propofe to make a *Property* of *every Article*, of *every Paper*, of *every Gentleman*, that enters their Doors. Was there ever fuch a modeft and reafonable Pack of Projectors known? efpecially confidering how little the Generality of them merit of the Publick, and how inconfiderable their *Expences*, *Stocks*, *Rifques*, and *Beginnings* are!

I might

[17]

I might mention in this Place the *paltry Spirit* of many of 'em, notwithstanding their exorbitant Profit: The *wretched Liquors* sold by some of them: Quarrelling with those of their Profession of honester Minds, for affording *Loaf Sugar* to Coffee; their pounding *Lump Sugar* for Tea, to pass it upon their Customers for *Loaf*: The *Pay* of their *Servants*, which many of 'em, (that perhaps themselves have become *Masters* by the Bounty of Gentlemen, scrap'd together in their *Servitude*) impose upon their Customers, conditioning with them to serve for their Vails, and even some of 'em *snacking* with the poor Fellows the Benefit of their *Box* at *Christmas*: But I would not be too prolix, nor say every *little Thing* that the *mean* and *low* Subject would naturally suggest on this Occasion: Wherefore, having *detected* and *retorted* their *scandalous Abuses*, and proved every Point I undertook, I will conclude this Article with turning a Sentence of their own upon them, as one might easily the whole stupid Pamphlet; *viz.* —— " 'Tis the Fate and Folly of all
" who practise and impose on the World with Success,
" that they never know when they are well; but by a
" wanton Abuse of the Publick Indulgence, provoke Peo-
" ple to fly in their Faces, rip up their Machines, and on
" the Foundation of Common Evils, to promote and esta-
" blish the Common Good." *Case, P.* 3.

And as they take Care to verify this Observation more than any Set of Men in Common Life, I cannot do better than to address the following Proposal to the Proprietors of Publick Papers, for putting a Check to the Injury they design Them, and for reforming the scandalous Impositions on the Publick; which I only offer as a rough Plan, to be alter'd and improv'd, as the Persons concern'd, who, no doubt, are better Judges than my self, shall think proper: But something of which seems to me to be absolutely become necessary.

I. THAT as the Attempt of these subscribing Coffeemen is calculated to injure the Proprietors of the Publick Papers, the said Proprietors, who are generally Persons of Reputation and Ability, will make it, as it is, one C O M M O N C A U S E against these Intruders, and contribute each so much *per* Share, as shall be thought sufficient to erect about Half a Dozen Coffee-houses, (to begin with) in the Neighbourhood of the most active Subscribers and Managers.

II. That these New Coffee-houses sell at Three-half Pence *per* Dish, the Liquors now usually sold for Two Pence; and for One Penny those that are sold for Three-half Pence;
and

[18]

and Punch at One Shilling *per* Quart lefs; all which may be fo well afforded, that a handfome Profit will accrue, which will foon reimburfe them the Money depofited.

III. That for a Diftinction from the Subfcribing Houfes, a Board fhall be affixed to their Sign with this Infcription, ALL THE PAPERS TAKEN IN HERE; and that the beft of all Sorts of Coffee-houfe Liquors fhall be fold there.

IV. That the fober decay'd Widows of reputable Houfe-keepers, or the ftaid deftitute Daughters of fome honeft unfortunate Families, too many of which will, doubtlefs, offer to the Knowledge of the Proprietors, or may be recommended by Gentlemen, who will take Pleafure to promote fo charitable and laudable a Defign, fhall be the Perfons fet up in thefe Houfes.

V. That two or three Perfons be elected by the Proprietors of each Paper, to be a Committee for managing this Defign to the beft Advantage, and to be re-chofen every Three Months by their refpective Proprietors; and who fhall regulate themfelves by a Majority of Votes in all their Proceedings relating to this Defign: Nine of whom to be a Committee to do Bufinefs, provided there be one Proprietor of moft of the Papers prefent.

VI. That the New Houfes fhall be taken in the Name, or by the Direction of fome one of the Committee, that in cafe of Death, Mifmanagement, or indifcreet Marriage, without the Confent of the Committee, whereby the Houfes may fuffer Detriment, they may interpofe to keep up the Credit of the Houfe: But that no Perfon fhall be difplac'd, except for wilful Negligence, difobliging Behaviour, *&c.* and that after three Months Notice; and the Confent of every Member of the Committee to be neceffary; and even then to be allow'd the clear Produce over and above the Charges of Management of the paft Trade, as a Recompence for their Trouble and Time, *&c.* and that they may be left in better Condition than at firft.

VII. That the Liquors fhall be contracted for, and fent in by the faid Committee, that they may be purchas'd at the beft Hand, and of unexceptionable Goodnefs; and that the faid Committee fhall infpect the Books of Accompt, to be kept by fuch Perfons, and their refpective Conduct, *&c.* as often as they fhall think proper, in order to keep them from running out, *&c.*

VIII. That

[19]

VIII. That the Proprietors of Papers shall reimburse themselves their Expences, in the first Place, out of the clear Profits, with lawful Interest for their Money; but not 'till the Trade is so far established, as that it may be done without Prejudice to the House.

IX. That the Committee of all the Papers shall have Power from Time to Time, as they see proper, to erect new Coffee-houses in such Places as may not detriment those set up on this laudable Establishment.

X. That the Meetings of the Proprietors of Papers, *&c.* in relation to the Concerns thereof, shall be, as often as possible, held at those Coffee-houses, in their Turns; and 'tis not doubted, but the Goodness of the Liquors, and the Excellency of the Design, in all its Parts, will induce many others to do the like.

XI. That such Papers whose Proprietors shall not think fit to encourage this Design, if any such should be, shall be the only ones omitted in the proposed Houses.

XII. That the Persons keeping these Coffee-houses, shall not particularly interfere with regard to Advertisements, that they may be desir'd to send to the Papers; but that they shall implicitely take the Direction of the Advertiser; and in case the Choice be left to them on that Head, that they shall faithfully recommend the Paper best likely to answer the Design of the Advertiser.

I will conclude with one Observation, That so far from Abuses and Impositions, there never was a Time, when the Proprietors of Papers exerted themselves so much, with a perfect Emulation, as it were, and to their very great Expence, to entertain the Publick, than at present, and for some Time past, and of Consequence when the Clamours of these People were more groundless.

F I N I S.

The case between the proprietors of news-papers, and the
coffee-men of London and Westminster, fairly stated.
Being remarks on their case lately publish'd. Wherein
The False Pretences, Wild Project, and Groundless
Complaints of that insolent set of Men are duly examin'd,
properly expos'd, and thoroughly confuted; and their
Calumny of Abuses and Impositions justly retorted. With
a proposal for remedying the flagrant, scandalous and
growing Impositions of the Coffee-Men upon the Publick.
To which is annex'd, I. Henley the orator and the Butchers
[...] II. A Whip for the Post-Boy [...] III. An Inspection
into the Spectator and other News-Papers [...] IV. Polly
Peachum's Child [...] V. The Reigning Devil, or Hell
Upon Earth: Giving an Account of the Women Mollies
[...] VI. The Cormorant of St. Paul's [...] VII. A Solution
and farther Observation not to be nam'd but understood
by those that are Masters of the Art of Thinking (London,
printed for R. Walker, [1729]), 23, [1]pp.; 8°. BL: 12330.
f.26(6). ESTC T19980. Extract, pp. 5–13.

This is extracted from a 23-page satirical response to the paper scuffle between
The Case of the Coffee-men (above, pp. 89–130) and *The case between the proprietors of news-papers, and the subscribing coffee-men, fairly stated* (above, pp.
131–51). The similarity between its title and that of the latter tract suggests that
it may be a satirical spoiler intended to be mistaken for the other text. The first
half is occupied with an account of the contest between the newspaper proprietors and the coffee-men, with both sides subject to ridicule. The satirist notes the

number of new weekly papers of entertainment that are offered to the public, and their increasing reliance on gossip and scandal, which suggests to the writer that the coffee-men's plan to start their own newspapers is poorly conceived. The satirist suggests further that both the coffee-men and newspaper proprietors rely on each other's business: that newspapers both disseminate and produce news in the coffee-room; and that coffee-houses rely on newspapers to attract custom. In this way both coffee-houses and newspapers profit from the circulation of lies and gossip. The coffee-men are further attacked for their custom of employing 'tempting, deluding, ogling, pretty young Hussies to be their Bar-Keepers' (pp. 166–7). The second half of the pamphlet is bulked out with a farrago of miscellaneous news and gossip, concerning, amongst other things, an altercation between the Dissenting minister John 'Orator' Henley (1692–1756) and the butchers of Newport Market; the state of the *Post-Boy* newspaper edited by Abel Boyer; the revival of the *Universal Spectator* by Henry Baker in 1728; London's underground homosexual culture of 'Women Mollies'; and an allegorical reading of a recent sighting of a cormorant (a symbol for the devil) perched on the cross atop the dome of St Paul's cathedral.

The book was printed by Robert Walker at the White Hart without Temple Bar, next to a building famed for its association with Chamberlen's 'Anodyne Necklace', a quack remedy widely advertised in the newspapers from 1715 on. Nothing is known of the author. Only one copy of the text is extant, in the British Library. Although the tract is undated, it may be dated to 1729 by its close allegiance to the texts to which it replies. An account of this tract, and *The Case of the Coffee-men,* is offered in Charles Wright and C. Ernest Fayle, *A History of Lloyd's from the founding of Lloyd's coffee house to the present day* (London, for the Corporation of Lloyd's by Macmillan, 1928), pp. 68–71, and, more briefly, in Jeremy Black, *English Press in the 18th Century* (Philadelphia, University of Pennsylvania, 1987), pp. 20–1.

THE

C A S E

BETWEEN THE

Proprietors of News-Papers,

AND THE

Coffee-Men of LONDON and WESTMINSTER fairly Stated, &c.

THE
C A S E

BETWEEN THE

Proprietors of News-Papers,

AND THE

Coffee-Men of LONDON and WESTMINSTER, fairly Stated.

BEING

REMARKS on their CASE lately publifh'd.

Wherein the falfe Pretences, wild Projects, and groundlefs Complaints of that infolent Set of Men are duly examin'd, properly expos'd, and thoroughly confuted ; and their Calumny of Abufes and Impofitions juftly retorted. With a Propofal for remedying the flagrant, fcandalous and growing Impofitions of the Coffee-Men upon the Publick.

To which is annex'd,

I. *Henley* the Orator and the Butchers, or the Butchers and *Henley*. II. A Whip for the *Foft-Boy*, to enable him to ride out every Day. III. An Infpection into the *Spectator* and other NEWS-PAPERS, without *News, Truth*, or even original *Nonfenfe*. IV. *Polly Peachum's* Child ; its Name, Father, &c. V. The Reigning Devil ; or, Hell upon Earth : Giving an Account of the Women Mollies ; and whether the Clergy pour more Prayers than the Army do Curfes, into the Ear of the Almighty. VI. The Cormorant upon St. *Paul's*, a furprifing Omen. VII. A Solution and farther Obfervation not to be nam'd but underftood by thofe that are Mafters of the Art of Thinking.

A Compound of Madnefs, of Mirth and of Wit,
If you buy you are fafe ; if you don't, you are bit.

LONDON: Printed for R. *Walker* at the *White Hart*, adjoyning to the *Anodyne-Necklace*, without *Temple Bar*. Price 6 *d*.

THE

CASE

BETWEEN THE

Proprietors of NEWS-PAPERS,

AND THE

Coffee-Men of *London* and *Weft-minfter,* &c.

FOR a People to found their own Praife, as being more wife and fagacious than the reft of the World, may juftly be call'd a Vanity, unlefs they can prove, by their Writings, and other tranfcendant Qualities, that they out-fhine the reft of Mankind, and have the Advantages of Nature in a fuperior Degree, which adapts their Minds to Improvements in Arts and Sciences.

Now

(6)

Now as daily Experience convinces the whole World, that we *Englifhmen* may challenge any Part of the Univerfe to cope with us in the Increafe of human Learning, or in Improvements or Inventions of any Kind whatfoever, we may without Vanity conclude ourfelves, (upon Proof of this Affertion) a very learned, wife, and contriving People.

For the Proof of this, I think I could give a thoufand Inftances, without going further than this Metropolis, exclufive of all the Arts and Improvements daily increafing in other Parts of the Kingdom; but I fhall only confine myfelf to a few fpecial Remarks, and leave the Judicious to determine betwixt our Parts and Policies, and thofe of our Neighbours.

It would be good Manners to begin with our Court-Politicians, they ftanding in the firft Rank; but as every old Trunk and Hat-Box can furnifh you with Speculations of this Kind; and as every *Saturday* ftill furnifhes the Town with whole Themes of thefe learned Lucubrations, I fhall rather chufe to animadvert upon our fhining Novelties, State-Politicks being almoft worne Threadbare, which obliges the Authors of thofe weekly Pamphlets to fall upon private

(7)

vate Perſons Conduct out of Malice, under the Pretence of being Publick-ſpirited, and aiming at the Good of their Country: However, this very Article is an Argument to prove that the *Engliſh* are a very cunning People. But to my Purpoſe.

Wit and Contrivance is ſuch a growing Commodity in this Iſland, that we ſee every Week a new Paper of Entertainment uſher'd into the World, with a promiſing View, and glaring Obſervations.

The *Athenians* are recorded a People who *ſpend all their Time in hearing and telling ſome new Thing* ; but what were they in Compariſon with our own Countrymen? who are ſo intelligent, that if an old Woman does but ſprain her Ancle going over a Stile in *Yorkſhire*, in two or three Days you have the whole Account of the diſmal Diſaſter in our News-Papers. This lucky Thought brings me to my Purpoſe ſooner than I could otherwiſe have reach'd it.

Amidst all this Induſtry and Aſſiduity of our News-Writers, one would think it were impoſſible any new Papers ſhould ſtart by way of Intelligence : Yet our Coffee-men are ſo vain as to think they can furniſh the
Town

(8)

Town with something more extraordinary than what we are at present Masters of; but I being a Cutler, invented a Pair of new-fashion'd Scissars to clip their Wings, that they shall not be able to fly out of their own Nests to annoy the Publick with their croaking.

I design'd at first to write a serious Essay on this Subject, and for my Text to have taken the two following Lines out of a famous Satyrist:

With dismal Coffee lo I chanc'd to nod,
And fall a Victim to the sleepy God.

But the Coffee-men pretending they have recover'd from a Lethargy, I shall attack them in another manner, and shew the exact Case, as it now stands, between the Proprietors of the present News-Papers, and the Coffee-men of *London* and *Westminster.*

THE Collectors of News, 'tis true, gather up most of their Intelligence from Coffee-houses; but what of that? They pay for their Coffee, and very often run the Hazard of broken Bones into the Bargain; which I think a sufficient Argument to entitle them to the Property of the Papers. Besides, is it reasonable to think, the Coffee-men should
make

(9)

make an Advantage both of their Liquor and Difcourfe? If their Houfes are the grand Magazines of Intelligence, muft they be the Intelligencers? They tell you a formal Story of the *Publick's being impofed on with Lyes and Fictions, inftead of News.* Suppofe this were true, what is that to the Coffee-men? Were it not for the Follies, Vices, and Extravagancies of Mankind, how would they fupport themfelves? Was nothing but Truth to be contain'd in the Papers, how would the Company who refort to their Houfes employ themfelves? one Story being oppofite to another, affords Matter for Argument, and Argument caufes Expences; otherwife Coffee-men might fhut their Doors up.

Now as what I have faid is undoubtedly true, are not the Coffee-men a Parcel of very filly Fellows to ftrike at the very Root of their own Livelihoods?

A handfome Lye well told makes a good Figure in a daily Paper; and I appeal to all who are converfant with Publick Intelligence, if their Minds are not more frequently awaken'd by a roufing fictitious Tale, than by little foolifh Truths not worth repeating: Befides, the Publifhers of the prefent Papers have this Advantage

B   of

(10)

of the Coffee-men, that they don't pretend
to be such zealous Tell-Truths as the Coffee-men pretend to be; they insert all they
hear, but the Publick may believe what
they please. But the Coffee-men are to
insert nothing that may call their Veracity
in question: Now I leave all the World
to judge whether it is possible two Papers
should be publish'd every Day by these
plodding Fellows, and all the Matter contain'd in those two Papers true.

THE *Scepticks* said there was no such
Thing as Truth in the World, and how
then can they pretend to insert nothing but
Truth in their Papers? It would be more
condescending, and generously spoken,
should the Coffee-men say they would fall
in with the same Methods practic'd by
the other News-Writers; and even upon
this Foundation they need not fear but
their Papers would be bought and read:
But as the Case now stands, I believe and
hope no-body will mind them; besides, the
present News-Writers have a vast Advantage over them; for it is a very idle,
foolish Lye indeed that cannot be believ'd
for one Day after it is told; and Men of
Business, or Men of Pleasure, (of which
the Company resorting to the Coffee-
houses is entirely compounded) never mind

or

(11)

or remember any Thing that is of above a Day's ftanding.

THIS, I think, is a fufficient Argument to prove the Coffee-men are acting upon a very fandy Foundation, and will no more be able to cut down the other Papers with Truth, than they can roaft a Surloin of Beef by the Heat of the Sun in *January*.

IT has been obferv'd, by a very able Divine, that Plays and Romances never come into the Hands of Chandlers, Grocers and Tobaconifts; but Sermons and Divine Difcourfes are fold to thofe People by Wholefale. Now I would ask what all this is owing to, but the Corruption of the Age, and a general Tendency the World has to Vice and Immorality, then why, in the Name of Folly, fhould the Coffee-men pretend to publifh Truth when no Body cares to read it? I thought to have cut and diffected their Propofals, *&c.* but I have other Matter upon my Hands, which is to prove, according to my firft Propofition, that we *Englifhmen* are the moft fruitful of Invention of any People in the Univerfe; and tho' I expofe the extravagant Humour of the Coffee-men, in offering to fet up News-Pa-

pers of their own, and depend so much
upon that Idle, *non Exiſtence* Truth, yet
I muſt acknowledge, however, that they
are not to be caſt out of the Number of
ingenious contriving *Engliſhmen*; for ſhould
I offer to do them that Prejudice, it
would ſenſibly weaken my firſt Propoſition:
But as I propoſed a Remedy for the flagrant ſcandalous and growing Impoſitions of
the Coffee-men upon the Publick, I ſhall
obſerve,

THAT though the News-Writers have
ſhuffled ſeveral Papers into their Houſes,
they have been even with them, Tit
for Tat, and raiſed the Price of Coffee
and Tea, *&c.* which, one would think,
ſhould take off the Edge of their Complaints, eſpecially conſidering, that if we
thruſt ſtill more Papers upon them, they
may ſtill advance the Price of their Commodities in Proportion. We are ſenſible
the Grievance would have been conſiderable if they had not ſo made themſelves
Satisfaction: But here is another Thing
which galls me moſt confoundedly, and
is very heavy upon ſome Hundreds beſides
my ſelf.

THEY take Care always to provide ſuch
tempting, deluding, ogling, pretty, young
Huſſies,

(13)

Huffies to be their Bar-keepers, as steal away our Hearts, and infensibly betray us to Extravagance. This has been a growing Evil for some Years, but is now got to its full Height; and the sly young Dogs the Coffee-boys, when you call to pay, desire you will please to pay at the Bar. This has often cost me a Compliment, which I invented for my Mistress, and very frequently a Glass or two of Ratifee, or Dr. *Stephens's* Water.

THESE young Gipsies steal our Hearts with such sly alluring Looks, that a Man must be a *Stoick* whose Blood is not put into a Fermentation at the Sight of them; and therefore I think it highly reasonable that the Punishment should be petition'd to redress the Grievance and insupportable Abuse on our human Frailty.

THE Impudence of the Coffee-boys is likewise insupportable; for, in Imitation of the real Gentleman, they have learnt the amourous Smirk, the antick Bow, the alamode Grin, and the Dogs strut like an Ensign at a Review, by which they bring the best of Gentlemen into Contempt.

James Salter, *A catalogue of the rarities to be seen at Don Saltero's Coffee-house in Chelsea. To which is added, a compleat list of the donors thereof* (London, printed by Tho. Edlin, 1729), 16pp.; 8°. BL: 1401.c.37.(1). ESTCT100196. Hünersdorff.

James Salter (d. 1728), a barber, opened a coffee-house on the corner of Lawrence Street in Chelsea in 1695, moving after a few years to Danvers Street, where he remained until 1715. He then moved to a building on the site of what is now Cheyne Walk (no. 18). His coffee-house (Lillywhite 352) became a favourite meeting place for gentlemen with an interest in science and antiquaries living in Chelsea, including Sir Hans Sloane, Richard Mead, Edward Chamberlayne and Nathaniel Oldham. Salter acquired his sizeable collection of curiosities by donation: Sir Hans Sloane is said to have given him duplicates from his collection, as did many other gentlemen and men of science. A poetical autobiography of the 'Museum Coffee House' appeared in the *British Apollo*, II (4 May 1709) – where Jemmy Salter is called the 'Chelsea Knacketory' – and *Mist's Journal* (22 June 1723). A description of a visit to Salter's Museum Coffee-house is given in Richard Steele's *The Tatler*, No. 34 (28 June 1709), where he notes that his 'Eye was diverted by Ten Thousand Gimcracks round the Room and on the Sieling' (ed. by Donald Bond, 3 vols (Oxford, Clarendon Press, 1987), vol. I, pp. 251–4). It is not clear how the coffee-house gained its Spanish nickname: one account has the name coined by a regular customer, Admiral Sir John Munden, who was a veteran of wars with Spain; another by Richard Steele because it had a satirical and Quixotic connotation. See Thomas Faulkner, *An Historical and Topographical Description of Chelsea* (Chelsea, T. Faulkner, 1829), pp. 378–83.

There is no reason to think that *A catalogue of the rarities to be seen at Don Saltero's Coffee house in Chelsea* is not an accurate description of the collection, despite the inclusion of many fakes, freaks and ephemera. The catalogue described a collection that included specimens of exotic flora and fauna, royal memorabilia, curious items of foreign manufacture, anthropological rarities, *lusus naturae* (natural wonders) and mechanical contrivances. Nonetheless, some of the exhibits were without doubt ironic: not least '56 Pontius Pilate's Wive's Chambermaid's Sister's Sister's Hat', or '242 Robinson Crusoe's, and his Man Friday's Shirt'. This combination of scholarship and jest made Don Saltero's famous as a place of entertainment throughout the eighteenth century, and as the century wore on, the coffee-house slowly lost sight of any distinction between science and charlatanism. In Fanny Burney's *Evelina* (London, T. Lowndes, 1778), when the Branghton girls mention Don Saltero's as a possible destination for a pleasure outing, it is another sign of their irremediable vulgarity (vol. II, pp. 105–13). In 1799 the collection was sold at auction (*Gentleman's Magazine*, 69:1 (1799), p. 160), and realised only about £50.

The *Catalogue* was issued nearly every year after 1729, with many small changes marking the slow evolution of the collection. The first edition was published by Thomas Edlin, at the Prince's-Arms in the Strand; thereafter the publisher was not stated. The *Catalogue* was sold at the coffee-house for three pence. The precise number of editions and reprintings is unclear: the printing in 1750 was called 'The nineteenth edition', and the last in 1795 named as 'The forty eighth edition'.

A
CATALOGUE
OF THE
RARITIES
To be Seen at
Don Saltero's Coffee-House
IN
CHELSEA.

To which is added,

A Compleat LIST of the Donors
thereof.

LONDON:

Printed by Tho. Edlin, at the *Prince's-Arms*
in the *Strand.* 1729.

TO ALL

My Kind Cuſtomers.

Gentlemen and Ladies,

I Have endeavour'd for ſeveral Years, to gather and preſerve Curioſities, for the Delight of the Publick, and have met with ſuch Succeſs, by the Aſſiſtance of ſeveral noble Benefactors (a Liſt of whoſe Names I have, as a Specimen of my Grati-tude, ſet down) that I can now venture to ſay the moſt Curious may be entertain'd in Speculation : I hope therefore, that this Catalogue may give general Satisfaction, nothing being ſet down but what is here to be ſeen, and that after the eaſieſt Manner, every Thing having the Number affixed, as in the following Pages.

Were I to give an Hiſtorical Account of ſeveral of theſe Things, it would ſpin this

to

to too great a Length, I muſt therefore beg the worthy Donors Pardon for not particularizing their Gifts.

The firſt Donor was the Honourable Sir John Cope, *Bart. to whom and Family I am much obliged for ſeveral very valuable Pieces, both of Nature and Art, eſpecially to the late* Sir John *for the unparalell'd Mill juſtly call'd* Art's Maſter-Piece, *and to the preſent* Sir John *for the* Perpetual Travelling Clock, *the moſt curious of the Kind in the World.*

A Com-

A Compleat LIST of the Benefactors to DON SALTERO's Coffee-Room of Curiosities.

SIR John Cope, *Bart.*
   and *his Sons.*
    Sir J. Munden.
Sir Hans Sloane, *R. S. P.*
Sir Thomas Littleton.
Sir Francis Drake.
Sir Robert Cotton.
Mofes Goodyear, *Efq;*
Edward   Chamberlayne,
   Efq;
Robert Woodcock, *Efq;*
Patrick Mien, *Efq;*
Octavian Pullen, *Efq;*
Lee Warner, *Efq;*
———— Hambden, *Efq;*
Charles Cox, *Efq;*
Henry Ballenden, *Efq;*
Thomas Lone, *Efq;*
Col. Lloyd.
Capt. Fofter.
Capt. Wild.
Capt. Bunfear.
Mr. Francis Elleker.
Mr. Henry Playford.
Mr. Jackfon.
Mr. Lanoy.
Mr. Palmer.
Mr. John Halley.
Lord Sutherland.
Brig. Hopkey.
Mr. Elers.
Mr. Pennyman.
Lord Strathnaver.

Mr. Pratt.
Capt. Hopkey.
Col. Spatfwood.
Mr. Gyhon.
Mr. Guiger.
Capt. Jones.
Capt. Tubly.
Doctor Clifton.
Mr. Meyo.
Mr. Mienfen.
Mr. Bafs.
Mr. Thomas James.
Mr. Bootle.
Mr. Arran.
Mr. Arnold.
Mr. Chaplin.
Mr. Barrow.
Mr. Pennant.
Mr. Blow.
Mr. Cuthbert.
Mr. Mead.
Mr. Merrick Cole.
Mr. King.
Mr. Owen.
Mrs. Williams.
Mr. Bennett.
Mr. Wilks.
Mr. Bayley.
Mr. Warner.
Mr. Barnadifton.
Mr. Owen Swan.
Mr. Sanguine.

A
CATALOGUE
OF THE
RARITIES, &c.

1 THE Model of our Blessed Saviour's Sepulchre at Jerusalem

2 Painted Ribbands from Jerusalem with the Pillar, to which our Saviour was tied when scourged, with a Motto on each

3 Box of Relicks from Jerusalem

4 Piece of a Saint's Bone, in Nun's Work

5 A Nun's Whip

6 A China Nun, very curious

7 Crucifix and Beads

8 The Four Evangelists Heads on a Cherry Stone

9 A Romish Bishop's Crosier

10 The Pope's infallible Candle

11 A Pilgrim's Staff

12 A Pilgrim's Bucket

31 The

(8)

13 The Fryar's Difcipline
14 A Coffin of State for a Friar's Bones
15 A Wooden Shoe put under the Speaker's Chair in K. James the IId's Time
16 Serratura Italiana
17 A Manatee Strap
18 A Female Embrio
19 An Embrio of a Seal
20 Forty-Eight Cups, one in the other
21 Amber with Infects in it
22 Skeletons of Mice
23 A ftarv'd Weafle
24 A ftarv'd Cat found many Years ago between the Walls of Weftminfter Abbey
25 A ftarv'd Rat
26 The Jaws of a ftarv'd Boar
27 A ftarv'd Daw
28. Skeleton of a young Swan
29 The Skeleton of a young Frog
30 Gold and Silver Ore
31 Several curious Medals
32 The Model of Gov. Pitt's great Diamond
33 Several very fine Shells, all mark'd 33
34 Several Sea Corals, all mark'd 34
35 Spider Shells
36 An Indian Crown
37 Guftavus Adolphus's Gloves
38 Harry VIIIth's Coat of Mail
39 Queen Elizabeth's Stirrup
40 Queen of Sheba's Fan
41 Katherine Q. Dowager's Coronation Shoes
42 King Charles the IId's Band which he wore in Difguife in the Royal Oak   43 Wil-

(9)

43 William the Conqueror's Flaming Sword
44 Oliver's Sword
45 King James the IId's Coronation Shoes
46 King William the IIId's Coronation Sword
47 King William's Coronation Shoes
48 King Charles the I. and his Sons, in a tri-form Picture
49 Queen Ann's Testament
50 Henry the VIIIth's Gloves
51 The Czar of Moscow's Gloves
52 King of Widdaw's Staff
53 Queen of Sheba's Cordial Bottle
54 Queen Elizabeth's Strawberry Dish
55 The Queen of Sheba's Milk-maid's Hat
56 Pontius Pilate's Wive's Chambermaid's Sister's Sister's Hat
57 The Emperor of Morocco's Tobacco Pipe.
58 Several Pipes used in different Countries, all mark'd 58
59 An Indian Pipe of Peace
60 Humming Birds
61 A Bird of Paradise
62 A Woodcock's Egg
63 Porcupines Quills
64 A large Porcupine
65 A Cuckow
66 A Flamingo
67 South-Sea Pidgeons
68 Sea Parrot
69 White Woodcock
70 A Pelican's Bill
71 A King's Fisher

72 A

(10)

72 A Soland Goose
73 An Albetrofs
74 An Oftridge's Leg
75 Oitridge's Eggs
76 Mango Birds Neft
77 A large Indian Batt
78 The Head of an Indian Crow,
79 The Head of a Cormorant
80 The Head of an Egyptian Hen
81 A Buftard
82 The Claw of an Eagle
83 Ruffs and Rhees
84 A Chinefe Pincufhion, finely wrought
    with Figures
85 A little Sultanefs
86 A Chinefe Almanack
87 Book wrote in Chinefe Characters
88 A Chinefe Dodgin
89 A Chinefe Knife and Fork
90 A Chin. Waftcoat to prevent fweating
91 A Chinefe Idol
92 A Camelion
93 A fmall Pair of Horns, and feveral fmall
    Legs of Guinea Deers
94 Serpents Tongues
95 Black Scorpions
96 White Scorpions
97 Centipes
98 Young Frog in a Tobacco-ftopper
99 The Back-bone of a Rattle Snake
100 A Claw
101 A Salamander

102 A

(11)

102 A Root of a Tree in the Shape of a Hog
103 A white Rat
104 The Scalp of a Buffalo
105 A Crocodile
106 A Snail Drake
107 Ball of Hair taken out of the Maws
   of Oxen and Calves, all mark'd 107
108 A large Pair of Buck's Horns
109 The Leg of an Elk
110 The Claw of a Ruffia Bear
111 A white Mole
112 Tusks of a wild Boar
113 The Head and Paws of a large Tyger
114 An Antelope's Horn
115 A Sea Unicorn's Horn, feven Feet and a
   half in Length
116 An Elephant's Ear and Teeth
117 An Elephant's Tail
118 Rattle Snake 10 Feet and a half in Length
119 Rattle Snakes, all mark'd 119
120 A Cockatrice Serpent
121 A young Leopard
122 A Gallo Wafp
123 A Bever
124 The Horns of a Shamway.
125 The fore and hind Paw of a large Seal
126 Rhinocero's Horns
127 Tarantulas
128 A flying Squirrel
129 Rattles of Snakes feveral, all mark'd 129
130 A large Worm that eats into the Keel of
   Ships in the Weft-Indies

131 A

(12)

131 A Piece of Worm-eaten Keel
132 The Rhinoceros Fly
133 A Stag Fly
134 Piece of Wood not to be confumed in Fire
135 Piece of the Asbeftus Stone
136 A Piece of Solomon's Temple
137 A Piece of the Briftol Rock
138 Several Petrefied Pieces
139 A petrefied Child, or the Figure of Death
140 Petrefiéd Plumbs and Olives
141 The Effigies of an Egyptian Mummy
142 The Hand of an Egyptian Mummy
143 Several Plumb-ftones, mark'd 143
144 Cocoa Nuts
145 Mufcovy Snuff-box made of an Elk's Hoof
146 A curious Snuff-box, adorned with Mother
      of Pearl Figures
147 Highlander's Snuff-box
148 A Gyant's Tooth
149 Caffada Bread
150 The Belts of Wampum, Indian Money
151 Indian Spoon of equal Weight with Gold
152 Indian Bows and Arrows, all mark'd 152
153 Indian Tammahacks, all mark'd 153
154 Calabafh very large : This is part of the
      Indians Food
155 Several of a fmaller fort, all mark'd 155
156 A Gurgulet that the Indians cool their
      Water with
157 Spanifh Golila or Band
158 Cedar Apple, gathered on Mount Libanus
                                    159 The

(13)

159 The Bark of a Tree, which when drawn appears like fine Lace
160 A Fan made of an Indian Leaf of a Tree
161 Indian Pouches
162 American Bags for the Hair
163 Moſcow Gloves
164 Turky Quivers for Arrows
165 A Micolet's Shoes
166 A Turkiſh Piſtol
167 A Turkiſh Fan
168 Indian Weapons
169 Shoes, Stockings, and Sandals, all uſed in diverſe Countries, mark'd 169
170 Terrapins
171 Indian Ornaments
172 A Swediſh Man of War
173 Indian Purſes
174 A Piſtol with four Boxes, taken from the French at the Siege of Namure
175 An Iſraelitiſh Shekel
176 A Braſs Cremona Violin
177 A Sea Turtle as it came out of the Egg
178 A ſmall Sea Hedgehog
179 Sea Horſes
180 A little Whale
181 A very ſmall Saw of a Fiſh and ſeveral larger, all mark'd 181
182 A curious Ball of Fiſh Bones found near Plymouth
183 A Whale's Pizzle
184 Tusks of Sea-Horſes
185 Sea Woolf

186 Sea-

(14)

186 Sea-Feathers feveral, all mark'd 186
187 A Star Fifh
188 Sword-Fifh and the Saw-Fifh, great Ene-
    mies to the Whale
189 Sea Porcupine
190 A Lanthorn Fifh
191 A Guoanna
192 An enamell'd Lobfter
193 Sea Armodilla
194 An Otter
195 A Toad-fifh
196 Sea Turtle
197 Sucking Fifh
198 King Crab
199 Large Porpoife's Head
200 Cuckold Fifh
201 A Mufcle-fhell from Port-Mahon, two
    Feet long
202 A Shark's Jaw, with 280 Teeth
203 Head of a Rackoon
204 A large Lobfter's Claw
205 A large Otter
206 Tail of a Dolphin
207 One Joint of a Whale's Back-bone
208 Large Alligator and her Eggs
209 King Crab
210 Bull Fifh
211 A John Doree
212 Jaws of a large Shark
213 The Mermaid Fifh
214 Quick a Hatch
215 Gonanna

216 Sea

(15)

216 Sea Turtle
217 Mola Fish
218 Milstone Fish
219 Armadilla
220 A Dolphin, with a Flying-Fish hanging
    at his Mouth
221 A young Shark
222 Lump-Fish
223 A Sea Hedgehog
224 Little Lobster
225 Sea-horse's Pissle that they make Cramp-
    rings of
226 Remora Fish
227 Spun Glass
228 A Reel in a Bottle
229 A Wooden Clock, with a Man a mowing
    the Grass from the Top
230 A Travelling Clock, that is 36 Hours,
    scending a little Hill
231 A Staffordshire Almanack
232 A perpetual Almanack
233 Lances all mark'd 233
234 Fish-weapons all mark'd 234
235 Swords and Daggers
236 A Flea-Trap
237 A curious Mouse-Trap
238 A Pair of Brashalls to play at Balloon
239 A Cannibal's Habit
240 Model of a Canoe
241 Some of the Cannibal's Dishes
242 Robinson Crusoe's, and his Man Friday's
    Shirt

243 The

(16)

243 The Ladle they ufed to eat Broth with
244 A Gourd
245 Locuft Beans
246 A Reel in a Bottle
247 King Henry the VIIIth's Spurs
248 The Rattle of a Rattle Snake, with 27 Joints
249 A Sheet of Paper from China twelve Foot long, and four Foot and a half broad

F I N I S.

Anthony Hilliar, *A Brief and Merry History of Great Britain, Containing an Account of the Religions, Customs, Manners, Humours, Characters, Caprice, Contrasts, Foibles, Factions &c., of the People. Written originally in Arabic by Ali-Mohammed Hadgi, Physician to his Excellency Cossem Hojah, late Envoy from the Government of Tripoli, in South Barbery, to this Court. Faithfully render'd into English by Mr Anthony Hilliar, Translator of the Oriental Languages* (London, J. Roberts, J. Shuckburgh, J. Penn and J. Jackson, [1730]), [iv], 52pp.; 8°. BL: T.857.(4). ESTC T106120. Extract, pp. 21–4. Hünersdorff.

Hilliar's *A Brief and Merry History of Great Britain* is a mock travel journal, satirising the forms and excesses of London life from the point of view of a fictional Ottoman physician, Ali Mohammed Hadgi, who is described as visiting London attached to the embassy of the government of Tripoly in South Barbary. The title announces that the story he relates is a 'brief and merry history', a code phrase which signals the work's allegiance to the genre of urban ramble literature made famous by Ned Ward and Tom Brown. The device of the oriental narrator was derived from the older spy tradition, of which *The Turkish Spy* (London, 1691–1718) is the most famous, and of which the *Persian Letters* (1721; trans. by Ozell, 2 vols (London, J. Tonson, 1722)) of Montesquieu (1689–1755) was the most recent example to gain renown. In his remarks on translation in the 'Preface', Hilliar plagiarises from the preface 'To the Reader' in volume six of *The Turkish Spy* (first published 1693), p. [vi]. In the *Turkish Spy* model, a fictional alien develops a sharp satire on occidental life and manners by drawing a contrast between the two cultures, identifying the ways in which Ottoman life is superior or more civilised. The writing itself has a structural irony, and makes use of techniques of defamiliarisation to render the reader's everyday life strange and surprising.

In this extract, Hilliar's Hadgi describes the coffee-houses of London, which he finds much less attractive than the English believe them to be. His account organises the coffee-houses according to their typical clientele, marking their characters onto the geography of the city. This topography of London coffee-houses is iconic rather than descriptive: he ascribes to each coffee-house a totalising and characteristic sociability, and exemplifies each place with a snatch of jargon emblematic of the discussions there. Each of these terms, almost incomprehensible to outsiders, is arranged so as to form a mini-narrative: a satire on the incomprehensible nature of urban life.

Nothing is known of the author, who appears not to have published anything else (and may be a pseudonym). The volume was published by a quadripartite of booksellers: J. Jackson, St James's Street; John Penn, Westminster Hall; James Roberts, Warwick Lane; and John Shuckburgh, Fleet Street, and seems to have been printed by Henry Woodfall (the ornaments in the volume are those used by him). It was reprinted in Dublin by James Hoey in 1730.

A Brief and Merry

HISTORY

OF

GREAT BRITAIN:

CONTAINING

An ACCOUNT of the Religions,
Cuſtoms, Manners, Humours, Chaꞌacters,
Caprice, Contraſts, Foibles, Factions,
&c. of the People.

Written Originally in *Arabick,*

By ALI MOHAMMED HADGI,

Phyſician to his Excellency COSSEM HOJAH,
late Envoy from the Government of *Tripoli,*
in *South-Barbary,* to this Court.

Faithfully render'd into *Engliſh*

By Mr. *ANTHONY HILLIAR,*

Tranſlator of the ORIENTAL Languages.

To which are prefix'd, the Effigies of the Author,
Curiouſly Engraven on Copper.

LONDON:

Printed for J. ROBERTS, near the *Oxford-Arms* in *Warwick-
Lane*; J. SHUCKBURGH, between the two *Temple-Gates,
Fleetſtreet*; J. JACKSON, near *St. James's-Houſe*; J. PENN,
in *Weſtminſter-Hall*; and Sold by the Bookſellers of *London* and *Weſtminſter.*

(Price One Shilling.)

[21]

There's a prodigious Number of Coffee-Houfes in *London*, after the manner I have feen fome in *Conftantinople*. The Outfides have nothing remarkable or worth defcribing, fo that I'll fpeak only of their Cuftoms, which deferve fome Notice, becaufe moft of the Men refort to them to pafs away the Time. Thefe Coffee-Houfes are the conftant Rendezvous for Men of Bufinefs, as well as the idle People, fo that a Man is fooner ask'd about his Coffee-Houfe than his Lodgings. Befides
Coffee,

[22]

Coffee, there are many other Liquors, which
People cannot well relish at first.   They smoak
Tobacco, game and read Papers of Intelligence : here they treat of Matters of State,
make Leagues with Foreign Princes, break
them again, and transact Affairs of the last
Consequence to the whole World.   In a word,
'tis here the *English* discourse freely of every
thing, and where they may in a very little
time be known ; their Character likewise may
be partly discovered, even by People that are
Strangers to the Language, if they appear
cool in their Discourses, and attentive to
what they hear.   They represent these Coffee-
Houses as the most agreeable Things in *London*,
and they are, in my Opinion, very proper
Places to find People that a Man has Business
with, or to pass away the Time a little more
agreeably than he can do at home ; but in o-
ther respects they are loathsome, full of Smoak,
like a Guard-Room, and as much crowded.
I believe 'tis these Places that furnish the Inhabitants with Slander, for there one hears
exact Accounts of every thing done in Town,
as if it were but a Village.

  At those Coffee-Houses near the Court,
called *White's, St. James's, Williams's,* the Conversation turns chiefly upon *Equipages, Essence,
Horse-Matches, Tupees, Modes, Mortgages* and
Maidenheads ; the *Cocoa-Tree* upon *Bribery* and
Corruption, Evil-Ministers, Errors and *Mistakes
in Government* ; the *Scotch* Coffee-Houses, towards *Charing-Cross,* on *Places* and *Pensions* ;
the *Tilt-yard* and *Young-man's* on *Affronts, Honour, Satisfaction, Duels* and *Rencounters.*   I was
informed that the latter happen so frequently,
in

[23]

in this part of the Town, that a *Surgeon* and
a *Sollicitor* are kept conftantly in waiting ; the
one to drefs and heal fuch Wounds as may
be given, and the other in cafe of Death to
bring off the Survivor with a Verdict of *Se
Defendendo* or *Manflaughter*. In thofe Coffee-
Houfes about the *Temple*, the Subjects are generally on *Caufes, Cofts, Claps, Demurrers, Rejoinders, Salivations,* and *Exceptions* ; *Daniel's*,
the *Welch* Coffee-Houfe in *Fleet-ftreet*, on *Births,
Pedigrees* and *Defcents* ; *Child's* and the *Chapter*
upon *Glebes, Tythes, Advowfons, Rectories,* and
Lecturefhips ; *North's, Undue Elections, Falfe-
Polling, Scrutinies,* &c. *Hamlin's, Infant-Baptifm,
Lay-Ordination, Free-will, Election,* and *Reproba-
tion* ; *Batfon's* the Prices of *Pepper, Indigo,* and
Salt-Petre ; and all thofe about the *Exchange*,
where the Merchants meet to tranfact their
Affairs, are in a perpetual hurry about *Stock-
Jobbing, Lying, Cheating, Tricking Widows* and
Orphans, and committing Spoil and Rapine on
the Publick.

In *London* and its Suburbs, they have about
threefcore Taverns to one Parifh Church; the
Mafters of them are generally more intent on
the *Strength* of their *Tables* and Chairs, than
that of their *Wines*, which are contrived fo
for more *fociable Entertainments*, and they often-
times procure their Guefts a great many very
painful Stools.

In the Evenings the Women pafs thro' the
chief Streets in Shoals, like Mackrel in hot
Seafons; and affociating themfelves with vicious Men, hurry into thefe Taverns in Pairs
and Couples, Male and Female, that a Perfon
unacquainted with this Cuftom, would imagine

3

[24]

gine they were apprehenfive of a fecond De-
luge. They acknowledge themfelves obliged
to the *French* for a very modifh *Diftemper* that
attends their Venereal Exceffes; the Youths
of the *Army* and the *Law*, are generally pretty
much affected with it, fome of whom I obferved, that have fcarce arrived to Maturity,
hardly able to hold a Pair of Colours, or fairly
march from one Guard to another ; and one
time a Man bearing a large Burthen on his
Body, paffing haftily through *Weftminfter-Hall*,
amidft a Crowd of young Lawyers, unhappily
beat about fourteen of them to the Ground,
by a flight Joftle ; a melancholly and afflicting
Sight to the Beholders !

The Life and Character of Moll King, late mistress of King's Coffee-house in Covent-garden. Who departed this Life at her Country-House at Hampstead, on Thursday the 17th of September, 1747. Containing a true narrative of this well-known Lady, from her Birth to her Death; wherein is inserted several humorous Adventures relating to Persons of both Sexes, who were fond of nocturnal Revels. Also The Flash Dialogue between Moll King and Old Gentleman Harry, that was some Years ago murdered in Covent-Garden; and the Pictures of several noted Family Men, drawn to the Life. To the Whole is added, an Epitaph and Elegy, wrote by one of Moll's favourite Customers. And a Key to the Flash Dialogue (London, printed for W. Price, near the Sessions-House in the Old Baily, [1747]), 24pp.; 8°. BL: C.133.dd.7. ESTC125312. Hünersdorff.

The Life and Character of Moll King is a coffee-woman's biography, a subgenre of the prostitute's biography. The book narrates the history of Mary or Moll King (1696–1747), later known as Mary Hoffe, an actual person, although some aspects of the narrative may be exaggerated or fictional. The text also offers an ironic description of the language encountered in vulgar coffee-houses, especially that variety of criminals' cant called 'flash'. According to the *Life and Character*, Moll was arrested more than twenty times by the magistrates under Sir John Gonson for running a disorderly house, but she successfully evaded conviction by exploiting a loophole in the law. Prostitutes who met with their clients at her house went elsewhere for sex; and as her coffee-house had no beds in it other than Moll and Tom's own, it could not be a brothel. Nonetheless, Moll was frequently indicted for offences at the Middlesex quarter sessions (see Helen Berry, 'Rethinking Politeness in Eighteenth Century England: Moll King's coffee house and the significance of "Flash Talk"', *Transactions of the Royal Historical Society*, 6th series, XI (2001), pp. 65–82; and Markman Ellis, 'The coffee-women, *The Spectator* and the public sphere in the early-eighteenth century', in *Women and the Public Sphere*, ed. by Elizabeth Eger and Charlotte Grant (Cambridge, Cambridge University Press, 2001), pp. 27–52).

Coffee-women's biographies (see also *The Velvet Coffee-woman*, above, pp. 39–88) identify the coffee-house as the location of a distinct urban sociability: coarse, secretive, and transgressive – a long way from the polite urbanity of the coffee-house in the Spectatorial model. In the coffee-woman's biography, the coffee-house attracts a clientele that is heterosexual, freely mixing distinct social classes, counter-hierarchical, disorderly and vulgar. Moll King's Coffee-house was one of the most notorious houses of entertainment in London. It spawned a number of satires, verses and prose fictions describing its distinct sociability and cultural allegiance: *Tom K—g's; or the Paphian Grove ... A mock-heroic-poem in three cantos* (London, 1738); *The highlanders salivated, or the loyal association of M—ll K—g's midnight club: with the serious address of the ladies of Drury, to the batter'd strolling nymphs of their community* (London, M. Cooper, 1746); *Covent Garden in Mourning, A Mock-Heroick Poem. Containing some Memoirs of the Late Celebrated Moll King* (London, B. Dickinson, 1747). It was also mentioned in several subsequent novels, verses and comedies: *Marriage-a-la-Mode: an Humorous Tale, in Six Canto's, in Hudibrastic Verse* (London, Weaver Bickerton, 1746); Tobias Smollett's *Roderick Random* (1748) and *Peregrine Pickle* (1751); and Henry Fielding's *The Coffee-house Politician; or, The Justice Caught in His Own Trap. A comedy* (London, printed for J. Watts, 1730).

Nothing is known of the writer. Little is known about the publisher, W. Price, a bookseller who published three scandalous criminal biographies 1747–8, and who claimed here to keep shop near the Sessions-House in the Old Bailey, the criminal court erected next to Newgate Prison. The ESTC lists only two surviving copies of this tract, one at the British Library, and the other at the Bancroft Library, University of California, Berkeley.

THE
LIFE *and* CHARACTER

OF

MOLL KING,

Late Mistress of KING's Coffee-House in *Covent-Garden,*

Who departed this Life at her Country-House at *Hampstead,* on *Thursday* the 17th of *September,* 1747.

CONTAINING

A true NARRATIVE of this well-known Lady, from her Birth to her Death; wherein is inserted several humorous Adventures relating to Persons of both Sexes, who were fond of nocturnal Revels.

ALSO

The FLASH DIALOGUE between *Moll King* and Old *Gentleman Harry,* that was some Years ago murdered in *Covent-Garden;* and the Pictures of several noted *Family Men,* drawn to the Life.

To the Whole is added,

An EPITAPH and ELEGY, wrote by one of *MOLL*'s favourite Customers.

And a KEY to the *Flash Dialogue.*

LONDON:

Printed for W. PRICE, near the *Sessions-House* in the *Old Baily.* Price Three-pence.

(3)

THE
LIFE, &c.
OF
MOLL KING.

 HERE is no need of make-
ing any Apology for fending
this little Tract into the
World, fince the Perfon who is
the Subject of it was fo univerfally known, efpecially to both
the Sexes who were fond of nightly Recreations.

We fhall begin with *Moll*'s Birth, which was
in the Year 1696, in a Garret in *Vine-ftreet*, in
the Parifh of St. *Giles in the Fields*, in *Mid-
dlefex*, where her Father followed the Bufi-

A 2

nefs

(4)

neſs of a *Shoemaker*, as a Chamber-Maſter, and her Mother ſold Fruit, Fiſh, and Greens about Streets, ſo that *Moll's* Education was not more polite, than that of the Nymphs of either *Billingſgate* or *Covent-Garden* Market. She was, when very young, obliged to get her Bread in the Streets with her Mother; for *Criſpin*, her Father, never regarded what became either of the Mother or Daughter, they were left to ſhift for themſelves, whilſt he jovially ſpent his Money amongſt his been Companions.

The Girl being tolerably handſome, and very ſprightly, one Mrs. *Atwood*, then of *Charles-Court* in the *Strand*, took her as a Servant, where ſhe continued but a ſhort Time, for being much us'd to the Streets, ſhe could not brook Confinement within Doors ; and ſo leaving this Service, ſhe betook herſelf to her old Calling of ſelling Fruit in a Barrow about Streets, without imbibing all thoſe Vices which are but too ſoon learnt by theſe Sort of People.

Amongſt the Market People, ſhe was generally belov'd for her Induſtry and Good-Nature, and had ſeveral Sweethearts before ſhe was 14 Years old ; but no amorous Addreſſes could move her, till one *Thomas King*, a young Fellow of her own Calling, courted her Love and Affections, which he in a ſhort Space of Time gained, and they agreed to be married.   Having

(5)

Having rais'd a little Money to defray the
Expence of their Wedding, they came to the
Fleet, and were tack'd together by one of
the *Couple-Beggars*, who ftroll in that Part
of the Town in great Numbers to ruin
young People ; But *Moll's* Fate proved very
happy, and fhe and her new Husband (who
at that Time amongft the Market People
went by the Name of *Smooth'd-Fac'd-Tom*)
liv'd comfortably for fome Years together,
till fhe was drawn away by a young Gentleman nam'd *Murray*, who is now in a very
high Station in one of the Publick Offices.
Not only the Gentleman here hinted at, but
likewife feveral others, as 'tis faid, fhar'd her
Favours, and fhe began to be of fome Confequence amongft the gayeft Ladies of the
Town; for tho' as we before obferved, fhe
was not fo happy as to have a liberal Education, fhe had very good natural Senfe, with
flighty Turns of Wit, and remarkably fober
at that Time of Day ; and whilft fhe faw the
Town Ladies get dead drunk with their
Sparks, fhe took care to keep herfelf cool,
that fhe might make her Property of both the
Gentlemen and their Miffes.

The firft Acquaintance of any Note that fhe
made was one *Nanny Cotton*, a great Companion of the famous *Sally Salisbury*, who was
very kind to her, and lent her a Sum of Money. During her Abfence from her Husband,
which

(6)

which was not a long Time, he became almoft diftracted, and courted her to return
Home at any rate, which fhe as obftinately
refus'd for fome Time; but by the Perfua-
fions of her Friends, and *Tom*'s kind Entrea-
ties, fhe was prevailed on to cohabit with her
Husband; and notwithftanding this Elope-
ment, fhe always declared that fhe tenderly
lov'd him; and would never have left him
one Hour, had not fhe been well affured that
he kept Company with a lewd Woman, who
once feverely beat her.

Indeed it muft be confeffed, that *Moll* was
never a common or reputed Pick-pocket;
and if fhe herfelf was to be credited, fhe never was liberal of her Favours to any Perfon
but *Tom King* her Husband, and Mr. *Huff*,
whom fhe married after his Deceafe.—It will
be more eafy for the candid Reader to judge
of the Truth of this, than for me to determine.

When this fair Damfel had compromis'd all
Matters in Difpute with her Husband, fhe
thought appearing again in the Streets would
be much beneath her Dignity; and therefore
determined to take a Stall in *Covent-Garden*
Market, which fhe promifed herfelf would be
the firft Step to her Preferment, as indeed, it
luckily happened. *Tom King*, at that time,
and during her Abfence, had been Waiter at
a Bawdy-Houfe in *Covent-Garden*, and fav'd

2

(7)

a little Money in that *honeft* and *genteel Cal-ling.*

Moll had exceeding good Succefs in her new Bufinefs, and in one Seafon clear'd upwards of 60 *l.* by felling fmall Nuts only ; fhe hav-ing bought up, very cheap, a large Quantity at a Time, when foon after the Price rofe fur-prizingly, of which fhe took the Advantage, and made a fine Market.

Her afpiring Genius, was, by the good Succefs at her Stall, raifed fomewhat higher, fo fhe had Thoughts of taking a little Houfe, or rather Hovel, in *Covent-Garden* Market, to fell Coffee, Tea, &c. and this fhe commu-nicated to her Spoufe, who very readily fell in with her Notion, and the Houfe was taken accordingly, at the fmall Rent of 12 *l. per Annum.*

In this Houfe they firft fet out with mak-ing Coffee at a Penny a Difh for the Market People, and Tea and Chocolate in Propor-tion ; and in a fhort Time their Bufinefs in-creas'd fo greatly, that they were obliged to take another Houfe adjoining, and afterwards a third, notwithftanding which they had fcarcely Room to accommodate their Cu-ftomers.

As their Bufinefs at firft confifted chiefly of fuch Perfons as came on Bufinefs to the Mar-ket, they were obliged to rife at One or Two o'Clock in the Morning, efpecially on Market
Days,

(8)

Days, and all the Fruit Seafon ; and as that Part of the Town is remarkable for the Rendezvous of young Rakes, and their pretty Miffes, fo they thought this a very proper Office to meet at, and to confult of their nocturnal Intrigues. Every Swain, even from the Star and Garter to the Coffee-Houfe Boy, might be fure of finding a Nymph in waiting at *Moll's Fair Reception Houfe*, as fhe was pleas'd to term it, and the moft fqueamifh Beau, furely, could not refufe fuch Dainties, and the very *fweeteft* too that ever *Covent-Garden* Market afforded.

Here you might fee Ladies of Pleafure, who appear'd apparelled like Perfons of Quality, not at all inferior to them in Drefs, attended by Fellows habited like Footmen, who were their Bullies, and wore that Difguife, the more eafily to deceive the unwary Youths, who were fo unhappy as to caft their Eyes upon thefe *deceitful Water-Wag-Tails*.

Tom King had not been but a few Years Mafter of this Houfe, before a great many Gentlemen of Fafhion, and fome of the gayeft Ladies of the Town, us'd to frequent this Houfe every Night, or rather Morning, for Company feldom began to come in till about One or Two o'Clock.

As there were no Beds in the Houfe, nor Room for any, (except that in which Mr. *King* and his Wife lay, in which they us'd

to

(9)

to go up a Ladder at their Bed-time, which Ladder was immediately taken away again as soon as they had entered their Apartment) so no Company could be accommodated with Lodging; they only met here, as before observed, to make Assignations, or when they were heartily drunk to stagger to some Bagnio for Quarters, which *Moll* generally us'd to recommend her Customers to, that they might (as she said) be us'd well; and a Servant with a Candle and Lanthorn was appointed to attend them; who, if he could conveniently, seldom fail'd of picking their Pocket; if the Fellow had no Opportunity so to do, the Miss generally had, and was sure never to go away empty-handed.

The People in *Covent-Garden* seeing how fast *Tom* and his Wife were getting Riches, there were several Houses set up in Opposition to him, but to no Purpose, for *Moll* was very obliging, and, when sober, behaved civil and courteous, more especially to the Gentlemen; but as to the Ladies she was never under any Pain of quarrelling with them; for she well knew, if she made the Gentlemen her Enemies, they would leave her House, and then the Misses must of Course follow them; so that such Behaviour would inevitably ruin her Trade.

She had a great many of the poor Females *under her Thumb*, as she term'd it, because

B

she

(10)

fhe lent them Money at a high Intereſt ;
but to do her Juſtice, thoſe who behaved
well, and paid her honeſtly, never wanted a
Friend ; for as ſhe was very punctual herſelf,
ſhe was a great Obſerver of Punctuality in
others;--- but notwithſtanding her Temper,
we do not find that ſhe ever put any one in
Priſon, unleſs they uſed her very ill.

Abundance of the poor Sort of Market
People in the Neighbourhood, ſhe lent Money to at the Rate of Two Shillings or Half
a Crown in the Pound ; but the Town Miſſes
were obliged to pay dearer, for ſhe made a
great Diſtinction between Induſtry and Vice ;
for ſhe was a Woman well acquainted with the
World, both in low and genteel Life, had not
her love of Wealth led her on to do ſuch
Things as were highly inconſiſtent with Morality, and very unbecoming her Sex.

The Houſe became ſo very famous for
nightly Revels, and for Company of all Sorts,
that it got the Name of a College, and it was
frequent amongſt the Players, and witty Beaux
to accoſt each other, with, *Are you for* King's
College *to Night, to have a Diſh of* Flaſh.
with Moll ?

This *Flaſh*, as it is called, is talking in
Cant Terms, very much us'd among Rakes
and Town Ladies, and can ſcarcely be underſtood but by thoſe that are acquainted with it.
                                                      This

(11)

This *Lingua* was very much in Vogue at *King*'s Coffee-Houfe, the better to conceal what was intended by thofe who fpoke it.

About 15 Years ago, there was a Dialogue printed in the Cant Language, and intitled, *The Humours of the Flafhy Boys at Moll King's*; and as it is now out of Print, and not to be had, we fhall give it here as a Specimen of the great Politenefs of thefe fort of Gentry. It is fuppofed to be fpoken by Mrs. *King*, and one of her beft Cuftomers, before her Houfe was frequented by People of Fafhion. The Party who begins the Flafh after Supper calls to know hisReckoning, and isfuppofed to have been *Moythen*, who was ftabb'd fome Time ago by *Dick Hodges*, the Diftiller.

Harry. To pay, *Moll*, for I muft hike.
Moll. Did you call me, Mafter?
Harry. Ay, to pay, in a Whiff.
Moll. Let me fee! There's a Grunter's Gig, is a Si-Buxom; two Cat's Heads, a Win; a Double Gage of Rum Slobber, is Thrums; and a Quartern of Max, is three Megs:—That makes a Traveller all but a Meg.
Harry. Here, take your Traveller, and tip the Meg to the Kinchin.—But *Moll*, does *Jack* dofs in your Pad now?
Moll. What *Jack* do you mean?
Harry. Why, *Jack* that gave you the little brindle Bull Puppy.

B 2

Moll.

(12)

Moll. He dofs in a Pad of mine ! No, Boy, if I was to grapple him, he muft fhiver his Trotters at Bilby's Ball.

Harry. But who had you in your Ken laft Darkee ?

Moll. We had your Dudders and your Duffers, Files, Buffers, and Slangers ; we had ne'er a Queer-Cull, a Buttock, or Porpus, a-mongft them, but all as Rum and as Quiddifh as ever *Jonathan* fent to be great Merchants in *Virginia.*

Harry. But *Moll,* don't puff :—You muft tip me your Clout before I derrick, for my Blofs has nailed me of mine ; but I fhall catch her at *Maddox*'s Gin-Ken, fluicing her Gob by the Tinney ; and if fhe has morric'd it, Knocks and Socks, Thumps and Plumps, fhall attend the Froe-File Buttocking B—h.

Moll. I heard fhe made a Fam To-night, a Rum one, with Dainty Dafies, of a Flat from T'other Side ; fhe flafh'd half a Slat, a Bull's-Eye, and fome other rum Slangs.

Harry. I'll derrick, my Blood, if I tout my Mort, I'll tip her a Snitch about the Peeps and Nafous. I fhall fee my jolly old Codger by the Tinney-fide, I fuppofe with his Day-Lights dim, and his Trotters fhivering under him.—As Oliver wheedles, I'll not touch this Darkee, I'll map the Pad, and fee you in the Morning.

This

(13)

This was Part of the Cant that the Gentry of *King*'s College were mighty fond of; and which too many People now scandaloufly affect to practice; but by Persons of Modesty and Understanding, thofe that are fo ridiculous as to ufe it, are looked upon not to be very well bred: It is not a Man's Apparel or well furnifhed Pocket that proclaim him a fit Member for a fober Company, but his Difcourfe and Behaviour; for it is notorious enough that we daily fee Highwaymen, Houfebreakers, Pickpockets, Money-Droppers, &c. who make the Appearance of Gentlemen, and gild their Vices with a gaudy Coat, that they may be the lefs fufpected.

We fhall now proceed on our Narrative, and tell what further happened to the Mafter and Miftrefs of this extraordinary Coffee-Houfe. The Money flowing in fo faft upon them, *Tom*, with the Confent of his beloved Helpmate, purchafed an Eftate near *Hampftead*, at a Place known by the Name of *Taviftock-Hill*, and on a Piece of Ground fit for the Purpofe, he built a very genteel Country-Houfe, and was determined to make as great a Figure as moft of the Mercers in *Covent-Garden*, often declaring that he got his Money more honeftly than any of them.

This rural Retirement was the Place where *Tom* ended his Days, a few Years ago; for having greatly impaired his Health by Drinking,

(14)

ing, and other Vices, he was obliged to be pretty much in the Country. His Spouse was quite of another Way of Thinking; she was an utter Enemy to Retirement, getting Money was all that she aim'd at, for said she, *I love to be in Town, because I shall see what my pretty Birds* (meaning her Customers) *are doing.*

One Day some young Gentlemen riding out towards *Hampstead* for the Air, as *Moll* was looking out of her Window, one of them said, loud enough to be heard by her, *Look yonder, there's* Moll King's *Folly*; she immediately reply'd, *No, ye Bantling, it's your Folly, and some more Jack-an-Apes as silly as yourself; for you know Fool's Pence flew fast enough about, and they help'd to build it.* This caus'd a merry Laughter among the Company and the young Spark was the Jest of his Comrades for some Time after; he being a Person remarkably fond of acting a Part in a Night-Scene.

Some Time after the Decease of Mr. *King*, his Spouse got into a great many different Quarrels, which cost her pretty handsome Sums of Money: Amongst others, she had an Information filed against her in the Crown Office, and an Indictment preferred against her in *Middlesex*, for violently assaulting and beating a young Gentleman in her own House, which Indictment she removed from *Hick's-Hall*

(15)

Hall into the Court of *King's-Bench* by *Certiorari*, thinking to evade the Punishment due to her Crime, on a Presumption that her Prosecutor would not follow her, on Account of the great Expences that generally attend such Suits; but in this she was greatly mistaken. For the Affair was prosecuted, and brought to a Trial before a Jury of the County, who, notwithstanding the Testimonies of all the Witnesses that she called to set aside the Evidence that had been given against her on the Part of the King, she was found guilty, and gave fresh Bail for her Appearance on the first Day of the next Term, when she was called on to receive Judgment on her Conviction, and the Persons who were her Bail delivering her into Court, her Sentence was, to pay a Fine of Two Hundred Pounds, to find Sureties for her good Behaviour for a Year, and to be committed to the Prison of the *King's-Bench* until the said Fine was paid, and Securities given as aforesaid.

As she always had a natural Aversion to part with Money, especially on such an Affair as this, she suffered herself to go to Prison, and said if she was to pay Two Hundred Pounds to all the insolent Boys she had thrash'd for their Impudence, the Bank of *England* would be unable to furnish her with the Cash.

The Offence being committed within the City

(16)

City and Liberties of *Weftminfter*, the Fine was the Property of the then High Bailiff, who well knowing fhe had Subftance fuffi-cient to pay it, would by no Means at firft mitigate the Sum, fo that fhe remained in Goal fome Time before fhe confented to dif-charge the Fine, and 'tis faid that the High-Bailiff compounded with her for lefs than Half the Sum fhe was mulcted.——Thus fhe obtained her Enlargement, and returned to her *lucky Office* in *Covent-Garden,* where, not-withftanding her Abfence, her Bufinefs was tranfacted to her Satisfaction, and Fool's Pence were pouring in upon her from every Quar-ter.

Her Confinement in Prifon coft her a very Trifle, for fhe had Vifitors enow, of both Sexes, who fpent their Money liberally enough which made her quite eafy under her Circum-ftances.

Upwards of twenty Indictments were foon after preferr'd againft her before the Grand Jury at Weftminfter-Hall for keeping a dif-orderly, ill-govern'd Houfe, but very few of them were found, becaufe it appeared to the Inqueft, that fhe had no Beds in the faid Houfe, and that the Parties who had indicted her had none of the beft of Characters, fo that fhe extricated herfelf from thefe new Dif-ficulties with very little Expence.

Seldom a Day pafs'd, but fome Warrant

or other was ferv'd upon her: Sir *John*
G—*nf*—*n* was indefatigable in paying her
nocturnal Vifits, but fhe generally found out
fome way or other to pacify both him and his
Mirmidons.

Being once fummon'd before the Bench of
Juftices, fitting at *Covent Garden* Veftry,
and examined as to the Irregularity of her
Houfe, fhe had the Affurance to tell their
Worfhips, that all the Complaints againft her
were without Foundation, and that her Houfe
was under better Government than any one
in the Parifh, as they would find, if they
would do her the Honour of paying her a
Vifit. The Colonel infifted on having her
bound over to the Seffions, and ordered the
Cryer to call for the Perfons who had made
Information againft her, which was accordingly done, but none of them appear'd! on
which fhe told the Bench, they might very
eafily fee through the Malice of her Enemies,
who were afhamed to look her in the Face:
—— At the fame Time fhe having taken
Care to bribe them to keep out of the Way;
And then fhe us'd to fay, *that fhe had bubbled
t he Bench.*

It is not at all furprizing how this Woman
efcap'd Punifhment fo often, when we confider, that all the Wealth of the Bagnio-Keepers
or the Bawds, about Covent-Garden, and indeed 'all Weftminfter, could not fubdue her:

C   Their

(18)

Their Women Lodgers were always on her
Side, becaufe fhe uſed to protect and defend
them againſt the Infults of thofe vile Harpies.
_The famous, or rather infamous, Mother
Haywood, well known in Covent Garden,
but lately deceafed, ufed very often in the
Night Time, to pay Moll a Vifit, but her
chief Errant was to look after her Girls, who
us'd frequently to defert to this Houfe for *a
Regale*, as they called it, and leave the old
Beldrum by herfelf to hunt for Wenches for
her Cuftomers. As thefe two old Sinners
were implacable Enemies, nothing was fo
agreeable to the Company in Moll's Houfe as
to hear their Quarrels and Bickerings. Moll
would tell her, how fhe frequently ordered
her Servants, when a Gentleman was in Liquor, to bring two or three Dozen of broken
China Punch-Bowls, and prefent them to his
View, when he arofe in the Morning; fwear-
ing, that he had broken them all the
Over-Night; at the fame Time calling before him one or two of her Waiters with
Bruifes and black Eyes, vowing that the Gentleman in his Liquor had beat them fo unmer-
cifully, that fhe did not expect their Lives.
The Gentleman greatly furpriz'd, would naturally ask, who he had brought in the Houfe
with him? The Reply was, that he had
brought a dirty Creature dead, drunk, whom
they had turn'd out for fear fhe fhould rob
                                          him.

(19)

him. This was all a Fineffe, the better to colour their Villainy: The Gentleman was robb'd, and had perhaps 20 *l.* to pay for Rack Punch, befides the Charge of the broken Bowls, and fomething for the Servants whom he had beaten. The Gentleman having no Money, was obliged to give his Note, perhaps, for 40 l. for which he never had 40 Pence, and fo got himfelf arrefted the next Day, or fometimes before he went out of the Houfe, and if he could not find either Money or Friends, all that was further to be done, the Bailiff convey'd him to Gaol till he gave Bail, or paid the Debt.

As none of thefe old Bawds or their Adherents, were a Match for Mrs. *King*, they have not for fome Years paft, dar'd to enter her Houfe, becaufe they not only betrayed their Ignorance, in not being able to difpute with her, but expofed themfelves greatly to the Infults of Gentlemen, who there publickly heard all the villainous Schemes of Extortion and Impofition which they practic'd, and which greatly intimidated Men from going into fuch Houfes; for *Moll* us'd to fay, *If fhe flung her Cuftomers now-and-then herfelf, fhe was not willing any body elfe fhould fling them.*

One *H —— k*, a noted Bagnio-Keeper, never was fo well match'd, as when attack'd by this Virago; She was well acquainted

C 2 with

(20)

with his Tricks, and told him of all the Sla-
veries he impos'd on unhappy Women, by
taking Coffee-Houfes, and putting them into
them as Miftreffes, for which they paid fometimes three Guineas a Week, but feldom lefs
than *two* ; and if they could not make good
their Payments, the *Marfhalfea* Prifon was
their next Quarters. If he lent them a few
Sconces, fome Decanters, two or three broken
back'd Chairs, aud an old Bed or two. not
all perhaps worth 10 l. they muft give him
a Note for 40 l. payable on Demand, and if
they did not behave to his Liking, the Note
was put in Force againft them, and a Prifon
was fure to be their Portion.

Of all the Fellows of this Sort, that live
by unhappy Women, fhe us'd to fay, none
was more cruel and mercilefs, than one they
call *Drury-Lane Populus*, (or by fome better
known by the Name of the *Covent-Garden
Porpus*) an odd Creature of the *Bum* Order,
remarkable for fhaking his Head : tho', faid
fhe, there is *Nothing in it*. This Fellow
much dreading the Sight of *Lucifer*, is now
fo religious as to go to Church, but it's
thought, by all his Acquaintance, that it is
not fo much for the Sake of his Soul's Welfare, as to fhew his fine Cloaths and his
Diamond Rings, obtain'd by Rapine, Plunder,
and at the Expence of the Lives of many
poor unfortunate Women. This Fellow,
with

(21)

with his *wagging Nod*, it's hop'd, will, fome
Time or other, die of a Suffocation in the
Road to *Paddington*; tho' he has had, for
feveral Years paft, a great Averfion to ridng
on the other Side of *Tyburn* Turnpike, becaufe his Horfe once happened to throw him
juft underneath the Gallows. —— He that has
been twice in *Newgate*, may very probably
come there a third Time; and if he fhould
be doom'd to the Gallows, he has only the
Confolation of riding thither in a Coach.

Then there's a *great* Brandy - Merchant,
who was, for his much greater Skill in *Rapping*, before he was properly inftructed,
made Overfeer of the Mob in *Kingfton* Market
Place. This was a Chap whom *Moll* never
lik'd. She faid, that he had liv'd long by
Oppreffion and Villainy; and that if he had
a keen Head to put the Dictates of his wicked
Heart into Execution, there would not be a
more dangerous Fellow in the four Quarters
of the World: This *honeft* Man, faid fhe,
will go thro' *Thick and Thin*.

As no body was better acquainted with
thefe Sort of Gentry, fo no one could give a
better Account of them; fhe knew them
perfonally, and could repeat the Tricks of almoft every one, even from the furtheft Part
of *Tothil-Fields* to *Limehoufe-Hole*, but to
defcribe them in this fmall Tract, would be
impoffible, tho' it is intended to write a fmall
Volume

(22)

Volume of them, that all Perſons may be
guarded againſt their nefarious Practices.

She had no more than two Husbands, viz,
Mr. *King*, and Mr. *Hoff*, the latter of whom
married her, in hopes of having the Fingering
of her Caſh, but in this he found himſelf mi-
ſtaken, for ſhe had taken Care to make a Widow's Will to her Son, who is a very hopeful
young Fellow, and on whom ſhe beſtowed a
liberal Education at *Eton* School.

For ſome Years paſt Mrs. *King* (for this
was the Name ſhe always went by) has been
in a bad State of Health, ſo that ſhe was obliged to retire to *Hampſtead*, where ſhe departed this Life on *Thurſday* the 17th of
September; and the following Epitaph and
Elegy were wrote by one of her favourite
Cuſtomers.

The EPITAPH.

Here lies my Love, who often drove,
   Wheelbarrows in the Street;
From which low State; to Billingſgate,
   With Wickedneſs replete.
She ſold a Diſh, of Stinking Fiſh,
   With Oaths and Imprecations;
And ſwore her Ware, was better Far,
   Than any in the Nation,
From thence ſhe came to be in Fame,
   Among the Rogues and Whores;
But now ſhe's gone to her long home,
   To ſettle all her Scores.

(23)

The ELEGY.

How vain the State of a bad Woman,
  How frail her Being, fleet her Breath;
Her Life but one contracted Span,
  At best Uncertain sure her Death.
Tho' strong her Make, her Mind at Ease,
  As if no Ill could her annoy;
Some latent Seeds of dire Disease.
  Doth quickly her fair Frame destroy.
Pleased with the Love of female Friend,
  We think the Bliss will still remain;
Her sudden unexpected End,
  Proves all our pleasing hopes are vain.
In the lov'd *Moll* were lately seen,
  This Case tho' common verified;
One Instance more to us thou'st been,
  That nothing here can long abide.
Thy Constitution strong and sound,
  Foreboded Years of Life and Health;
But soon received its mortal Wound,
Thy Strength availed not in thy Wealth.
One Week we saw thee Blith and Gay,
  Who in the Night, us Spirits gave;
The Next a lifeless Lump of Clay.

A KEY to the *Flash Dialogue.*

To hike, is, To go home. — *A Grunter's
Gig,* a Hog's Cheek. — *Si-Buxom,* Six-pence.
— *A Cat's Head,* a Half-penny Rowl. —*A
Whyn,* a Penny. — *A Gage of Rum Slobber,*
a Pot of Porter. — *Thrums,* Three-pence.
Max.

(14)

— *Max.* Geneva. — *Meg*, a Half-penny. — *A Traveller*, a Shilling. — *Kinchin*, a little Child. — *Dofs*, to fleep. — *Pad*, a Bed. — *Grapple*, to lay hold on. —*Trotters*, Legs. *Bilby's Ball*, Tyburn-Houfe. —*Ken*, a Houfe. — *Darkee*, the Night. — *Dudders*, Fellows that fell Spital-fields Handkerchiefs for India ones. — *Duffers*, Thofe who fell Britifh Spirituous Liquors for Foreign. — *Files*, Pick-pockets.—*Buffers*, Affidavit-Men. —*Slangers* Thieves who hand Goods from one to the other, after they are ftole. — *A Buttock*, a Whore. — *Porpus*, an ignorant fwaggering Fellow. — *Rum* or *Quiddifh*, Good-natur'd. — *To puff*, to impeach. — *Clout*, a Hand-kerchief. — *Derrick*, to go away. —*Sluicing her Gob*, wetting her Mouth, or drinking. — *Tinney*, the Fire. — *Froe-File-Buttock*, a Woman Pick-pocket — *A Fam*, a Ring. — *Dafies*, Diamonds. — *T'other Side*, South-wark. — *Half a Slat*, 10 s. 6 d. — *Bull's Eye*, 5 s. — *To tout the Mort*, to find out the Woman. — *Snitch about the Peeps and Nafous*, a Fillip on the Nofe and Eyes. — *Old Codger*, an old Man. — *Day-lights*, Eyes. — *Oliver wheedles*, the Moon fhines. — *To nap the Pad*, to go to Bed. —

F I N I S

Arthur Murphy, '[Account of Jonathan's Coffee-House] Numb. 5, November 3, 1753', pp. 31–6; '[Proposal for a Female Coffee-House] Numb. 15, January 5, 1754', pp. 85–90, in *The Gray's Inn Journal. By Charles Ranger* (London, printed by W. Faden and J. Bouquet, [1753–4]), 52v.; 2°. BL: Burney. ESTCP1786. Extract, pp. 31–6, 85–90.

Two essays from a satirical essay-periodical written by Arthur Murphy (1727–1805) using the persona of Charles Ranger. The periodical in general offered a wide-ranging and gentle satire on the follies and peccadilloes of London society, especially those of literary and theatrical interest. The essays excerpted here both have their focus in coffee-house sociabilities of the early 1750s. Murphy follows the model established by Addison and Steele in *The Tatler* and *The Spectator*, by using a narrative persona – in this case Charles Ranger – as an organising structure for the diversity of material. But Murphy's essays diverge from the Spectatorial focus on the moral reform of society, and instead each offers a sharpened satire against particular subjects. The first, extracted here, satirises the mysteries of the securities market in stocks and shares conducted at Jonathan's Coffee-house in the City, especially the role of Jewish stock-jobbers in providing liquidity in the market. The second is directed specifically against Arthur Macklin's scheme for a reformed and genteel coffee-house and lecture room (later known as the British Inquisition, and located in Covent Garden), and more generally ridicules Macklin's notion that women might take an active part in the political and intellectual public. In addition, each essay is suffixed by a more miscellaneous collection of satirical portraits, collected under the title 'True Intelligence', in parody of the form of contemporary newspapers.

Arthur Murphy was born in Ireland, and came to London in 1751 where he commenced writing for Henry Fielding's *Covent-Garden Journal*. In 1752–3, he wrote 49 essays in a column entitled the 'Gray's-Inn Journal' in a weekly newspaper called the *Craftsman*, whose fictional editor was 'Joseph D'Anvers' (so as to distinguish him from 'Caleb D'Anvers', the fictional editor of Nicholas Amherst's long running *The Country Journal; or The Craftsman* (1727–50)). On 29 September 1753, he began publishing his essays under their own independent title, *The Gray's Inn Journal*, using the pseudonym of 'Charles Ranger', continuing for 52 numbers until 21 September 1754 (although confusingly the first three numbers of this separate publication were numbered 50–2, so as to underline their continuity with *The Craftsman* series). Murphy's periodical was published by William Faden and J. Bouquet, printers who were renowned for the high quality of their work (Faden was the publisher of Johnson's *Rambler* and *Idler* essays). The day after the last essay was published in 1754, Murphy made his debut as an actor at Covent Garden, and in later life he gained fame as a dramatist. Several weeks after the conclusion of *The Gray's Inn Journal* in 1754, the publishers issued a complete bound set of the 52 essays, with a title-page and contents list. In 1756 Murphy published a two-volume set in octavo entitled *The Gray's Inn Journal* (London, printed by W. Faden for A. Vaillant in the Strand, 1756), combining both sets of essays, adding three more, and drastically revising their order, dating and text. The two essays excerpted here are also found in these volumes: 'Account of Jonathan's Coffee-House: No. 19, February 25 1752' (vol. I, pp. 122–9) and 'Proposal for a Female Coffee-House: No. 61, December 15, 1753' (vol. II, pp. 50–6). Further revisions and redatings were made for the *Works of Arthur Murphy*, 7 vols (London, T. Cadell, 1786). For the complicated publication history see Roy Aycock, 'Arthur Murphy, the *Gray's-Inn Journal*, and the *Craftsman*: some publication mysteries', *PBSA*, 67:3 (1973), pp. 255–62.

THE

GRAY's INN JOURNAL.

By *CHARLES RANGER*, Esq;

NUMB. 6	*To be continued Weekly.*	Pr. 2 *d.*

SATURDAY, NOVEMBER 3, 1753.

Gray's Inn, Nov 3, 1753.

Ecce iterum Crispinus,   JUV.

SOME Time ago I entertained the Public, with a Scene from a Dramatic Piece, entitled the TEMPLE *of* LAVERNA, which was fo favourably received, that I am inclined to think the Readers of the GRAY's-INN-JOUR-NAL will not be difpleafed to fee fomething more of that Performance,

SCENE. II.

A Number of JEWS *circumcifed and uncircumcifed form a Clufter in the Middle of the Temple, from whence the following confufed Sounds iffue, viz.*

TICKETS — Tickets — Lottery-Tickets — come, who buys 300 for all this Month? — I fell a hundred for next *Monday* at 15 *s.* 6 *d.* — What do you fay, *Adam* ?

Adam. Come I'll give you 15 *s.* for a 100 next *Monday* —

—— No Mafter *Adam,* I have my Eye-Teeth as well as you,

or

or any Man in the Houſe; do you think I don't know, what is
a doing? Altho' Mr *Slyboots* lies by, I can ſmoke his Agents.

Moſes Noiſy. I tell you what, I want 500 for *Wedneſday* Morning
to compleat my Commiſſion, and in a Word I'll give 14*s.* 6*d.*

All. Hoot him, hoot him, mind *Noiſey*, mind *Moſes.*

Enter a Country Gentleman, in Boots with his Friend.

Country Gent. Is it here?

Fr. Yes, Sir.

Country Gent. Woons, what a Place it is!

Fr. Come Sir, you had better ſit down, and make your Obſervations upon this Scene, which you were ſo very deſirous to be
a Spectator of.

[*As ſoon as they are both ſeated the Waiter comes up and demands
Sixpence each.*]

Country Gent. Six-pence Mon! for what? to ſee theſe Monſters,
I ſuppoſe.

Waiter. Sir, it is uſual, every Gentleman pays Six-pence, who
ſits down.

Country Gent. Nay, Friend, I ſhan't diſpute it with you—It is
not the firſt Tax you have raiſed upon me.

Fr. Hark ye, Mr. *Trueblue*, you had better not ſpeak in that
Manner; ſee how they ſtare.

Country Gent. S'blood! let'n ſtare? what care I? I expect no
Place; and, woons! I think a Mon, who pays half his Eſtate in
Taxes, ſhould at leaſt be allowed to ſpeak his Mind.

Fr. Not quite ſo loud, I beg, Mr. *Trueblue*—You don't mind
them but they all know me, and I would not willingly draw upon
me their Ill-will.

Country Gent. Well, well, well —to oblige you — But, which is
the Mon, who does what he pleaſes with the great Mon at the
other End of the Toon— Woons I cannot remember his Name—
Lord, we drink Confuſion to him very often in the Country— He
is richer than a *German* Prince, they ſay —

Fr. Caiphas, you mean?

Country Gent. Ay, ay, *Caiphas* is the Mon —which is he, pray?

Fr. He is not come yet, but it is probable, you will ſee him
preſently.

[*Here the Jobbers grow very clamorous crying in harſh diſſonant
Tones,* — Tickets — India-Bonds — Reſcounters— Conſolidate.]

Country Gent. As I am an *Engliſhman*, this is a perfect *Babel* —
Reſcounters, Conſolidate, woons, theſe Fellows have certainly made
a Compact with the Devil, and thoſe are the Words by which
they call him to their Aſſiſtance.

Fr. No, Sir, no —Thoſe are the Names of the ſeveral different Stocks.

Country

No. 6.   THE GRAY's INN JOURNAL.   33

Country Gent. Blefs me, Friend *Worthy*, it is a melancholy Thing that our poor Country fhould be drained of her Wealth and Power, by fuch infernal Leeches. Ah! many a Time and oft, have my Lord *Turncoat* and I talked over thefe Things in the Country— We have fat together, and drank *The true Intereft of Great Britain*, and *Old England without Taxes*, until we have been both ready to cry — But no Mon is to be depended upon I fee — he is gone off, and as deep, I warrant in the Mire, as any of them.

Fr. I believe Mr. *Trueblue*, you never faw fo many *Jews* together before.

Country Gent. No, never to be fure — but we fhall foon have them fwarm in all Parts of the Kingdom now, that they are naturalized — Woons! if they come among us, I know what—Let them take care Care of themfelves, I fay; their Betters have been properly treated there, I can tell them—Let them look to it—but prithee, Friend *Worthy*, is the Report we have in the Country true? why, they fay, Mon, that there will fhortly be laid a Fine upon any one, who is convicted of going to Church. Woons! if that fhould be the Cafe, notwithftanding the Love I have for *Old England*, I am determined to fell my Acres, and retire to fome *Chriftian Proteftant* Country, for I would not become a *Jew*, nd not to be a Minifter of State.

Fr. Hufh! who have we here?

Enter Lord Bowfprit, *and Mr* Servile.

L. Bow. (*Looking at his Watch.*) No, he is not come yet; it is not quite Twelve.

Servile. Pray, my Lord, how long have you been acquainted with *Caiphas?*

L. Bow. Ever fince the Year forty-fix. I leave a Sum of Money in his Hands, which he jobbs for me, and furnifhes me with an Account at the Years End. I would have you do the fame.

Servile. I fhould like it very well, my Lord; but it does not fuit me to lodge a large Sum with him.

L. Bow. If that be your only Objection, he can act for you in another Shape, he can buy and fell Stock, for your Account, without Money, this we call *Bulls* and *Bears*.

Servile. Yes, but, my Lord, I think there is an Act of Parliament againft that, is not there?

L. Bow. Yes, there is fomething of that Kind; Sir *John Banard's Act* they call it; Sir *John* you know is a particular Sort of Man, and confults the Intereft of the Public, but thofe chimerical Projects of his do not coincide with the prefent Syftem, by any Means—He is a very fingular Sort of Man, what they call a Patriot; indeed he has been always the fame.

Servile.

34   THE GRAY's INN JOURNAL   No. 6.

Servile. I wonder what he gets by that, I was my self a Patriot
for two Seffions, but I found there was nothing to be got by it, and
fo I entered a Volunteer under the oppofite Banner.

Enter Caiphas, *(upon which a general Silence enfues.)*

Caiphas. Has any Body enquired for me ? — Hah! my Lord!
Yours !

L. Bow. Mr *Caiphas*, I am your moft obedient humble Servant
— Give me Leave, Sir, to introduce this Gentleman to your Acquaintance, he is a particular Friend of mine, Mr *Servile.*

Caiphas. I am glad to know any Friend of your Lordfhip's —
Has this Gentleman any Inclination to do any Thing in our Way ?
you need but let me know.

Servile. Under your Direction Mr *Caiphas*, I fhould like to job
a little.

Caiphas. Its enough — call upon me To-morrow Morning —
I'll put you in the Way.

Servile. I fhall be for ever obliged to you, Mr *Caiphas.*

Caiphas. Say no more — You are my Lord *Bowfprit*'s Friend
that's enough.

Fr. to the Country Gent. Well, Sir, what think you of the renowned *Caiphas*, that is the wonderful Perfonage, whom you have
heard fo much of.

Country Gent. I proteft, I cannot conceal my Aftonifhment —
why, I expected to fee a Giant, Mon — woons, is it poffible that
Old England fhould be bamboozled thus !

L. Bow. Mr *Caiphas* I am glad to hear that you begin to be
pretty quiet in the City now. The Clamour againft your People
fubfides, I am told, you need not be under any Apprehenfion, it
will die away entirely in a little Time, I dare fay,

Caiphas. I do not care much, my Lord, whether it dies away
or not, Money is my Religion ; and if I can but bring together
enough of that, I dont' care a Pinch of Snuff for any Sect, or
any Party whatever.

[*Several* Jew-Brokers *fhew great Surprize, at over-bearing this,
upon which* Caiphas *turns about, puts out his Tongue, and winks
at them.*]

L. Bow. Nay, I think you would be right in that, Mr *Caiphas*,
for why fhould a Man of your Senfe lie under any Difadvantage,
for Punctilio's or Form ? We have done all we could to ferve you ;
we are not fo tenacious of Religion, but we can admit yours a-
mong us ; and Money certainly is a very good Religion — that
is the Maxim of a wife Man.

Caiphas. Well, well, we will talk more of this another Time —
will you dine with me at the KING's-ARMS ? I am obliged to go
now to the *South-Sea-Houfe*, but, I have ordered an excellent *Ham*
for

for Dinner, and if you and your Friend will dine with me, we will be joyous.

L. Bow. Ham, Mr *Caiphas!* Come, come, that is a good Sign— I find you are coming over to us — you will foon be as good a *Chriftian* as any of us.

Caiphas. Nay, my Lord, thofe Things I laugh at — I tell you what, it is clear to me, that *Mofes* never was in *Weftphalia*, or he would not have prohibited *Pork*, ha! ha! ha!

L. Bow. Ha! ha! ha!

Servile. Ha! ha! ha!

Caiphas. Well, my Lord, your Servant, Mr *Servile*, your's
[*exit* Caiphas.]

L. Bow. Now that you know him, *Servile*, be fure to cultivate your Acquaintance with him, depend upon it, you will find it your Intereft.

Servile. I fhall not neglect it, believe me, I will be at his Houfe To-morrow Morning by eight o'Clock — but we have no farther Bufinefs here, let us go.

L. Bow. With all my Heart.
[*exeunt L.* Bowfprit *and* Servile.]

Country Gent. Woons! this Place has ftruck fuch a damp upon my Spirits, that I fhall not be myfelf again, until I get into Company with a Set of honeft Fellows, and drink THE OLD CONSTITUTION, in a Pint-Bumper.

Fr. Come, come, if you grow melancholy, we muft quit thefe Gentry.

Country Gent. Woons! I wifh, I could blow them all up, and then I fhould have a clear Eftate — Let me give them one hearty Curfe, and then we will go.

Fr. No, no, no, let us leave them quietly.
[*Forces the* Country Gentleman *out, upon which the Scence clofes.*

****

TRUE INTELLIGENCE.

From my Regifter Office, Nov. 3, 1753.

THIS Week was iffued from the Prefs, a very notable, curious, elegant, polite and fenfible Pamphlet, in which the Author has found the Means of conferring his Praife and his Cenfure in the oppofite Extremes of judicious Extravagance, which, without Doubt, will moft certainly anfwer his Purpofe of exalting his Favourites and deprefling the Objects of his Severity. In this extraordinary Production many delicate Animadverfions are indifcriminately thrown out upon three Characters, all highly eminent in their Profeffion, and (if I may indulge myfelf in a little Vanity) the Author of this Paper is difhed up at the End of it, *Pour faire bon bouche.* This Part however
ever

36　THE GRAY's INN JOURNAL.　No. 6

ever of the Performance is fhort of the Delicacy which runs through the reft of his Raillery, as in this Place, he has not hefitated to offer to the Public an impudent and fcandalous Falfehood. The Writer of the GRAY's INN-JOURNAL is above entering the Lifts with a Man who dares to think one Thing and tell another ; He will juft obferve to Mifs *Noffiter*, that fhe had better let *Honeft Ranger* kifs her Hand than any Fellow of them all ; and he difdains to make any other Reply to the Perfon, who has once been guilty of an Impofition on the Public, as it is not to be doubted but he, who can publifh a Falfity upon one Occafion, will entrench himfelf at all Times behind a thoufand others ;

> *Deftroy his Fib and Sophiftry in vain ;*
> *The Creature's at his dirty Work again.*
>
> POPE.

Bedford Coffee-Houfe, Nov. 2, 1753.

Wit and Humour, and Sprightlinefs, and Pleafantry have fubfifted here for a long Time paft, until fome certain Wits interrupted the Stream of our Happinefs by difplaying a good Deal of *falfe Fire*, and obtruding upon the Company fome *Flourifhes*, which were not at all approved by the fenfible and judicious. It is however hoped, that thefe contending Genius's will adjuft their Differences, without difturbing the Harmony fubfifting between the Reft of the Gentlemen who frequent this Place.

Drury-Lane Play-Houfe, Nov. 1, 1753.

On *Monday* Night laft was prefented here, the Tragedy called VENICE PRESERVED, when Mr *Moffop* performed the Part of *Pierre* with that Gallantry and heroic Ardor, which is the Characteriftic of that Confpirator, and Mr *Garrick* and Mrs *Cibber* mutually exerted their excellent Art, at touching the compound Paffions of the human Heart; and, it is no Wonder that in fome Scenes the Emotions of the Audience run fo extremely high, as they were acted upon by the two beft Tragedians in the World. Since that Mr *Foote* has again drawn together a very fplendid and numerous Audience, by his appearing in the Character of *Fondlewife*, which whole Incident is reprefented by this Performer and Mrs *Pritchard*, with as much Pleafantry as has been known on the Stage.

LONDON: Printed for W. FADEN in Wine-Office-Court, Fleet-Street; and J. BOUQUET, in Pater-Nofter-Row ; where Letters to the Author are taken in.

THE

GRAY's INN JOURNAL.

By *CHARLES RANGER*, Efq;

NUMB. 15   *To be continued Weekly.*   Pr. 2*d*

SATURDAY, JANUARY, 5, 1754.

Gray's Inn, *Jan.* 5, 1754.

Quales Threiciæ cum Flumina Thermadoontis
Pulfant, & Piƈtis bellantur Amazones Armis.   VIRG.

PAID a Vifit, a few Days fince, to a
Lady, for whom I have always entertained
a very high Efteem, on Account of a
pleafing Turn of Converfation, and many
other good and agreeable Qualities, which
fhe is poffeffed of. Mrs *Millefont* (for
that is her Name) was never known to
have the leaft Propenfity to Scandal or Detraƈtion ; fhe is ena-
moured of the Virtues of her Neighbours, and whenever fhe
cannot fay fomething handfome of any of her Acquaintance,
fhe is fure to be filent, without attempting to help about a lame
Story by Innuendos, Winks, Nods, or any other female Artifice. She does not concern herfelf with the impertinent Knowledge of, who and who were together at the Mafquerade ; who
were feen to interchange a few fond Regards at the Theatre,
or who has lately had an Ill-run at Play; Politenefs, Good-
nature and Affability are her charaƈteriftic Perfeƈtions, and
fhe is ready to fee and allow Wit and Beauty in others, as
well as in her own Daughters; though in my Opinion, it is a
rare Thing to fee them equalled by any of their Sex. Both
the young Ladies are tall and graceful; elegant in Shape and
delicate in their Features; extremely like each other in the
Turn of the Face, and ftill each of them forming, if I may

be allowed to ufe the Painter's Expreffion, a different School
of Beauty.

HARRIET, being two Years elder than her Sifter, is
rather more formed, and in higher Bloom than *Charlot*; but the
latter promifes to be rather fuperior when arrived to Maturity;
when every Grace, which is now but growing up, is fufficiently
unfolded, and all her Charms arrive to their full Perfection.
Harriet feems to be fenfible of the approaching Eclipfe which
her Beauty muft fuffer very fhortly from the more ftriking
Eclat of her Sifter; but fhe perceives it without feeling any In-
citement to Envy, or a Dejection of Spirits. On the contrary
fhe rallies herfelf with a great Vivacity, and will fairly own that
fhe is upon the Look out for a Man for herfelf, before *Charlot*
becomes fo mifchievous a Beauty, as to engrofs the Attention of every Beholder; and then, fays fhe, " I fhall lofe
" all my Admirers, and fo I'm refolved to get married
" out of the Way." Upon this Plan fhe has directed herfelf for fome Time paft, without throwing off the juft Degree of Reftraint which her Delicacy prefcribes to her upon
every Occafion; but at the fame Time, there is fuch an Ema-
nation of Spirits in her Eye, and fuch a Sprightlinefs in
her every Gefture, that I fhall think it a very great Impu-
tation on the Tafte of her Admirers, if none of them fhould
happen to propofe for her. Though *Harriet* at prefent
throws the Dart like a Tyrant, as the Poet phrafes it, I am
convinced when fhe refigns her Perfon, fhe will bid adieu to
what the *Beaux* call her Haughtinefs, and her infolent Airs.
I am perfwaded that her good Senfe will then lead her to imitate
the Gentlenefs and amiable Difpofition of *Charlot*, who does
not aim at being fo fierce a Beauty as *Hariet*, but is chiefly
defirous to be Miftrefs of willing Hearts. She does not endeavour to kindle her Eyes into that Glare of Fire, for which
many others are remarkable, but unambitioufly fhe lets them
fhine in their own native Mildnefs; and were *Horace* to know
her, he would never put his famous Queftion to her; *Cui
flavam religas comam?* for fhe was never known to fet her Cap
at any Man, and her Converfation is always fo negligently
fenfible, that fhe cannot be fufpected of ftudying to be brilliant,
and if fhe captivates every Heart, it is without any premeditated Defign. In fhort, the Difference between thefe too
young Ladies is this; *Charlot*'s Charms have a conftant Ema-
nation, and *Harriet*'s Beauties are in a perpetual Exertion.

I spent an Hour in the moft agreeable Manner with this
Family, when at Length the Difcourfe, after having been band-
ed about between the Opera and the Burletta, refted for fome
Time upon *Shakefpear* and other celebrated Dramatic Poets. I
was pleafed to be engaged on thefe Topics, when the eldeft Sifter,
in her giddy Manner, interrupted us by afking me, " Pray Mr
" *Ranger*, can you tell me fomething about *Macklin*'s new
" Scheme; I was at his Benefit, but I was fo ftupid, I did not
" under

" understand the Hint in the Epilogue you printed. Pray what
" is the Man about ?"——To this I replied, that I really was
not sufficiently in the Secret of his Scheme, to acquaint her
with the whole Scope of it ; that he has built two magnificent
Rooms, and intends to furnish them in an elegant Manner ; the
Apartment on the Ground-Floor to be a public Coffee-Room,
and the other to receive such of the Nobility and People of Fashion
as may think proper to subscribe to his Undertaking. " Well,
" I vow and protest, (says *Harriet*) it's a vexatious Thing to
" see how these Men are always contriving Places for their
" own Accommodation, without Troubling their Heads about
" the Women. The odious Things are always herding with one
" another, and the Ladies are sequestred from all the Joys of
" these convenient Meetings. Does not one hear them eternally
" saying with an Air of Indifference, Ma'am I must go to the
" Coffee-House, and so saunter away with a Tooth-pick in
" their Mouths ?—Whip me; but I wish the Women would
" agree to have a Coffee-House of their own, to be revenged of
" the Fellows—Lord Mr *Ranger* it would do charmingly ; don't
" you think so, Sister ? — It would so tantalize the Creatures,
" to see us going into a Place, where none of them can gain
" Admittance—they would be so proud to wait at the Door
" to hand us to our Chairs ; and it would be such a Pleasure
" to go and meet one's Acquaintance without going constant-
" ly in a stiff Dress to Routs and Drums ; dear *Ranger*, you
" must give us an helping Hand ; you must give us an Essay
" upon it you, wild Devil." With this she tapped me on the
Shoulder, in her lively agreeable Manner, and insisted with all the
Rhetoric of a Romp; that I should propose her Scheme to the
Public, which I assured her I should take the first Opportunity to
perform.

I HAVE ever been of Opinion, that, in the general, Coffee-
Houses are no very great Advantage to young Men, most of
those Places being frequented entirely by Bucks, Bloods, and
Rakes of all Denominations, from whom there is nothing to
be acquired except a Swagger in the Gait, a drunken Tot-
ter, a noisy riotous Deportment, a Volly of Oaths, and a
total Want of what is called Good-Breeding. I know at this Instant several young Gentlemen of Birth and Fortune, whose whole
Lives are spent between the Tavern and the Coffee-House, without
having any Connections in genteel Families, or any Acquaintance
with the amiable Sex, without which no one can ever properly
be said to relish Society, or to possess that Polish in his Manners,
which is necessary to distinguish the Gentleman. Perhaps this
Opportunity of detaching themselves from the Ladies in Coffee-House Clubs is the Cause of that Aukwardness, which is frequently remarkable in Persons of Condition, when by some Dis-
after they are compelled to endure polite Company. On this Account

count I am apprehenfive, that a Rendezvous of this Nature might have fome ill Effect upon the Deportment of the Fair, and I muft therefore declare, that, in my Opinion, the beft Way for both Sexes to enjoy the Elegancies of Life, is to mix with one another without forming any Parties of Separation.

It is however poffible that this Scheme may be carried into Execution, and no Doubt it will be attended with many notable Advantages. The Convenience of meeting People of Fafhion, without the neceffary Parade of going to their Houfes, will certainly be very great, and Appointments with each other may be fixed with Eafe by the Means of this Inftitution; as for Inftance a Memorandum-book may ferve for the following Purpofes.

"Lady *Laft-ftakes* came according to Appointment to meet
" Lady *Betty Modifh*; is gone to fee *Barry* in the dying Scene
" of *Romeo*; will be here again after the Play, when fhe will
" be glad to have a Party of *Picquet* with Lady *Betty*, and fpend
" the Remainder of the Evening."

" Miss *Madcap* called here about fix o'Clock in Hopes to fee
" Mifs *Limber-Tongue*; is gone to confult Mrs *Sermon* in *Naked-*
" *Boy-Alley*, after which fhe intends to fee *Harlequin Fortunatus*,
" and will call here again, and begs Mifs *Limber-Tongue* will
" leave Word where fhe may be heard of."

" Miss *Tattleaid* begs to fee Mifs *Graveairs*; has a Million
" of Things to fay to her, and particularly fomething fhe heard
" laft Night at Lady *Hurly-Burly*'s."

Such Proceedings as thefe will inevitably do Honour to the amiable Sex, and as they may judge it neceffary to *claim an equal Empire o'er the World*, I beg Leave to offer them a few Rules, which may ferve to conduct a female Coffee-Houfe with proper Regularity.

A System of Rules, &c.

I. That each Lady fhall pay *Six-pence* at the Bar, whether fhe drink *Tea, Coffee, Chocolate, Capillaire, Citron-Water*, or *Ratafia*, &c.

II. That the Actreffes fhall be admitted to this Coffee-houfe, by which means the Ladies will enjoy equal Pleafure with the feveral Gentlemen of Fafhion who are fo happy in the Converfation of his Majefty's Company of Comedians.

III. If a Quarrel fhould arife between any of the Ladies, they fhall not fall to pulling Caps in Company, but take another Opportunity to vindicate their Honour.

IV. If any Lady is difcovered with a Pair-royal of Aces in her Pocket, or endeavours to ufe any finifter Artifice at Cards, fhe fhall be expelled the Club, with as much Strictnefs as if it happened at *White*'s.

V. If

No. 15. THE GRAY's INN JOURNAL 89

V. IF any young Lady offers herself to be chosen into the Club by Ballot, a single white Ball shall be sufficient to admit her, it being improbable that a real Beauty will obtain that Favour from any one of her Sex.

VI and Lastly. THAT it shall be deemed meritorious in any Lady to brag of her Intrigues, her Amours, and her Designs with any young Man, who shall shall frequent Mr *Macklin*'s Coffee-House, by which Means the Ladies, may in Imitation of the laudable Practice among the opposite Sex,

> *Talk of Beauties, whom they never saw,*
> *And fancy Raptures, which they never knew.*   Z.

****

TRUE INTELLIGENCE.

From my Register-Office, Jan. 5, 1754.

I Have lately received several Remonstrances from the Ladies relating to the Inconveniencies they suffer in Hackney-Coaches for the Want of a String to stop the Coachman when Occasion requires it. One complains to me of having received a Black-eye, by an unlucky Jolt, when going to call to the Driver out of the Window: A second had her Head-dress totally discomposed, at a Time that she had a Mind to look as handsome as she possibly could ; and a third, in a fair Italian Hand, which is scarcely legible, mentions to me, that those *Limbs framed for the tender Offices of Love*, are so shattered, that they refuse the gentle Office of carrying their Burthen. In short, I am so importuned by my Correspondents to redress their Grievances, that I must now put out an Order to all whom it may concern, to provide the Ladies with the small Convenience abovemention'd.

To all Masters of Hackney-Coaches, &c.

Crusty and Ill-beloved,

WHEREAS we are advised that many Inconveniencies are endured by the lovely Part of the Creation, the female Sex, for the Want of a String to your Carriages, by the Help of which they might retard the rapid Driver, without running the Risk of a Black-eye, or a fractured Skull ; and whereas it appears to us highly just, that you should oblige the said Ladies in so necessary a Point, this is therefore to order all and every one of you to furnish your Vehicles with proper Accommodations, on or before the 25th of *March* next ; and whoever is found Delinquent after the said Time, shall have his Number taken by our Emissaries, and shall be prosecuted with the utmost Severity in our Court of Censorial Enquiry. Given under our Hand in *Gray's Inn, January* the 1st, 1754.

CHARLES RANGER.

Advices from *Dublin* inform us, that the Ladies of that Kingdom made very great Rejoycings on Occasion of a late Victory obtained there, in which they look upon the Honour of the Country to be materially concerned

90 THE GRAY's INN JOURNAL. No 15.

ned; and it is hoped that all Animosities will shortly be quieted by *his*
Grace * the Dutchess *of Dorset, &c.*

    * *This is a short way the Gazette has found of mentioning* his Grace the
Duke of Dorset, *and* her Grace the Dutchess of Dorset.

                    Wapping, Wind, N. N. W.

    Last Week *put in here Samuel Foote*, and *Charles Ranger, Esqrs*; They
behaved very well, of their own Accord, otherwise we should have made'n
steer another Way, tho' had we known Mr *Foote's* Intentions, we wou'd
ha' sent' in *bound for London*, with his *Topsails lower'd*, and t'other fresh Water Spark too. They should have had a *Broadside*, or so, and may hap,
ha' found that they had come to a bad Market. Tho' Mr. *Foote* may
divert the People farther *up-land*, we had aughten to run a muck and
tilt at us, as they say he intends to do very shortly in the Part of BEN in
the Play of *Love for Love*. Let'en, let'en do't; tho'f we don't often go
so far *inland*, we may *bowl up* to see him, and if he makes us laugh, why
we love a Joke as well as another, an that be all. He *rigged* himself here
in *flying Colours*, and bought Lieut. *Halfpay's* Hat and Wig off his Head, and
he is equipped for a Voyage up the Streights, an he had but a good
Cargo and a tight Vessel. However we shall all be *aloft* to see him, and
so we wish' in a good *Voyage*, and safe into Harbour again, for we hear
he spends his Money as fast as ourselves, and *cracks his Jest* with as much
Ease as we *crack a Bisket*, and so we ha' no further Malice to' en ; give an
take an that be all.

      Literary Bill of Mortality for the Year 1753.

Encreased in Offerings of Pamphlets to *Cloacina*, this Year, one thousand
    seven hundred and fifty three.

Encreased in periodical Papers, all neatly printed on a Sheet and half of
    fine Writing-Paper, Thirty-seven.

Abortive, Five hundred Plays, including Tragedies, Comedies, and one
    Parody of five Acts on Boadicia.

LONDON: Printed for W. F A D E N, in *Wine-Office-Court*, *Fleet-*
Street ; and J. B O U Q U E T, in *Pater-Noster-Row.*

George's coffee house. A poem (London, printed for the author, and sold by T. Osborne; R. and R. Dodsley; W. Owen; C. Moran; and Mrs. Cook, 1761), vii, 18pp.; 4°. Cambridge University Library: 7720.c.396. ESTCN7197. Hünersdorff.

A substantial verse satire on coffee-house conversation, debate and gossip in the early 1760s. Written in a gentle parody of heroic measure, the poem begins by surveying the literary politics of the period, making passing reference to a great many actors and playwrights famous in the theatre, as well as sundry poets and critics. Formally the poem must be counted as mock-epic (it begins by invoking the Homeric muse), but structurally it is more akin to the mock georgic strain, modelled on Gay's *Trivia* (1716). This satirical survey occasions the muse's peripatetic tour of the London coffee-houses, taking in a series of different coffee-house scenes, and briefly commenting on their distinctive discursive sociabilities. From page 251 onwards the scene settles into one coffee-house, presumably George's Coffee-house, Temple Bar – although identification is unclear, as the poem refers only to a widow coffee-woman and a servant named Will. In describing the conversation at George's, the poem satirises the follies of a group of army officers against a backdrop of the European and American campaigns of the Seven Years' War (1757–63). The poem is not substantially a satire on George III, as claimed by Hünersdorff.

Nothing is known of the author. Internal evidence suggests the poem was composed during the summer of 1761: there are numerous references to political and military events of the period April to July of that year, especially the Battle of Belleisle and the abandoned negotiations for a peace treaty between Britain and France. The text was printed 'for the author', meaning that the author took the risk of its publication by advancing money to cover the publication expenses. It was sold by a consortium of booksellers: Thomas Osborne in Gray's Inn, Robert Dodsley in Pall Mall, William Owen in Temple Bar, C. Moran at the Piazza in Covent Garden and Mrs Cook at the Royal Exchange. The poem was probably quite successful, because a second edition, with the emended subtitle 'A Satire', was printed in 1763, also 'by the author'. A copy at the Houghton Library, Harvard University, Cambridge, MA (EC75.A100.761g) has extensive manuscript annotations, as if for a revised edition, although the second edition makes no changes to the first other than the subtitle.

GEORGE'S

COFFEE HOUSE.

A

P O E M.

——————— *Arma virumque cano.*   VIRG.

L O N D O N:

Printed for the AUTHOR, and fold by T. OSBORNE, in
Gray's-Inn; R. and R. DODSLEY in *Pall-Mall*; W. OWEN,
Temple-Bar; C. MORAN, at the *Piazza, Covent-Garden*;
and Mrs. COOK, at the *Royal Exchange.* 1761.

(Price One Shilling.)

Where may be had the King of PRUSSIA's Letter to his
Friend MAUPERTUIS.

(iii)

P R E F A C E.

I Know many men in the world who are immediately prejudic'd againſt a work if it appears abroad without a *Preface* ; nor will they peruſe the ſheets, till they have read a pompous dedication, or a prefatory preamble twice as long as the work itſelf.

FIRST, they muſt know the deſign of the AUTHOR, how he came to undertake the ſubject ; where the MUSE firſt inſpir'd, whether walking, riding, ſailing, or ſetting, in Town or Country, by the ſide of a murmuring rill, or in the clouds of the fumigating Sons of *Mundungus* ——In this, I fear I ſhall diſappoint many ſuch my readers, being rather modiſh than explanatory ——for ho Perſon can be

A 2   ſo

iv   P R E F A C E.

fo ill-naturedly cruel, as to accufe me of having no
Preface at all.

My Jade of PARNASSUS has levell'd at no particulars; if one's pleas'd, and another benefits from
her *Chanfon*, fhe's highly rewarded for her Journey,
and the fame hackney PEGASUS that brought her
from the limpid fpring of HELICON, will jogg her
back again, without the wifh of a feed from your
terreftrial livery ftables — and fuppofe, fhe rubs her
back on her return, through the badnefs of her feat
or faddle — it's your bufinefs not to touch — for a
gaul'd horfe will winch.

As for the name of the Author, his birth, refidence, or employ, is very immaterial — His MUSE
was a fcullery *Wench* in the Kitchen of the wits
of King CHARLES the Second, but when Ros-
COMMON, BUCKINGHAM and WILMOT, withdrew
behind the Curtain, fhe made her exit in the mob
of their Caravan, and hired herfelf as houfe *Maid*
in the family of the HELICONIDES, where fhe long
                                                      liv'd.

P R E F A C E.   v

liv'd a moſt laborious life, till in my pilgrimage
up to MECCA, I paſs'd near the place of her
abode, to lave in the CASTALIAN ſpring, where I
firſt diſcover'd, and moſt Donquixotly fell in love
with her roſy cheeks, jetty locks, and innocent
graces —and for to elope with her my INDAMORA,
exercis'd an art, or rather an innate talent (peculiar to a County of this realm) ſtole an hackney
Pegaſus of the family's — and brought my CLIO
off. ——— Other particulars relative to her and my
ſelf you'll excuſe, but if you're a Buck of the
Turf the pedigree of her PALFREY may be a-
greeable.

Young PEGASUS was got by ORONTOPHITUS, be-
longing to the tutelar Saint of England, on which
the Champion ſlew the fiery dragon; his Dam
PANSOPHIA, that beat the famous *Veni, vidi, vici,*
Mare of Julius Cæſar's; his grand Sire BUCEPHA-
LUS, his maſter Alexander of Macedon, who with
him beat the globe, and at his death, built the
City *Bucephala,* near Hydaſpes, to his memory.
His

vi   P R E F A C E.

—— His grand Dam Lais that won immenfe fums at
Corinth —— His great grand Sire BELLEROPHONTISI-
BUS, which Bellerophon run againft the *Chimeræ*,
and heat hollow.—— His great grand Dam SEMI-
RAMIS, that diftanc'd the *Perfian Cyrus* on the
plains of Perfepolis —— His great, great grand Sire
BOSPORUS, run againft time in the *Vià Laǔtis* ——
but Jupiter betting confiderably againft him, fent
a gad fly to fting him, and threw his rider —— His
great, great, grand Dam, after winning many plates,
was the principal Hunter in ACTÆON's ftables ——
His great, great, grand Sire, the off Stallion in
PHAETON's car —— His great, great, great grand
Dam AVIS, that won a flying match againft *Priam
of Troy* —— His great, great, great, great grand Sire
PEGASUS VOLATUS, generated from the blood of
MEDUSA, and for his fwiftnefs was made a con-
ftellation :

PEGASUS *æthere fummo veloces agitat pinnas, & fidere gaudet.*

For every generous mind muft agree, nothing's fo
neceffary as a Latin fentence —— nor can it be juftly

P R E F A C E.   vii

ftil'd a *Preface* without it — but to convince the
world, how cautious I am of offending — give me
leave to fay with the only Poet. of the age —

    " Great are his perils in this ftormy time,
    " Who rafhly ventures on a fea of rhyme,
    " Around vaft furges roll, winds envious blow,
    " And jealous rocks and quickfands lurk below.
    " Greatly his foes he dreads, but more his friends,,
    " He hurts me moft who lavifhly commends.

C. CHURCHILL.

From my moving Villa
  of SANS SOUCI.   The A U T H O R.

GEORGE'S
COFFEE HOUSE.

RMS, and the Men I sing — the Men of war
Who pay their teasters at the Widow's bar;
Not that my Muse to any means offence,
Unless they bilk th'old Lady of her pence;
If such`a thing there is, or has been done,
The crimes so great, that Satyr cant't be dumb:
Yet such a thought my Muse scarce entertains.
Can it be want of pocket, pray, or brains?
For surely those who crowd that gloomy Place,
(Whose cloaths like Birth-day BEAUX, are spread with lace)
Can ne'er be guilty of that bilking crime;
Than she means harm, in this her harmless rhyme;

B

For

(2)

For CLIO knows, and fhe can only tell,
Oft there fhe's mus'd when tongues fupply'd a bell;
And if you'll credit but a Mufe's words,
They bawl'd fo loud — fhe always thought them LORDS ——
And what confirm'd her in this fhallow cafe,
Was to fee Men, bedizen'd fo with lace:
She hopes the BEAUTIES who frequent that houfe
Will pardon her, for fhe's an harmlefs moufe;
Long, long, fhe wander'd round this dirty town
For a bare fubject to pick up a crown;
Read every fhop, and 'moft ev'ry CANTO,
From witty CHURCHILL to the SCOTCH PORTMANTEAU.
Here in large letters, which oft' made her fmile,
Star'd TRUTH in RHYME, and there the foft BELLISLE
Next came the MINOR——Wilkinfon'd and ftale,
Then th'ANTI-ROSCIAD without head or tail.
Near VIC—s hiftory, with occafional notes,
Crowded with dry theatric anecdotes,
Nay what is more, with Irifhcifms full,
And to kill all, tautologically dull.
There the APOLOGY unequall'd fhines,
And his foft Mufe contemning CRITICKS dines.
Here poor RELIGION, refts on ROBSON's Pfalms,
There TARRATARIA frights with mad alarms.
High on a ftring, and ftitch'd in dirty blue,
Hung the pedantick, monthly mean REVIEW,
Like a cag'd Mag-pye let the witling prate,
He'll ftarve for corn, he fcatters thro' the grate. ——
Lo! read by all, and direful to tell,
Glar'd the untimely death of poor Mifs BELL.

Here

(3)

Here a Divine prefents his HYMN to HOPE,
There ELOISA's letters —— not by POPE.
Next Mr. OAKLEY in the JEALOUS WIFE,
Adds to a piece of true domeftick life:
Had fuch great Actors with poor MACKLIN been,
Might he not, think you, left the fecret Screen?
There in a corner, hardly read by three,
Peep'd a tranflation from the SANS SOUCI.
Here an affair periodically dull,
Without a title —— with the Moon in full.
She peep'd about, and really much furpriz'd,
Still no CHURCHILLIAD —— fo long advertiz'd,
A prudent Author, and a Wit reclufe,
To keep in Embryo —— the Mountain Moufe.
May a poor Mufe attempt to fay, or fing,
Dull FLORA, why! addrefs fo wife a King.
FIZGIG's a thief, a murd'rer, in this cafe
He's kill'd a Monkey —— nay and ftole his face;
Suppofe it's fafhion —— why? filch CHURCHILLS AD?
Fye! rob' a Wit, to cloath a Dunce that's mad.
Here large black letters moan RICHARDI NASH,
There pious PENTECOST —— Parnaffian trafh,
But to allure each walking Jackadandy,
The yawning frontifpiece of TRISTRAM SHANDY.

THE more fhe fought the greater was her lofs
From Aldgate bars to CHARLES at Charing-crofs;
But this alone did not, alas! fuffice,
In ev'ry Coffee-houfe fhe employ'd her eyes:

B 2   Sunk

(4)

Sunk down to JONATHAN's among the ftocks,
But found too dull a Samenefs in thefe blocks:
If ought feem'd confequential, wife, or new,
It was, fome plodding, dirty bearded Jew:
Who with his finger on his lip, ftood mute
Awhile, and then declar'd he'd feen Lord B—TE;
A Congrefs muft be —— and the DUTCH that chance,
BUSSY's arriv'd —— HANS STANLEY's gone to FRANCE.
The Bait went down, the Buz foon general grows,
And feventy dead — to ninety-two arofe:
One hour expir'd difpels all foggy fears,
And GIDEON grins at felling off his bears.

  LOYD's the next object of her city theme,
Where underwriters o'er their coffee dream.
Dead in a crowd of mercenary Bears
She fat, attentive to their Sea affairs,
Till one broke filence nubilous with cares.
From BELLISLE, HODGSON is repuls'd they fay
How fhall we this prodigious charge defray
Had I been there, I'd took it in a day.
Thus rant the Heroes of Plebeian pen,
Who if more filent, might be deem'd more men.—
A Cit roll'd in, with pork, and porter big,
Hid like a Lady-Lobfter in his wig,
A Draper — always at his prayers, or pipe,
Abroad a grumbler — and at home a gripe.
To him one prop'd as impudent, as dull,
Bawling —why Sir, you'll not infure from HULL!

                                                        He

(5)

He anfwer'd nought—but turn'd upon his toe,
Hung his moift lip—and waddl'd—to and fro.

To the JERUSALEM o'er the Pavement next
She fkim'd away—and NABOB CLIVE her text;
Small here the ftir, few objects for a theme,
Unlefs my Mufe, a guinea pig had been.——
Poor Girl fhe over piles of LEDGERS wept,
Then quite dejected thro' CHANGE ALLEY crept—
Until fhe reach'd, that Fabrick of plumb cake,
Where hoggifh Sons of Cuftard annual rake,
She foon reviv'd—the wing as foon affum'd,
And o'er the TRAYTORS heads, elated plum'd;
Then funk gradatim to St. CLEMENT's wall,
At her beloved SOMERSET to call,
There a droll groupe prefented to her view,
Cit, Soldier, Lawyer, Parfon, Sailor, Jew,
But for a poem, this medley would not do.
What her attention chiefly drew afide
Were prentic'd Prigs—who rare a buttock eyed,
Stuff'd into boxes in their Sabbath cloaths,
With bufby Bobs—true mark of Counter Beaux;
Who for the day had ruralizing been,
In alehoufe windows—merely to be feen,
At *Stepney, Chelfea, Red Caps* or the *Hill* *,
Where all they'd fpent, and yet without their fill:
Where fhould they come then to fupply their wants
But here?——where beef kind EDMONDS gratis grants.

A

---

* *Hampftead* or *Highgate.*

(6)

A filky Doctor then fhe glided down,
And foar'd to Tom's (where firft your Honours thrown)
Bett on the Baron, found fhe was not right,
The Gov'ner holding all the cards to' night.
Then chang'd the bett, and on a four foot Buck —
Againft a Coan of feven, fhe try'd her luck;
Doubtlefs the former muft have had the game,
But he 'kept praifing of his conftant flame,
Or raving loud, theatrically fpout,
" Ye Gods ! fuch hair — it's fhocking to come out ;
" Or foftly warbling fome Italiek ftrain,
Thump his dear craw — then *dimning* — yield the game.
It vext her fore, to think a Mufe's fkull
Should be   good money on an head fo dull —
Enrag'd at which, fhe out the window flew,
Titt'ring to think fhe'd bilk'd the little Jew.
Straight to St. Paul's, fhe bent her rapid flight,
All growing duller at th'approach of night,
There fnug fhe fat, all feeing, and unfeen,
Reflecting where to go, and where fhe'd been ;
At laft the Bedford fill'd her anxious head —
So from the Church to the Piazza's fped.
Awhile in cloifter'd flights fhe kept the plume,
And with an Author pop'd into the Room —
Here fhe beheld, a low, odd motley crew,
Criticks, Clowns, Poets, Fiddlers, Painters too,
Pimps, Players, Gamblers, Whitfieldites, and Turks,
Sprung from the O'neales, M'Dugglis and the Burks.
Pale here the Mimic turn'd, if what he'd faid,
Amongft his nonfenfe, touch'd the man in Red,

Here

Here he repairs poor witling for to fee
The fate of infant modern TRAGEDY;
Not that he wish'd that PROVIDENCE *was dead*,
For age trots on, and he may want his bread.
HOGARTH here creeps fometimes, to fteal a fneer,
And COLEMAN jealous of his wife to hear,
Nay poor hifs'd JACKSON from an houfe full cram'd,
Would know — but dreads the LIBERTINE is damn'd.
Biting his nails, a penfive figure, talk'd
Of ROSCIADS, NAIADS, 'POLOGIES — then walk'd:
What could this be fo very mad and rare;
But at a nearer ken — the young VOLTAIRE ——
Nothing delighted but the Hero's ftile,
So made her exit with the DESART ISLE.
But in the crowd the Mufes Midwife loft;
So in a Pet, o'er RUSSEL-STREET fhe croft;
And fcuded back to the PIAZZA hall:
(By MACKLIN firft intended for a ball)
Large there the furniture, the guefts but fmall;
But what there were, feem'd the ST. GILES's race,
In bob-wigs fome, and fome in MONMOUTH lace;
Thefe Sons too apifh for my Mufe's Pen,
She left their GUILDHALL, for the Widow's den;
(What is, is dull, no fpirit for juft Satyr,
Unlefs it's wit the echo's of a waiter.)
But why fhe likes her low'ring roof, to fay,
Is hard — unlefs like Owls fhe hates the day;
For all muft own, who do frequent that place,
There's fcarcely light, to fhow a brilliant lace;

Alas!

(8)

Alas ! the Widow's eyes has loft their fire ——
But fay, why wont fhe raife her Manfion higher ?
Unto the hand of time, fubmit we muft,
And WALGRAVE — like the' Widow, muft be duft.
Surely all Poets like not gloomy fcenes,
For moft 'their' lays are flowers, and purling ftreams,
Whether fatigue here ftay'd the Mufe's feet,
She'll not confefs, but here fhe took her feat,
And with her pencil thefe mementos drew,
The Widow feated fully in her view,
Drefs'd in a decent, yet becoming woe,
Snarling at Will — or fnuffing with a Beau.
But fhe, good Lady, had not time to fay,
The pains her toes endure a winter's day,
Till fome rude Youth, in boifterous accent hails !
Widow fome Coffee — d——n your toes and nails.
She with her ufual foftnefs, known to few ——
" Said I'm not deaf — perhaps it's fo with you.

THE next who came a pretty contraft made,
A fine fpun Youth, moft tuliply array'd,
From noble blood — the Beau I'm fure muft fpring,
Man, Cit, or Ruftick, never got the THING ——
Hair moft cobwebly, inexprefsly neat,
No Park bought nofegay half fo fine or fweet ;
Legs, O ye Fair, would really charm ye all,
Compleatly modifh ; fhapelefs, long, and fmall ;
But when he mov'd a pretty mincing pace,
Added to all the reft, the lovelieft grace ;

He

(9)

He fpoke, but oft' before it reach'd the ear,
Two monofyllables were loft in air.
" *Wadow* — a jelly warm — it's monftrous chill,
" I've really walk'd — but find *me migty* ill,
" I *caint* conceive how I abroad could ftare
" Without my flannels, Muff, Surtout, or chair:
" The Widow heard, but mutter'd with a groan,
" Such Things as you had better kept at home.
I've feen a Youth, but whether this or no
I'll not affert — but was in fact a beau,
Breakfaft being o'er, his hands more foft than filk,
Lave with a cambrick handkercher in milk,
I'll grant you leave, from this to ISPAHAN,
To find a thing more trivial if you can,
Much lefs than Woman, in the fhape of Man.

NEWS of the day fhe having juft run oe'r,
Paus'd on fome politicks a little more,
When lo! the door a folemn opening made,
And in his plad ftruts in an HIGHLAND blade;
Suppofe no plad! — the leer the *mon* betray'd.
'Tis really ftrange, but yet like Jews, this race
Bear all the map of SCOTLAND in the face.

ON metopofcopy reflecting, till
The door burft open with the echo — WILL!
" A dram Boy, give me, for I'm plaguey queer,
" And is the mail from IRELAND my dear?
" For one dear letter on this felf fame day,
" I'd give, do you fee my foul! a full month's pay.

C

One

(10)

One left his chair, and to the Widow's ear
Stole up to know, who was that *very dear* —
When she abruptly anfwer'd in an huff,
" An IRISH GAMBOLER, and took her fnuff.
The Widow then a little while withdrew,
For things more decent out of public view,
When up, in red, and fac'd with blue, a Smart
Props in the bar, to play the Widow's part;
Shadows in all, you'll find have fhadows too,
And Monkies mimick Monkies out of view.
Here as on Guard as trivial they appear,
Equally trivial, from the Van to Rear,
The power they have, they fhow it for the worfe,
Stopping a Beggar's bundle, or an Horfe,
FISHER, or HERMITAGE, they'll grant a pafs,
Deny a Brother, as they would an Afs;
I always ftudied to oblige the CORPS,
In point of duty, and in point of Whore,
Now fhall my ftudy and my duty be,
To thwart their wifhes, as they've thwarted me.——
Near on the right, now rofe a great difpute,
ON—W, want GR—LE, HOL—SE, wan't B—TE;
Quick turn'd my Mufe, and found them yet'ran Stagers
Twifting the Court, in full forbidding majors.
One kindly whifper'd — with a friendly fmile,
" God waft our Heroes fafe from hard BELLISLE.
" Zounds, bawls the next, Sir — would you them have quit
" Their ground — while there remains a foe to fpit.
A third reply'd, and with a gen'rous grace,
" Think on the Worthies butcher'd in that place.

" Grant

(11)

" Grant them, ye Gods! this fiege with glory o'er,
" And ev'ry merit, give to every CORPS.
" Don't let our wounded Heroes want their bread,
" And ftile all merit, that appear in red :
" Nor O! ye BRITONS, once forget the wounds,
" Your Children got, extending of your bounds ;
" Think how they bled to raife BRITANNIA's name,
" And fell in Legions, to fupport her FAME.
" And thou great LEGISLATOR hear the words
" Of him, who long follicited thy LORDS,
" And generous MONARCH now at once fupprefs
" The vulgar theme of every City prefs ;
" To Nobles give, whate'er their Virtue gives,
" But more to MERIT, then fhe now receives ;
" Banifh Dame Intereft, venal, dirty Whore,
" And give to Merit, MERIT's due, or more,
" Thee, glorious PRINCE, whom ev'ry Virtue warms,
" Whofe parent conduct, ev'ry BRITON charms,
" Whofe greateft ftudy, is his KINGDOM's eafe,
" And ever happy in the power to pleafe.;
" In Counfel learned, meek in regal ftate,
" To pardon hafty, and to punifh late.
" Give MERIT rank, in INDIVIDUALS too,
" Reward the red Coat, nor forget the blue.
" But this is fad — to fee a virtuous Youth,
" The Son of GLORY, LIBERTY, and TRUTH,
" Purchafe his rank, perhaps with all his ftore,
" Then waft him hence to diftant INDIA's fhore ;
" There let him fight till cover'd o'er with fcars,
" An individual in your GALLIC wars,

C 2   " Re-

(12)

" Return unknown, neglected let him lay,
" And ftarve, forgotten, on his poor half pay.

Just now the poft deliver'd at the bar,
His anxious parcels from the Seats of War,
And held the converfe of this good, old man,
Who drew his fubject from a virtuous, plan.
" A mail from Germany fqueaks out a Sage,
" Well! does the Prince the Marshal yet engage?
" A grand ftagnation feems in our affairs,
" To ftrike a blow, is more than Broglio dares:
" How fo! cries one, in flefh prodigious big,
(A Doctor by th'immenfity of wig)
" Think on his numbers, don't contemn a foe,
" Who at this Juncture's five to one, I know.
Words foon grew high — my Mufe had little fears,
When Phyfic, Law, and War, were by the ears,
All talk'd together, equally all big,
From the rofe bag to the full bottom'd wig,
The din ftill rofe, the Widow left her bar,
And fwell'd with fury join'd the clam'rous war.
With an intent this tumult to appeafe,
And with her Chocolate fons eftablifh Peace;
But all in vain — till in a Navy Blade
Enter'd, whofe funny phiz declar'd his trade,
Though few come here, unlefs they wifh to pafs
For Soldiers — and in all affect the afs:
Defpife the blue, the red coat to affume,
While Captain, Captain, echoes round the room

Big

(13)

Big and important with the news, to tell
HODGSON's victorious, PALLAIS, PALLAIS's fell.
The theme soon chang'd, joy smil'd in every face,
And a new lustre glar'd on ev'ry lace.
So great, so sudden, were the news to all,
Together, Widow, Will —Will, Widow bawl,
For Coffee, Punch, Tea, Doctors, Capillaire,
To drink brave HODGSON, Widow do you hear?
Nay some, so absent in their honest joy,
In Coffee toasted round the BRITISH boy.
Behold! how soon evaporates all this,
In silence first, succeeded with an hiss:
When a gay *Aid de Camp* declaring stood,
" PALLAIS was FRENCH — but yet this news were good,
" But all was yet in sacred silence cool'd,
" Till the *Gazette*, thro' PITT the whole reveal'd.
Now in suspence this gaping Room was left,
Yet not of ev'ry ray of hope bereft,
Those then who could, their seats again assum'd,
And their grave noses o'er their Coffee fum'd.
When in creeps *Lynch* with bow, and solemn air,
Stuff'd full off books his coat, his face with care:
Addressing first your *Honour* with a grin,
To feel your pulse, and how you like the *Sin*.
Sometimes in haste an Hermit he'll surprize,
And lewdness cram into his virgin eyes.
" Here's the CHURCHILLIAD, Sir, at last abroad!
" And 'Squire MURPHY's NAIAD Fleet-ditch ODE,
" CHURCHILLIAD, *Lynch*, — you surely must be wrong,
" O! let me chant the smooth Parnassian song!

" It's

{ 14)

" It's profe for *footh* — in rhyme it firft was writ,
" But fo inferior to the ROSCIAN wit,
" That quite incens'd the Sons of DRURY rofe,
" And chang'd harfh jargon, into venal profe ;
" I bought it —— read it, and condemn'd it too,
Not for it's merits, or it's being new. ——
The nut-brown NAIAPS *of the fable flood,*
Are not more blefs'd with mire, than he with mud ;
It's been a School-boy's rule for ages long,
That CLOACINA help'd the Poet's fong.
But fince the fmell, has no effect on you,
Who knows what wonders eating it may do ?
A fair angelick Sifter of the NINE,
Read thy SEWER ODE before fhe went to dine ;
But at the table, with a female's will,
Declar'd the various filth had made her ill. ——
Youth *Lynch's* pamphlets eagerly embrace,
And always buy when frontifpieces grace :
But if you want fair *Leda* and her Swan,
Or the *Cafcade* and *Angler*, he's the Man,
Or for your watch fome wanton piece of joy,
None can fupply you like the *Naked Boy*
To him fucceeded a red foggy Dame,
With fmuggl'd baubles for the BEAUX of fame,
Who in your hands will ruffles, ftockings thruft,
" *Take them your Honour — for you know I truft.*
Sometimes about a ghaftly figure — *purs*
" *Garters* your Honour — buy a pair of fpurs ?

My

(15)

My Clio now on impofitions mus'd,
Till by the noify phyfick Quorum rous'd,
Who in debate again were clofely fet;
Paying with head and fift, the national debt.
Finding thefe Medici the tongue affume,
Stole to that opaque corner of the Room,
Where a fring'd Curtain in theatrick tafte,
Excepting twice a-day is neatly trac'd;
Once when the Widow quits the mob to dine,
Then drops, this dufty fable red Ensign,
Or if fome Romeo's at his Juliet fad,
Then it divides, the gloomy, from the mad.
Here by two Youths, fhe calmly fat her down,
Who'd dearly purchas'd with their limbs, renown.
One, with a figh pathetically faid,
As penfive oe'r the daily news he read,
" The brave, the laurell'd, great Lord Downe is dead.
" Refleft unhappy Brother Suff'rer now,
" What glories living, wreath'd his honour'd brow,
" And yet with all his virtuous generous deeds,
" Like a plebeian, view the Hero bleeds!
" Can we repine, unhappy wounded friend?
" When British Nobles quicker deaths attend.
" At Minden had I tenfold tortures known,
" Smiling I'd bore them, to have fav'd my Downe :
" But fate ordain'd, and lo! the bullet fped?
" Behold! the Hero with the mighty dead.
" By the fame hand thus Kings and Beggars fall;
" Yet ftill it's glorious bleeding on a Gaul.

THUS

(16)

Thus like a fecond Mucrus, Cordus fpoke,
A Britifh plant, fprung from a Britifh Oak:
Th'attempt was great to ftab the Clusian Chief,
And what he bore, e'en ftaggers our belief;
Yet tell thofe Shades, the braveft Romans gone,
Britain like Rome has Sons as brave at home.
Behold the Theban † with his bearded fpear!
Nay, his laft martial declaration hear.
Though Mantinea deathlefs made his fame,
Yet on his plan, Wolf rais'd a greater name;
Rome's, Athens, Sparta's, Macedonia's men
Were brave — but Britons are as brave as them. ——
Weep o'er that fcene, where Quebec's Hero lies,
Lo! bleeding Downe between two Soldiers dies;
To fave their Ifle, from rapine, war, and luft.
They fell unnumber'd with the brave, and juft.

Britons, for fhame, let publick fpirit warm
Your fouls, to cherifh him who's loft his arm,
Or if a leg — th'unhappier is his lot,
But never let his fervice be forgot;
Study to make them happy in thefe days,
And bind their brows with never fading bays.
Small are the premiums in thefe rigid times
For wounded Heroes, and for Poets rhymes;
Such partial favour in preferments feen,
At leaft where my hard fortune's ever been,

---

† Epaminondas.

That

(17)

That on my word, furpriz'd I fhould be not,
If from the *Crofs* CHARLES o'er the *Bridge* fhould trot.
For without *Intereft, Merit* ever may
Knock at my LORD's — the Porter give his pay.
Are not thefe things though fhocking to the ear?
Efpecially friend, when from a BRITISH PEER.
Look fome days back ——— when a few GALLIC boats,
Muft crofs the CHANNEL to cut all our throats.
Where are our Soldiers? where our Sailors fay?
Will they defert us, in the needful day?
At once there's nought fo great as *City* fear,
A *Cow* on 'CHANGE an *Earthquake* may appear.

BUT above all, ye! fympathetick FAIR,
Make them the objects of your love, and care,
Reflect like SPARTAN Virgins, if you can;
They bled for you, which makes them more than Man:
To every Hero yield your Virgin charms,
Grant them the circling of your fnowy arms,
And from your lips this maxim let 'em know,
That you'll be kind, if they will beat the foe. ——
Such deeds as thefe will raife your Sexes fame,
And make you greater than the ROMAN name.
Infpire our Youth with courage more than man,
And conquer BROGLIO on a female plan;
With joy the Vet'rans may the papers con,
And hand the deeds from father down to fon,
Crowd to the Widows, quaff their doctors down,
And every *Chriftmas* fpare poor WILL a crown. ——
                    D.

(18)

My Mufe requefts — againft that forry day,
Not to defert her, on pacifick pay.
Although it's dear, whole threepence for a difh,
Yet for that money Sir, what would you wifh.
All fhe can fay — and Widow hear her prayers,
Before thy dark tribunal fhe declares,
What fhe can give, is, when thou'rt dead fome rhymes,
But will not bilk thee at the worft of times.
" Though with thy Kings, thou does not blend thy duft,
" Yet fhalt thou have a monumental Bust,
" And thofe who've drank thy Coffee, raife their eyes,
" Then ftrike their breafts — read —*Here the.Widow lies*.
" Who in her life her bleffings never fpar'd,
" But equal all her tongue and coffee fhar'd,
" Sprung from the loins of ADAM and of EVE,
" And older too, if *Heralds* you'll believe.
Say, can the mighty BL—K—EY higher foar?
But when exalted at an alehoufe door.

LONG may fhe live, the fubject of my page,
And GEORGE and GEORGES feel the golden age

F I N I S.

E R R A T U M.
Inftead of MACDUGGLIS.—*read* M' DUGGLE's.

Memoirs of the Bedford Coffee-House. By a Genius, 2nd edn (London, J. Single, 1763), 144pp.; 8°. BL: 12314. ee.11. ESTCT101296. Extract, pp. iii–59. Hünersdorff.

An anonymous prose satire on the theatrical critics who gathered at the Bedford Coffee-house in Covent Garden in the period 1751–61. Much of the satire is directed against individuals, such as Dr John Hill and his periodical *The Inspector*, and actor and critic Arthur Murphy. The satire recalls literary scandals and slights stretching back a decade (on p. 275, the writer states that these memoirs date from 1751 onwards). This local satire has some particular interest, but also casts light on the critical practices of the day. The sociable habits of the gentlemen who assembled in the 'dominion of wit' in Covent Garden contributed many important ideas and habits to the practice of literary criticism as it is understood today. Nonetheless, there are also enlightening differences: the judgement of criticism in the 1750s was first communal and sociable, made in a face-to-face encounter between members of a known coterie, before it was passed on to the public. Criticism was sociable, and its sociability was formed in the coffee-house.

The first edition was 144 pages in length, and was published by 'J. Single in the Strand'. A second edition was published 1763, also by Single, with 'many additions', taking the page length to 210 pages (ESTCT129526, continuing from pp. 140–206), but making no changes to those pages included in the first edition. Publication of the latter was listed in the 'Monthly Catalogue' of the *London Magazine*, November 1762 (p. 632). There was no earlier edition in 1751, as suggested by Arthur Sherbo, *New Essays by Arthur Murphy* ([East Lansing], Michigan State University Press, 1963), p. 196, n.70. The printer 'J. Single' was probably fictitious: his only publications on the ESTC are the two editions of the *Memoirs*, and a satire on John Shebbeare (*A Seventh Letter to the People of England* (London, J. Single, 1758)). The *Memoirs* is listed as one of the 'Books printed by Geo. Burnet at Bishop Burnet's Head, near St Clement's Church, in the Strand', appended to *The Parasite*, 2 vols (London, G. Burnet, 1765), vol. I, p. [191]. Nothing is known of the author. In the concluding dialogue of the text in both editions (not reprinted here) William Hobster, the proprietor of the Bedford Coffee-house, is reported as saying that he was a 'little man in black' (p. 141), while another coffee-house 'genius' recalls that he 'used to see the rascal scribbling in the next box, and be very attentive when any body was talking, or anything was going forward' (p. 141). Manuscript additions to the British Library copy of the second edition (BL 12330.bb.33) identify many of the protagonists in the satire. The review in Tobias Smollett's *Critical Review* commented that the author 'has selected a subject entirely suited to his talents. A dull, pert attempt, to be witty and satirical, is the character of this motley production' (14 (December 1762), p. 479). The review in *The Monthly Review* (27 (December 1762), p. 478) observed that it was a 'light and frivolous subject', but that the 'materials are put together in a lively manner; the style, tho' incorrect, not being totally destitute of spirit, nor of that variety of expression so necessary in delineating a variety of characters'.

MEMOIRS

OF THE

BEDFORD

COFFEE-HOUSE.

By a GENIUS.

LONDON:

Printed for J. SINGLE, in the Strand.

MDCCLXIII.

[Price Two Shillings fewed]

To the MOST

Impudent MAN alive.

Illuftrious SIR,

IT is with the higheft fenfe of your merit, that I take the liberty of dedicating the following fheets to you, as the propereft perfon to fecure this work from the fneers of felf-imagined wits, and the attacks of pfeudo-critics. So modeft a performance requires a doughty champion to protect it from the rage of folly and impertinence: And who fo fit as you, Sir, *The moft impudent Man alive?*

I mean not to flatter you, or adulate your parts and abilities, great as they are: I leave that to fycophants and

a 2 mercenary

D·E D I·C A·T I O·N.

mercenary dedicators. The world is already fufficiently acquainted with you and your virtue, to need no comment from fo bafhful a pen as mine. The purport of this addrefs is, therefore, only to intreat your countenance, fo effential in all great enterprizes, in the profecution of this work; which will confer an ineftimable obligation on,

S I R,

Your humble Admirer,

The Blufhing A U T H O R.

(1)

MEMOIRS

OF THE

Bedford Coffee-Houſe.

T is ſurpriſing that this place, ſo replete with matter, and ſuch a field for obſervation, ſhould have hitherto eſcaped the pens of all our hiſtorians, noveliſts, and me-moir-writers. This ſpot, which has been ſignalized, for many years, as the emporium of wit, the ſeat of criticiſm, and the ſtandard of taſte, is likely to be obliterated to poſterity, if ſome ad-

B   ᵥenturous

(2)

venturous bard fhould not deign to
tranfmit its anecdotes to that period,
when we may reafonably fuppofe, thro'
the natural viciffitude of things, no
veftiges of it can poffibly remain. With
this laudable defign, I have ventured
to take up the quill, which, though
feeble, will exert itfelf to convey an
impartial idea of this receptacle of modern genius's, to point out the various
changes it has underwent for thefe ten
years laft paft, relate the moft interefting hiftories of thofe who have frequented it, and depict a lively defcription of thofe fcenes which have
rendered it the moft celebrated.

The fituation of this place neceffa-
rily makes it a convenient affembly for
thofe who frequent the theatres, as well
as thofe who exert their talents to
pleafe the public in dramatic performances;

(3)

ances; and, for the fame reafon, it may be looked upon as the centre of gravitation between the court and city; the noxious effluvia of St. Bride's is here corrected by the genuine Eau de Luce from Pallmall, and the predominence of ambergrife at St. James's is qualified by the wholefome tar of Thames-ftreet. Nor does the converfation receive a lefs happy effect from this junction; the price of ftocks, and the lie of the day from the Alley, are foftened by the *bon mot* of Lady Dolabella, which fet every foul at the Duchefs Trifle's rout in a titter; or the duel that was fought this morning between Captain Terrible and Lord Puncto, when both of them were mortally wounded *in the coat.* By this fortunate menftruum in converfation all political controverfies are prevented;

B 2 and

(4)

and one fcarce knows here how affairs
go in Germany, without a mail is in
that day, and the Doctor is under fome
apprehenfions for the King of Pruffia.
In that cafe we are generally diverted,
in every fenfe, by a ftory from F—te,
or the purfuit of a moufe by fome
Knight Errant, famous in chivalry.
By thefe means (though politics are
feldom brought upon the carpet) a
battle in Saxony, or a rout in Weftphalia, have been accurately illuftrated,
to the pleafure and fatisfaction of all
bye-ftanders. A ftudent never launches
from Oxford or Cambridge ; a lawyer's clerk never claps on a fword, or a
haberdafher's 'prentice a cue-wig, but he
makes his appearance here. In a word,
a blood never comes upon the town,
or a hero never goes off the ftage,
without taking his degrees here. It is
here

(5)

here that modefty and bafhfulnefs, which diftinguifh the young men of fpirit of this age, are firft acquired: It is here they receive their finifhing ftroke of education, and ftart genius's, critics, bucks, fops, and fools.

Though it muft certainly be acknowledged, that *dramatic affairs* are here the *affairs of ftate,* and it is of more vifible (ay, and real) importance to the majority, whether the *little man* ftill remains at the *helm,* than whether Mr. P— is *in* or *out* of the adm——n; there are matters of other confequence tranfacted here. There is fcarce a quarrel of any import, that has not had its rife, its progrefs, or its iffue here: the heroes generally make their appearance, at leaft once upon this ftage (fo near and fo analogous to the others); and fhould they be fo unfor-

B 3   tunate

(6)

tunate as to lofe fomething in point of *fame*, they generally make it up in point of *noife*. This may be called the theatre of valour and punctilio, and is the proper fpot for a court of honour; a thing fo much wanted, and fo little underftood in this kingdom.

Another clafs who refort hither, make very little noife, either at the Bedford, or in the world, though their fole bufinefs is to be heard and attended to : I mean we gentlemen authors, who fcrawl upon our knees for want of a table, run a tick at the chandler-fhop for our paper, and have fcarce intereft with our landlady for a dinner. I fhewed this very piece, when I had got thus far, to mine ; and I fhould have went without a meal, had it not been upon the Bedford Coffee-houfe fcore.—O ! Mr. Hobfter,—you know

not

(7)

not what obligations I have to you !—
How often have I went on truſt with
you for a ſupper ! How often have I
had coffee and bread and butter in lieu
of a dinner ! How often have I ſkulk-
ed out of the back-door, when I have
had no money to pay ! What pro-
vender ! what ſupplies do I ſee *in fu-
turo* upon the credit of your houſe !
But, I ſay, no more as to ſelf. A poor
author is but a bad theme.

In the year 1751, from whence I
date theſe memoirs, Dr. H— commenced a new paper under the title
of *Inſpector*, which he uſhered into
the world with panegyrical remarks
on Mr. Grey's elegy in a country
church-yard : the paper ſucceeded beyond the author or the publiſher's
moſt ſanguine expectations, as long as
he remained incognito ; but a certain
B 4 natural

(8)

natural vanity, which that gentleman could never furmount, prompted him to reveal the author of fo well receiv-ed a piece; and from that moment he made himfelf anfwerable for what was publifhed under his fanction. In the courfe of his lucubrations he had at-tacked fome private characters; but as this was done under a mafked battery, he efcaped with impunity. A duel that happened at the Braund's head in Bond-ftreet, gave him occafion to cenfure a Lady's conduct, who was entirely blamelefs; the world took fhare in her injury, and he loft credit in proportion, with them. The laft refource of proftitutes is to fupport themfelves by the means they have been debafed; and, forry I am to fay it, the Doctor adopted this maxim, which coft him not only his literary,

but

(9)

but alfo his perfonal reputation. Mr. B——, an Irifh merchant, who had travelled abroad, and was on his return to Ireland, in London, had been reprefented to him as a proper chara&ter for ridicule; the Do&tor, without hefitation, drew him at length. Mr. B—— prefently knew himfelf, and wrote to the Do&tor, infifting upon a public declaration, that the chara&ter there drawn was not meant for him. Mr. H——, inftead of complying herewith, publifhed his letter, which was not exempt from fome grammatical and orthographical errors: this fo exafperated Mr. B——, that he pofted the Do&tor at the Bedford, threatening him with bodily corre&tion wherever he met him: and he was as good as his word; for, a few nights after, meeting him at Ranelagh, he found

B 5   an

(10)

an opportunity of pulling off his wig, and buffeting it about his face, which the Doctor bore with all the philofophical refignation of a Diogenes.

However, the Doctor endeavoured to palliate his conduct upon this occafion; and reprefented, *in his paper*, that he had been attacked by feveral armed men in one of the bye-walks, who had ufed him fo ill that his life was in danger :—But this only ferved to increafe the ridicule againft him, and, inftead of re-inftating him in the good opinion of the public, brought upon him a fhoal of farcafms, which, at length, obliged him to drop his paper. He did not, however, accomplifh this, before he had endeavoured to corrupt Mr. Fielding, who then wrote the Covent-Garden Journal, fo far as to want him to commence an
imaginary

(11)

imaginary literary war, which he thought would be the means of still supporting his paper; but this Mr. Fielding refused, with a juft fpirit of refentment.

Thus ended the *Infpeĉtor*, which had given rife to this *reign* of the Bedford; had placed there the Lion from Button's, which proved fo ferviceable to *Steele*, and once more fixed the dominion of wit in Covent-Garden.

In the courfe of thefe papers, the Doĉtor had taken occafion to animadvert upon the conduĉt of the managers of the theatres; particularly with refpeĉt to a rival pantomime, which then engaged the attention of the town; and Mr. Woodward, who performed Harlequin, found himfelf criticifed in his conduĉt, for having

B 6   taken

(12)

taken notice of a perfon, who threw
an apple from one of the boxes. This
Woodward very fmartly refented in a
letter to the Doctor, which the world
attributed to Mr. Garrick.

The reign of wit and pleafantry did
not, however, ceafe at the Bedford
upon the demife of the Infpector; a
race of punfters next fucceeded; a particular box was allotted for this occafion, out of the hearing of the Lady
at the bar, that the *double entendres,*
which were fometimes very indelicate,
might not offend her.

Errato was born and bred an apothecary; from a fmattering of the
claffics, and the reading of minor authors, he fancied —nay, he believed
the world fancied him a wit; and he
endeavoured to fupport both the opinions. He had, notwithftanding, hop-
ped

(13)

ped up and down the Bedford for
fome years, without being noticed for
any thing but the fize of his periwig, and the width of his mouth:
but a lucky accident, as he and his
friends thought it, brought him into
fome repute. Dr. H— and he had
a little altercation; which was, however, always conducted like men of
letters, without coming to blows or
fword-drawing; and, upon an egregi-
ous pun that *Errato* made in the Doctor's hearing, he applied to him Dennis's axiom, that " he who would pun,
" would pick a pocket;" which ex-
cited Errato to call for the *Infpector*
to go backwards with him. This nettled
the Doctor; and he took his revenge,
by publifhing, in the fame paper, a letter that came to his hands, written by
Errato to Mr. L— the finger, all in

puns,

(14)

puns, to beg an order. This immor-
talized Errato ; and he was, from this
moment, univerfally ftiled the *punning
apothecary.*

Mr. *Town* was fecond of the group.
This perfon, who had become poffeffed of a genteel fortune, from a ftrong
impulfe of being acquainted with actors, and a defire of being thought
judicious in theatrical performances,
with a very flender knowledge of his
own or any other language, had ufur-
ped to himfelf the power and authority of deciding the merits of all theatrical productions, and all new actors.
He had the addrefs to enforce his prerogative fo far, that, when any new
piece was reprefented, he was fur-
rounded in the pit by a fet of young
templars, and danglers about the other
inns of court, who call themfelves
                                 ftudents,

(15)

ftudents, together with merchants clerks, and journeymen mercers, who formed a cabal upon thefe occafions, to pronounce peremptorily upon the merit of the production ; but in doing this they did not pretend to have any opinion, but only to eccho that of Mr. Town, who gave the word, and judgment was accordingly pronounced. This judgment was always ratified immediately after the performance at an affembly held at the Bedford, which was thenceforward, without appeal, irrevocable.

Philocleus was an Irifh ftudent, brought up to the law: he was genteel in perfon, and had that eafy infignificant manner, which the unfkilful take for addrefs. He had an early attachment with the theatrical world; and, by an interefted connection with

the

(16)

the tall actor, he was always partially influenced in his favour, and for
whatever regarded him : but this was
never fo vifible as in his efpoufing
the caufe of Mifs Noffiter, on her
firft appearance in the character of
Juliet. A critique was wrote upon
her performance, which the public
voice gave to Mr. M—y, and this was
fufficient for *Philocleus* to call him to
an account,—fo great a champion was
he for the *Noffiterian* caufe.—Several
conferences were held at the Bedford,
in which fome table-orations were
made by *Philocleus*, to prove that he
would never forgive the author of that
libel : nor was his oratory deftitute of
merit or invention ; he introduced a
new figure—a powerful *Profopopæia*—
that had entirely efcaped Demofthe-
nis, Cicero, and all the moderns, which
I know

(17)

I know no other name for than the *Glaſſiopoeia*. This was of great ſervice in enforcing his argument and concluding the debate, at leaſt, for the evening; for a gentleman having been very attentive to his rhetoric, though on the other ſide the queſtion, was convinced of the ſtrength of his reaſoning by a glaſs of capilaire, which waſhed his face and cleared his underſtanding. This ſtroke was the very eſſence of gymnaſtic oratory, and was claſſed with the *brandiſh*, which was alſo then firſt introduced with great ſucceſs, and without any other ill-effect than that of ſlightly wounding one Auditor. It is ſurpriſing that Mr. Sheridan and his late contemporary orators ſhould not have taken the leaſt notice of theſe two new *figures*, ſo happily
pily

(18)

pily invented and applied by *Philo-cleus.*

When the debate had come to this pitch between the contending parties, it was conceived nothing but death could end the difpute, and that the literary world muft have loft a bard by the conflict. But Providence orders every thing for the beft; for no fooner had Ranger prepared his weapons (which biographers fay was the firft time of his publickly appearing with a fword) but Philocleus was convinced of his error, and fatisfied that Ranger could never have penned the perform-ance. This lucky and unexpected re-conciliation the Republic of Letters has much reafon to be thankful for, as, in cafe of any accident happening to Phi-locleus, they would have been depriv-

ed

(19)

ed of that masterly performance of his, which Mr. B—y, with much labour and affiduity, brought upon Covent-Garden ftage. This tragedy will remain a lafting ornament of Britifh or Irifh genius, as Philocleus's friends take particular care to have it bound with the beft editions of Shakefpear.

It was at this period that Mr. M—y firft wrote in the *Craftfman*, which, from the moft efteemed political paper, in the hands of Bolingbroke, Pultney, and the reft of the anti-league, was now dwindled to a mere common place country journal, with fcarce an advertifement tacked to it, to give it the form of a news-paper. In this condition it fell into that gentleman's hands, who once more revived its fame, not as a political or party paper, but

as

(20)

as an inſtructive and amuſing publication.   To him we were firſt indebted
for what was called *true intelligence,*
which contained a criticiſm upon theatrical affairs, and ſatirical obſervations
upon the moſt reigning topics of con-
verſation.   His *news for a hundred
years hence,* was a very fine ſtroke upon
the Jew bill: this, and ſome other
pieces of the like kind, made him firſt
be taken notice of as a public writer;
and, upon ſome difference between him
and the publiſher of the Craftsman,
he ſet up a paper upon his own bottom, which he called the *Gray's-Inn
Journal* (a title he had added to that
of the Craftſman) and which he continued with the ſame ſpirit till he
came upon the ſtage, firſt in the character of Othello. The world has ſince
been ſufficiently acquainted with this
gentleman

(21)

gentleman to need no farther comment upon him, or his writings.

Specio was a doubtful character : a mixture of the fop and floven, of the wit and gamefter; he for fome time puzzled the world to decide upon his vocation, and had he not too early dif-covered himfelf to be the fucceffor of Mr. M—y in the Craftfman, he might have paffed unnoticed as a genius, or a darling of the mufes. The *juice of criticifm* firft recommended him to the publifher; and had he continued the true intelligence with any thing of the fame fpirit as was in that receipt, the paper would not have languifhed a twelvemonth in his hands. He has fince written fome fugitive pieces, the titles of which are fcarce remembered by any but him and his publifhers, and he is now concerned in one of the new Magazines.

(22)

Magazines. *Specio*, with thefe trifling abilities, was now in the meridian of his wit and gallantry; he was, at leaft, a fourth rate punfter, though he would fcarce give up the palm to the great Errato, whom he envied and abufed. A bumper extraordinary made him the greateft whoremafter of the age, with the powers of a Valetudinarian; and his fuccefs in intrigue would have made one fancy him an Adonis, did not his face bear a great refemblance of that animal's which fo much refembles man.

Mopfy, the *beau* of the age, muft certainly find a place in this lift of genii. With parts to have done credit to a much more ufeful life, he was the dupe of abandoned women, and the ri-dicule of more abandoned men. His greateft ambition was to be well dreffed,

and

(23)

and his greateſt luſt to ſay *a good thing*
at the Bedford, which he himſelf approved by ſmacking his box, and taking a pinch of ſnuff.   His whole life
might be epitomized in one day.   He
roſe about noon, breakfaſted, dreſt;
whilſt his man was curling his hair, he
read ; not that he gave any attention
to his author ; but that, in caſe any one
ſhould drop in, it might corroborate
what he thought *a bon mot*, and which
he often repeated, " Whilſt the outſide
" of my head is ornamenting, I do not
" neglect the inſide." When dreſſed, if
fine weather, the park was the conſtant
place of his reſort : when he had ſhewn
himſelf here for an hour or two, he
dined at a tavern or chop houſe, looked over his liſt of women, pitched upon
one he had not lain with, and ordered
the tavern-waiter to get her ready by
ſuch

(24)

fuch an hour.   After having fauntered
at the play or coffee houfe, till the hour
of appointment, he fupped with his
girl, and paffed the evening with her
at a bagnio, or his chambers.   Thus he
lived, thus he died, without a friend,
with fcarce an enemy but himfelf; pro-
feffing in his laft moments, that, did he
know one perfon who really efteemed
him,   he would bequeathe him his
whole fortune, which was very confiderable; but, as he did not, he left it
to a diftant relation, whom he had never feen.

Harmonicus was born a mufician,
though his father was an upholfterer:
his merit and abilities were paffed all
doubt, and could be exceeded by nothing but Handel and his own vanity,
which did not only induce him to believe, that he was a great mufician,
but

(25)

but that he was a great wit, a great poet, a great fcholar; things which one fhould imagine, from the common run of the mufical world, were incompatible with harmony: however, he had a fmattering fufficient to initiate him amongft the board of wits, and he took his place accordingly. *Harmonicus* was a man of great intrigue, though he admired his wife even to a fault; he has been known to be the only facinated auditor, whilft fhe was finging in a public place, and he the only man in a fuit of velvet in the dog-days. But let it be remembered, that *Harmonicus*, though amorous, was of a cold conftitution: he had every feature of a rake, without the ability of being vicious; his imagination truly feculent, was curbed by the morbid habit of his body.

C

Thus

(26)

Thus have I already convened the Infpector, Errato, the Town, Philocleus, Ranger, Specio, Mopfy, and Harmonicus, the eight principal members of the bawdy-box; and I fhall now give a dialogue, pretty nearly as it paffed between thefe eight wits, on the utility of whoredom, and the propriety of fornication.

Inf. Marriage is not only a holy inftitution, and what every man who profeffes himfelf a Chriftian fhould advance; but it is alfo a very wife regulation, and politically juft; otherwife how could we determine the right of inheritance, and the legality of fucceffion?

Mopf. The Turks have as many wives as they can fupport, and a man's riches at Conftantinople, are always known by the number of his concubines :

(27)

bines: a cobler at the Porte, is happier than a duke here; and yet there is never any difpute concerning fuccef- fion, or inheritance, among the fub- jects.

Rang. The reafon is obvious: Our laws and the Mahometans are very dif- ferent; the eldeft fon does not there fucceed to the title and eftate by inhe- ritance, nor is the legality of birth of any confequence.

Er. Ay,—ay,—the *eftate in tail* there, is all they inherit.

Spec. A broad-backed Janiffary might make his fortune at Peterfburgh, if he were properly introduced into the clofet.

Har. By fornication I do not under- ftand the act of generation, which can never be a crime, as it is certainly na- tural, and productive of good to fociety,

C 2

in

(28)

in supplying it with members; but it is the abuse and prostitution of this act that renders it criminal; and it is blending morality with custom, to talk of the policy or legality of the deed.

Phil. Continence was looked upon as a virtue in all ages; the greatest heroes have piqued themselves upon it; and every thinking man must agree with the Doctor, that where celibacy is not to be arrived at, the most eligible state is that of marriage.

Town. Many considerations enter into the argument; a man's situation in life; the advantages and disadvantages he may derive from marriage; his connections and expectancies; his own disposition and power of constancy; meeting with an object suited to his mind.

Er. The object must certainly be the woman,

(29)

woman, or the money: if it is the woman, you muſt as certainly meet with her, or elſe you could not marry her:—if it is the money, a prudent man will make ſure of it before he ties the indiſſoluble knot. With re-gard to connection, we may ſuppoſe that *middling*; and, as to expectancy, if he marries for love, that will *center* in the firſt night's conſummation.

Spec. Marriage is certainly to be pre-ferred, where fortune and affections ſuit; but as there are ſo few ten thou-ſanders, and ſo many Xantippes, with-out my being the leaſt of a Socrates, I believe I ſhall go on in a regular courſe of fornication, to avoid the felicities of matrimony; which are too highly co-loured for me ever to think of copy-ing.

Inf. You talk like young men un-
C 3   experienced.

(30)

experienced. I have been married, though now single; and I place amongst the happiest of my days, those which I passed with my wife; and I have the highest expectation from such another union.

Rang. I believe, Doctor, you will not, with all your sanctity, pretend to alledge your constancy; and, if one may judge by the rapturous stile of the letters you have published, Mrs. Diamond gave you higher notions of bliss and extasy than Mrs. H—— did.

Er. Such valuable jewels are only worn for ornament. Mrs. H—— was a piece of domestic furniture for use.

Inf. You press very hard upon me, Gentlemen; but please to remember, that Mrs. H—— was dead, before ever my connection with Mrs. D—d began.

Er.

(31)

Er. But pray, Doctor, was Mrs. H—defunct, when she discovered you in close embrace with Mrs. A—, whose story you introduced in your assumed character of Mr. Lovell, whose adventures you have given the public.

Inf. It is all a fable, invented to hurt her with the world; and particularly Mr. C—y, who is upon the point of marrying her.

Er. If it be a fable, it is you yourself that have applied the moral, and therefore ingross all the scandal.

Har. Pray, Gentlemen, let's avoid touching upon private characters in this disquisition. The Doctor is but a man, and fallibility is his lot. We are not talking of what we do, but what is the most eligible to be done.

Town. From the present nature and disposition of things, it would be as

C 4   fruitless

(3²)

fruitlefs to think of preventing fornication, as it would to fupprefs eating;
be it a vice, it is a neceffary one, which
the moft polifhed ftates have winked
at, and which has its ufe not only
in banifhing greater and unnatural
crimes, but alfo in promoting the fafety
of virgins, and preventing fatal attacks
upon the marriage-bed.   Were there
no proftitutes, the profligacy of mankind would foon find means to create
them; and many a virtuous daughter
and chafte wife would fall a victim
to the Sabine-like brutality of luft.

Rang. All that can be thought of
as a remedy, is the proper regulation of this vice, which fhould not
be fo openly and publickly practifed:
our ftreets fhould be cleared of proftitutes, who are guilty of the greateft
obfcenities in the open day, and at
night

(33)

night lay wait for their prey of unwary youth, or the more mature, overcome with the fumes of wine. If they are a neceſſary evil, they ſhould be conſider- ed as ſuch, and kept within proper bounds; particular ſtreets ſhould be al- lotted for their reſidence, and any found out of their diſtrict ſhould be ſeverely puniſhed.

Spec. If we go ſo far in their re- gulation, it would be better to go a ſtep farther; eſtabliſh public ſtews at once, which might anſwer every end of whoredom, and, in a great mea- ſure, prevent many of the inconveni- ences that reſult from it. Proſtitutes, regiſtered, and claſſed, as they are at Venice, would prevent many frauds and robberies committed in our brothels; and, if they underwent an examination every day, with regard to their health,

C 5   and

(34)

and were feverely chaftifed upon de-
ception, the venereal diforder would
be greatly reftrained in its progrefs,
and nobody would have reafon to complain, without it were the doctors and
furgeons.   I have thrown together the
hints of a treatife, which I intend foon
to give the public upon this head.

Mopf. This will be a very ufeful
work to the public. Pray, remember
to fettle the price of the ladies according to their different claffes, as well as
the rates of bagnio-bills, both which are
infupportable.   I have one in my pocket, that I paid this morning, which
I think ought to be taxed. *(Reads)*

No.

(35)

Nº. IV.	*l.*	*s.*	*d.*
To Bread and beer —	0	2	6
Soals and dreffing —	1	5	0
Scotch collops —	0	9	0
Tarts — —	0	3	0
Wine — —	1	4	0
Fire — — —	0	3	0
Wax-lights —	0	2	6
Ribbon for night-caps	0	5	0
Houfe — —	0	10	0
Breakfaft — —	0	4	6
Chair-hire —	0	6	0
Paid at the bar *(to a Lady returned —)*	1	1	0
	5	14	6

Infp. Five pounds fourteen fhillings and fix-pence, for a night's lodging, befides the prefent to Madam!—A very moderate bill, indeed!

C 6   *Har.*

(36)

Har. Pray, Sir, how many ladies had you?

Mopſ. Only one for the evening, who was in the houſe when I went; the other I ſent away after ſupper.

Spec. And yet here is chair-hire for half a dozen, a mile from Covent-Garden. This is abſolutely an impoſition, and cognizable by any magiſtrate, even though he lived in Bow-ſtreet.

Er. No, no; it is not worth while troubling his Worſhip with ſuch trifling matters.——Have your bill taxed by the trade, I am ſure they will do you juſtice; but take care that neither Mrs. D—g—s, Mrs. G—-d, nor Mrs. B—t, are impanelled, for they would have charged you double; and, you will find, they will diſcover ſome neceſſary articles have been omitted;
ſuch

(37)

fuch as, *birch to light your fire with*;

" To rouze the Venus lurking in your veins,"
(As *Armſtrong* has it)

a dozen or two of jellies, white gloves, and cold creams, to prevent heats in the morning, with along ſtring of *etcæteras*, which we may ſuppoſe are here all flung in amongſt dreſſing of the *ſoals*.——

(Juſt as *Mopſy* was going to reply to this Pharmatic wit, his prime mi-niſter, Jack H-rr-s, appeared at the bar, to give him intelligence of a lady that he had, with great art and perſuaſion, prevailed upon to wait at the next door, till he ſtept in to ſee for the beau.—— This ſummons ſaved him ſome bluſh-ing, a good deal of humming and hawing, and at leaſt an ounce of ſnuff, to prove, as he declared after-wards, he intended, that he did not know what *Errato* meant.)

——What! Mopſy's gone, without
having

(38)

having fix-pence of his bill ftruck off
for exorbitancy?

This learned converfation might, in
all probability, have continued much
longer, if it had not been interrupted
by the intrufion of *Pertinacio*. This
gigantic figure had borrowed fome low
wit, from frequenting the clubs of
choice fpirits, and had lately come to
an affluence upon the demife of his
father, who had laboured in the humble vocation of a carpenter, and he
piqued himfelf upon being " a chip
" of the old block." He, neverthelefs, put on the gentleman in every
thing but his behaviour, which was
always farcaftically impertinent towards
the evening, when his head was filled
more with the fumes of wine than
ideas. In thefe moods he had lately
made his appearance at the Bedford,

had

(39)

had faid rude things to many, and *impromtus* to all ; and was pro-nounced d—mned fmart and clever. He told the Doctor to-night, that his wig fat better than he had feen fince he had it dreffed at Ranelagh ; and en-quired whether his barber Mr. B— was in town ? He afked Errato, whether he killed more with his phyfic than he made fick with his puns ? — He was going on at this humorous rate with the whole room, when he unluckily met with a perfon, who diftinguifhed be-tween wit and impertinence, and very juftly thought that no man had a right to abufe a whole affembly for his amufement; and, taking Pertinacio by the collar, he told him very plainly, and without equivocation, " That, if he " did not defift from his ill-timed and " infolent raillery, he fhould give him

that

(40)

that chaftifement he deferved." In faying this he gave him a very hearty fhake. Pertinacio took the hint, ftifled his wit, and made a precipitate retreat, without examining the fitting of either his own or the Infpector's wig.

This giant being thus eafily demolifhed, the coffee-room remained quiet for fome evenings; wit, pleafantry, and punning, refumed their ancient feat, and M—ft—p, for a time, was the principal theme. His friends cried up his voice and perfon, his expreffion and accuracy; his opponents difcovered he was aukward, affected, and left-handed; had a morofe caft with his brow, which could never be foftened to fuit a pleafing character. The *Town* was, however, entirely on his fide, though *Philocleus* would not admit him into any kind of competition with B—y.

F—te

(41)

F—te had given tea, gained a fortune
and fpent it, had turned matrimonial
procurer with a fuppofed conjurer, and
acquired another, which was diffi-
pated as quick as the firft : his genius
was, as ufual, his laft refource; he had
planned the fable of a new comedy,
to accomplifh which he made a tour
to Paris, to catch the manners of thofe
flighty metropolitans ; and, upon his
return, finifhed his piece, called the
Englifhman in Paris, which is the beft
written, and has the moft merit of any
of his performances. This piece was,
as ufual, critically difcuffed here: the
friends of the author praifed the language, admired the novelty of the
thought, and the national moral it con-
veyed : his antagonifts faid the incidents were frivolous, the characters
outré's, the language bombaft in fome

parts,

(42)

parts, and low in others; the plot ill-
concerted, and the *dénoüement* forced;
and, above all, that he had no prece-
dent for calling a performance that
confifted but of two acts, a comedy.
Thefe fentiments did not, however,
prejudice the public enough to condemn the work, which met with the
approbation it deferved, and once more
recruited the finances of this uncommon genius.

About this time feveral new characters appeared upon the theatre of
the Bedford. A flying fcuffle between
a crazy knight, and an officer of the
guards, had made every one take particular care not to have his fword in-
voluntarily drawn from him. This affair was thus circumftanced: the knight
was ftanding by the fire-place, when
the captain approached, who, by turning

(43)

ing round, accidentally threw down a coffee-pot from the ftand, which, in fome meafure, wetted his legs. This he conftrued into a direct affront; and, without afking an explanation, flew to a Gentleman's fword, who was ftanding by an adjacent box, drew it, without afking his leave, and wounded the Captain, before he was apprifed of his intent, fufficiently to draw and defend himfelf. The confequence of this, after the evening, when furgeons attended, and pronounced the wounded Gentleman out of danger, was, that the knight was tried by a court-martial, and declared unfit to ferve his Majefty hereafter in a military capacity, though he had, till then, bore his commiffion in the army.

Several fkirmifhes of lefs importance occurred about this period; but

as

(44)

as they moftly ended in a twitch by the nofe, or a gentle kicking, we fhall pafs them over in as much filence as they were taken, in order to introduce the following new characters.

Spintilo was bred a haberdafher : he had tagged laces, and fold mittens, with the greateft fuccefs, for fome years, in Cheapfide. Unluckily he had a fortune left him, which was his ruin : he commenced Gentleman, found out the beft wafhes for making hands white, and removing freckles ; took lodgings in Covent Garden ; and, for the firft time, put on a fword and embroidery. Spintilo was not by nature deftined for a rake; yet he profeffed debauchery: he was under the middle fize, remarkably flender, but more remarkably foppifh. Every woman he faw was a conqueft; every equipage
the

(45)

the model of his own. With such talents and remarkable parts, it is not furprifing that Spintilo fhould run out his fortune, confifting of no lefs than five hundred pounds, in two years ;— it is not furprifing that he fhould not have married a lady with twenty thou-fand pounds ;—it is not furprifing that he fhould take refuge in the verge of the court, and ftill be a fop :—but it is furprifing he fhould get inlifted for a foldier (confidering his height) ; and (confidering his courage) that he fhould ever have the heart to go to Germany.

We fhall illuftrate this character with the ftory of one of his intrigues, which he ufed to relate himfelf. Saun-tering one day, about noon, in Hyde-park, he overtook a lady, accompanied by a black boy in livery : her lap-dog

run

(46)

ran away, and the fervant could not catch it; but he fortunately caught it, and brought it to the lady, who teftified her fatisfaction fo much, that, in a difcourfe which enfued, fhe afked him home to dinner. He found her houfe as elegant as her perfon, and her repaft worthy of both; fhe informed him fhe was married to a governor of one of our Weft India iflands who was abroad, but whom fhe expected home foon; that fhe was adored by her hufband, who was as rich as Crœfus. In faying this fhe dropped fome hints that fhe had no fmall regard for our cavalier, whom fhe artfully complimented upon his elegant addrefs, the gentility of his perfon, and the choice of his cloaths. Spintilo was in raptures; he could not eat for joy; he faw nothing but gilt chariots and birth-day fuits before him; he
knew

(47)

knew not how to recommend himfelf the moft; he pulled out his beft fcented handkerchief, afked her if fhe approved the odour, and begged he might procure her fome; he propofed a party to Ranelagh; a jaunt to Richmond; a journey to Scarborough. He befpoke two new coats that very day; and laid out all the money he could borrow, in a fnuff-box, which he prefented the lady with the next time he faw her; he run in debt forty pounds with a jeweller for trinkets, which he, with great perfuafion, prevailed upon her to accept.

He now thought himfelf at the eve of all his happinefs, and expected every day to receive fome prefent of great value, with notes for two or three hundred pounds inclofed. He could not devife the reafon of the delay, as he
had

(48)

had thrown out some hints that his
steward had been greatly disappointed
by his tenants failure of paying their
rents, on account of bad crops : however, he concluded he had been back-
ward in point of gallantry, as he had
scarce done more yet, than kiss the
lady's lips. Spintilo resolved upon a
bold attempt; and, though he was
conscious of his manly inabilities, which
had hitherto deterred him from at-
tacking the lady's virtue, fired with
wine, he pressed her to a close embrace: she, at first, appeared greatly
surprised; but, by degrees, softening
to his desires, she promised to make
him happy the ensuing night.

Never did a night of bliss so terrify
a lover. He rose early in the morning, came to the lady's, to know if
she was still in the same mind. Sorry

to

(49)

to find she did not yet relent, he examined himself over and over, but could
not be convinced he should be able to
give her the satisfaction she expected.
The appointed hour too early came;
and he wrote a card, to make an apology for not waiting upon her, being
taken suddenly ill; but then feeling
his purse, and thinking all his expectations would be destroyed by this apology, he took three cordials extraordinary to strengthen his courage, and
repaired to the place of rendezvous.

When he entered the room, he found
the Lady reclining on a sopha, reading Dryden's translation of *Ovid's art
of love:* she asked his opinion of some
lines, and desired him to read them
to her, which the more perplexed him,
as he had somewhat neglected his
studies, and had not the happiest

D   knack

(50)

knack at pronunciation; however, he got over the lines, and thought it was time to make an attack, in form, upon the Lady. " Madam," faid he, " why fhould we lofe time in perufing " the theory of love, when we may " fo eafily obtain the practice?" In faying this, he threw her on her back upon the Sopha, and made way with his hand to the feat of pleafure, which might an anchorite have warmed. But Spintilo experienced not the power of her charms; for when he had thus far obtained, he found himfelf the only obftacle to enjoyment. He was now humming and hawing for an excufe, whilft his enamorata lay thus expofed, when the door opened, a middle-aged man entered: the Lady fwooned, and Spintilo, unufed to fuch frights, actual-ly —— his ——. The perfon who

came

(51)

came in, recoiled fome few fteps with amazement; but foon recovering, drew his fword, and would have made an end of our hero, had not the fervants interfered, and prevented this fatal cataftrophe. Spintilo had, before this time, learnt this was the Lady's hufband, to whom he fell upon his knees, protefting his innocence, in faying, he vowed, before G-d; "that it was not in "his power to injure him if he would." The Gentleman had the curiofity to examine; and finding fo fmall a pretence to virility, gave credit to his affertion, and difcharged him with running the gauntlet thro' the hall, where every one of the fervants (the cookmaid and fcullion not excepted) had a kick at his breech.

Dorimont was florid and comely, toafted by the women, and envied by

D 2   the

(52)

the men. Dorimont dreffed well, and piqued himfelf upon keeping good company; he was heir to five thoufand a year, which he had already antici- pated by loans, at *cent. per cent.* The ladies reaped the benefit of his credit, and did him the honour to drink his health in his own wine. He appear- ed one night at the Bedford, and a certain genius undertook to perfuade him he looked very ill : — no man was ever more terrified with the thoughts of ficknefs than Dorimont; he turned pale upon the information, and look- ing in the glafs, perceived the very vi- fible alteration. He was eafily pre- vailed upon to retire into the adjacent room, where a perfon with a phyfi- cal periwig foon came, and recom- mending phlebotomy as the moft ef- fectual method of recovery, his coat was taken off, his fhirt-fleeve turn- ed

(53)

ed up, and all the apparatus prepared; dreading the fight of the operation, he turned his head afide, when,
lo! a tooth-pick was the lancet,
and a glafs of warm red tea poured
over his arm, the iffuant blood. Dorimont, with the affiftance of a glafs
of water, efcaped fainting, which was
more than he had ever done upon a
like occafion before. His arm was
bound up; the ufual chirurgical fee
paid, and he began to fancy that the
lofs of a little blood had done him
good. After this it would be needlefs to fay Dorimont was no genius;
he, neverthelefs, affifted at the board
of wits, and, though he had a natural
impediment in his fpeech, has been
heard to pronounce *damnation*, with as
much emphafis as any man living,
upon a new play or a new actor.

D 3   Dorimont

(54)

Dorimont was not thought to be naturally very courageous, but he was
much inclined to have the world believe him fo: fame, ill-natured fame,
whifpered that he had received fome
twitches by the nofe, and had once
fairly and philofophically underwent
that ignominious chaftifement of kicking, fo fatal, as *Hudibras* has it, to the
feat of honour. Thefe reports had
come round to him, which fet him
upon employing a certain wit, who
acted in the humble character of a
toad-eater and *fycophant*, to devife a
means of wiping off this flur which
was thrown upon him. Punctilius,
after fome cogitation, told him, the
only fure method would be, to have
an affair with fome perfon, whom he
fhould force to a fubmiffion. Dorimont fhook his head at this advice,
and

(55)

and plainly made the submission himself.—" Sir, continued Punctilius, I
" don't mean you should run any risk.
" I'll fix upon a man whom you may
" be sure of conquering:—only have
" resolution enough to bear up to
" the last; and, in case of extremity,
" draw your sword, if he should have
" courage enough to do the same,
" which I very much doubt; I'll take
" care to have chairmen ready to beat
" down your swords with their poles,
" and no harm shall come of it."

Dorimont swore he would do it, if
Punctilius could hit upon a proper object: Q—n had lately given the salutary advice of *soaping his nose to Poltronius*, upon having it once twitched
in the public assembly at Bath, and he
was judged the very man they wanted.
Dorimont took an opportunity of throw-

D 4

ing

(56)

ing a difh of fcalding coffee over his legs, without making him any apology. Poltronius afked him what he meant by it? and infifted upon fatisfaction. They went out under the piazza, fwords were drawn and brandifhed at a cautionary diftance.——Dorimont was, however, apprehenfive, as the chairmen did not immediately interfere, upon Poltronius's making fomething of a half-lounge, and called out, " Where are the chairmen ?—" Who " calls chair," was the immediate reply.—" An't you hired?" continued Dorimont.—" No, your Honour,' rejoined honeft Teague.--" Damn Punc- " tilius (bawled Dorimont) I thought " he had hired you." " Sir," cried Punctilius, " through the arches, you " have got into the wrong piazza :" By this time Dorimont's real chairmen

had

(57)

had taken the alarm, and this affair ended *greatly* to both the combatants *honour*, without the leaft effufion of blood.

About this very period another ren-counter had like to have happened, and proved as fatal in its effects as the preceding. *Didlius*, a confummate fop, whofe beauty had never been noticed by any but himfelf, and which, indeed, he was at fome pains in difcovering, if we may infer from his frequent ap-plication to the looking-glafs; had more than once broke a Gentleman's fhins with his fword, in this infpection, at the fire-place; and, being fo very intent upon his dear face, though at other times a mighty polite man, he al-ways omitted apologizing for the of-fence; which fo irritated the Gentle-man, who was rather of a captious

D 5 turn,

(5⁸)

turn, that, without faying a word, he rofe up, went to the bar, and taking the meffage-book, which may be ftiled the Bedford Coffee-houfe Journal, he wrote the following laconic and polite billet.

" This is to acquaint Mr. Didlius, " that he is a puppy and a rafcal."

(*Signed*)   ——   ——

After which he left the book open, and feated himfelf at the window next the bar, expecting Didlius to perufe his note; but he had bufinefs of more importance to attend, he had a girl in keeping, who perfuaded him fhe was fond of him, to meet in the upper-boxes, fo that he only ftept in to adjuft his folitaire, and was gone in a trice. Though this curious card efcaped Didlius's perufal, it prefently attracted a circle round the bar, who firft reading

the

(59)

the infcription, and then looking at the author, were conjecturing what muſt be the event, and *ſudden death* was pronounced *nem. con.*

It was not till next day that Didlius was apprifed of the infult, when he took an opportunity, in the abfence of every one but the waiter, to anfwer this epiftle in as laconic a manner as it was written, though the ftile was very different.—*He eraſed it with a copious penful of ink.*

Having mentioned the Bedford Coffee-Houſe Journal, it may not be improper to convey a better idea of it than the tranfcript of this note can ; wherefore I fhall make no apology for the following extracts.

The British coffee-house. A poem (London, printed for the author, and sold by W. Nicol; W. Flexney; J. Ridley; and C. Moran, 1764), [4], 24pp.; 4°. BL: 1487.r.6. ESTCT63317. Hünersdorff.

A substantial but anonymous Wilkes-ite verse satire on Scots in politics composed in heroic couplets. Formally the poem is a kind of mock epic, depicting the arrival in London of Sawney, a ragged Scotsman seeking advancement, although the conceit is not developed consistently. The poem surveys the Scottish influence in court politics by following his journey around the coffee-houses of London, or more particularly, the political houses of the Strand and Charing Cross. There he visits, amongst others, Slaughter's, the Turk's Head, Will's Scotland Yard and finally the British Coffee-house (from p. 349), which was in these years closely associated with Bute's political interest (mentioned as such in *The North Briton*, No. 46). The political allegiance of the poem is with Wilkes and the Whigs, especially in their attack on the Tory ministry of John Stuart, Earl of Bute, 1762–3, which they routinely depicted as crypto-Jacobite and politically corrupt. The poem also celebrates key figures in the Whig pantheon of military and naval heroes, such as Cumberland, Anson and Granby. The poem is a contribution to the campaign to fan public hostility towards Bute and the Tories more than it is an attack on Scottish manners (although it is that too), an allegiance signalled by the epitaph quoted from Charles Churchill's anti-Bute satire *The Prophecy of Famine* (1763).

The author is unknown. The poem was reviewed in Ralph Griffiths's *Monthly Review* without enthusiasm, as was to be expected of that journal: 'Abuses the Scotch in the old strain: These dirty Scriblers have no invention: nothing but an eternal round of hunger, and filth, rags, – rags, and filth and hunger' (30 (1764), p. 157). It was also reviewed with hostility in *The Critical Review*: 'The author's ability in poetry does not even qualify him for the very lowest and most detestable of all offices, that of abuse' (16 (1763), p. 479). The poem was published for the author by four established publishers associated with the Whig interest: William Nicol, W. Flexney, J. Ridley and C. Moran, and was advertised by Moran with other anti-Bute satires.

THE

BRITISH

COFFEE·HOUSE.

A

POEM.

To that rare Soil, where Virtues cluft'ring grow,
What mighty bleffings doth not England owe;
What *Waggon-loads* of courage, wealth and fenfe,
Doth each revolving day import from thence?
To us fhe gives, difinterefted friend,
Faith without fraud, and STUARTS without end.

LONDON:

Printed for the AUTHOR:

And Sold by W. NICOL, St. Paul's Church-yard; W. FLEXNEY, in Holborn;
J. RIDLEY, in St. James's-ftreet; and C. MORAN, under the Great Piazza,
Covent-Garden.

M DCC LXIV.

Price One Shilling and Six Pence.

B O O K S Publi/hed and Sold by C. M o r a n.

GEORGE'S Coffee-houfe.   A New Edition.
Sydenham.   A Poem to Mr. Pitt.
The Meretriciad.   The Fifth Edition.
The Firft and Second Parts of the Temple of Venus.
An Addrefs to the Two Reviews.
The Triumph of Brutes.   A Scots Satire.
        And all other publications extant.

In   the   Prefs,

And   will   be   publifhed   with   all   convenient   Speed,

In   two   Pocket   Volumes,

VOYAGES and Travels, or a Collection of Letters to a
        Gentleman in London, written in Europe, Afia, Africa, and
America.——Containing an Account of many Things never yet laid
before the Public; particularly a copious Defcription of the Eaft-
Indies, Manners, Religion, and Cuftoms of the Natives.——The
burning of an Indian Woman of Quality——and fome Miracles per-
formed by St. Thomas the Apoftle, when preaching the Doctrine of
Chrift.   Of an Hermit, on an uninhabited Ifle in the Weft-Indies.
—Of Eaft Friezland,—And Lifbon at the Time of the Earthquake.

[1]

<hr>

THE

BRITISH

COFFEE-HOUSE.

M USE *speak the* Scots, *who since* Colloden's *woe,*
      So many Towns, such change of fortunes saw.
But tell the truth, for thou or none can'ft tell,
How Charley *triumph'd,* and how Charley fell?
How he hung wanton upon Jenny's * charms,
How wanton both curfed Britifh Billy's arms;
The ftrange reverfe of Fortune muft be faid,
How WILLIAM triumph'd, and how Charley fled:
That WILLIAM who chaftis'd the rebel hoft,
And with blue bonnets ftrew'd the bloody coaft:

<hr>

* Cameron.

B   That

[2]

That WILLIAM who repuls'd the northern Loon,

But not the *Stuarts*, nor the chair of *Scoon*.

That Royal WILLIAM with fuch good poffeft,

To make him dear to all the brave and beft ;

His mercy ev'n offending *Scots* muft own,

For WILLIAM fprung from a forgiving crown :

Rebels his valour, *Whig's* his truth proclaim,

The KING his virtue, and the world his fame.

SING ——, how in rags ambitious SAWNEY came,

Without one merit how he rofe to Fame ;

How he commenc'd an Author without wit,

How two *Reviews* applauded what he writ ;

How without one defert he creep'd to Court,

And being a Scotfman how he got fupport :

Thefe, thefe relate,——thefe moft minute affairs,

And then, O ! mufe you'll have a Kingdom's cares.

THE morn was raw,——The Hills were clad in fnow,

When Sawney's *ey'n* firft dawn'd upon the mow ;

He rofe, he fhook, he crack'd, he claw'd his hair ;

But one fhake more, had fhook his body bare :

To

[3]

To work he went,—but dreams perplex'd his head,
" If he faw London he fhould eat white bread :"
The hungry thought fo prey'd upon his brain,
He left his work, and backwards trudg'd again :
Rapacious lice themfelves not half fo keen,
When blown to Sawney, from a beaft more clean :
Prophetic Daddy heard the dream reveal'd,
And with his kiffes blefs'd the hopeful *Chield.*

   N E w clad, (as Scotland cloaths the high-cheek'd things
That come to London upon Raven's wings)
Poor Sawney was :—His bonnet had been blue,
Freckles evinc'd his bum ne'er breeches knew ;
Nine lank red hairs afide down dangling hung,
Pendent his arms, which as he ftrode *fwang fwung :*
Legs without calves, but ftill fubftantial legs,
His face with dufky fpots like Turkey's eggs :
His coat of northern cut,——of colour rare,
Whilom it had bore fome,—but now thread bare :
He could not boaft the luxury of fhoes,
But ftamp'd as plain a Scot, as Heaven ftamps Jews.
                                                      This

[4]

This *Hebrew* form an open cart afcends,

A cart for ever bears him from his friends :

A cart, O ! would a cart receive the whole,

The noofe I'd faften, and I'd afk no toll :

I mean the fordid many——blot, on blot

Deface the word, that wounds an honeft Scot.

Here Sawney found three low, three highland Loons,

Ganging their gaits to crave fome little boons,

" *For ken ye men, how fimple 'tis to lofe*

" *For want of beging, liquor, food and cloaths :*

" *Mc Donald faid, for fee ye all, he'll raife*

" Fortunes by names, and not by worth, or praife :

" Right, right, replies Mc Duggle, fo I ween,

" For elfe fuch lads the Campbells ne'er had been.

Thus to the crowded CAPITAL they run,

Thofe to undo, who cannot be undone :

For her infatiate, proftituted whomb,

To fome's a cradle, and to fome's a tomb :

Rapacious fwallows, like the common feas,

Fools of all climes, and Knaves of all degrees.

What's Irifh intrepidity of face,

To this itinerant, venal, daring Race,

A

[5]

A *decent* fhare muft be allow'd to Burk,
But ftill the Scot's beats all the brafs of Cork.

THESE fix, I fay, thefe very wretched fix,
Whom CHARON will deny to crofs the Styx,
Were found fo wretched poor at BERWICK toll,
To leave for all in pledge, *one mill, one doll:*
Yet boafted ftill their noblenefs of blood,
Tho' crept from Scoundrels from the very flood;
The good old Woman wept, and wifh'd them luck,
The waggon rumbl'd, and they claw'd *the Yuck.*
So very dull, yet ftill fo full of fpite,
So very vain, with yet fo little right,
So full of filth, and yet fo full of pride,
Tho' at each jolt a rag forfook each fide:
In fpite of dirt yet pedigree would glide,
From whom defcended, and to whom allied:
Tell me my Mufe, alas! thou haft no guile,
Is there a Campbell not a-kin t' Argyle?
It's all one blood,——which ebbs from vein to vein,
And fills alike the vaffal, and the Thane:
Coufin they always claim as interefts fuit,
I've met ten fcores a-kin to th' Earl of Bute.

C

Mute

[6]

Mute Sawney fat amidſt theſe various themes,

Yet glow'd in heart, as he approach'd the Thames ;

His great prophetic ſoul declar'd him made,

White-bread like oyl upon the ſurface play'd ;

But various things unſung of earlier days

Crow'd in his mind,——as oft at boyiſh plays

He march'd a Serjeant,——or in turn a drum,

From which ſome good his ſire declar'd muſt come.

Can none remember, I remember well,

Adds the ſage Father, where the Scriptures tell

That mighty Cyrus, when a Boy would play

As thou doth SAWNEY.——Theſe for ever ſtay.

With our young Hero,——whoſe ambitious mind

To luſt and woman was alike inclin'd.

Revolving thus, the driver ſtops, and bauls,

" *Behold ye gentlemen our great St. Paul's ?*"

St. Paul's it was from Highgate's lofty top,

Where northern Boobies kiſs the horns, and ſtop.

The ſeven gaz'd, nay, they had gazed ſtill,

Had not the waggon rumbl'd down the Hill.

EACH when arriv'd declar'd he had no plan,

Yet each would be a great *exceeding* man,

Dubious

[7]

Dubious which way to act, which way to take,

Jock took his ftick, and thus prophetic *fpake.*

" In antient times, e'er Scotfmen writ, or read,

" Or thus like Gypfies ftrol'd abroad for bread,

" When Scotland held her Kings at HOLYROOD,

" Nor mixt, with Englifhmen her purer blood,

" E'er that good chair which FERGUS *caw'd* his own,

" Was dragg'd to London from it's ftate of SCONE ;

" If any doubts arofe, the good *mon* took

" (As I do know) his 'ftaff, his fword, or crook

" And let it fall,—that very way it fell,

" Declar'd the good man's journey, ill or well :

" Mine's this my friends, St. Andrew guide ye ftill."

The ftick, prophetic pointing Holborn-Hill.

The reft purfued the maxim near or far,

Some went thro' Aldgate, fome through Temple-Bar.

Excepting Sawney,——he'd a nobler fcheme,

Luft was his ftudy,—woman was his theme.

The reft, like old LUCRETIUS' fyftem rofe,

By chance—to victuals, and by chance to cloaths.

Make through this fewer of Scotsa ftrict report,

You'll find the fix in office, or at C*.

Unhappy

[8]

Unhappy Country, over-run with thefe,
A greater curfe than Egypt found her fleas.
Half fkill'd in letters—whether black, or gold,
Sawney went on as paffing many told.
Some fent him here, fome there, as humour hit,
Some put him right, and bleft his want of wit;
If he made ufe of his unnatural tongue.
" *Follow your nofe my friend, you can't go wrong :*"
Thus like a *tennis-ball* poor Sawney's pride
Was bandy'd up, and down, from fide, to fide.

A LARGE fafh'd room at th' end of Cecil-ftreet
Firft drew his eyes,—and firft receiv'd his feet :
Which as his head went forward flew behind,
For Sawney fprung from a fubmiffive kind.
Here Yorkfhire Bucks, who not fo wife as rich,
Bellow the merits of a-horfe, or bitch :
For wealthy Heirs as modern *breeding* runs ;
Pafs common fenfe for Horfes, hounds and guns ;
Launch into follies of a great expence,
And fink Eftates,—without the *aid* of fenfe.
" Zounds, cries a booted 'Squire what have we here?"
When Sawney bow'd, and grin'd from ear to ear ;

The

[9]

The way enquired, which the 'Squire declar'd

Was two miles more—when Sawney turn'd, and ſtar'd

FRONTING ſteep Meretricious Catherine-ſtreet

A Turk's head ſtands,—a Turk's head round, and great ;

Where many a-head as truely great, and round,

As truly thick,———and truly full of ſound

Are daily ſeen,—of no peculiar kind,

Unleſs peculiar, heads without a mind.

Tho' truth forbid, ſo kind, ſo juſt a muſe,

Should blame the widow of ſo good a houſe :

A gentle widow, and as gentle gay,

As full of merit, and as full of play

As widows are.—A woman, bleſt to pleaſe :

Tell me a *bar* where eloquence wiſh eaſe

United flow like her's ? ſhe has a tongue,

Ye Gods ! ſhe has,—as ſoft as ever rung :

I love your houſe,—your ſign, the whole for you,

I love your broth,—I love your coffee too :

Widow, exceſſive love's exceſſive rage :

In bar, in pulpit, off or on the ſtage :

Love made me ſcrawl—be kind I beg to-night,

And bid the Waiter ſet poor Sawney right.

D   Not

[10]

Not right to principle, for that's forgot,

For ev'ry Tory is at heart a Scot :

A curſe ſufficient,——it's by all agreed :

Who will not curſe the reptiles of the Tweed ?

A ſwarm beyond whatever Nilus bred,

Tho' heaven aſſiſted to devour their bread.

    L o ! what a wond'rous revolution's here,

Whigs go to plough, and Tories rule the ſphere :

In times to come will this be underſtood ?

" A Wɪʟᴋs impriſon'd for his Country's good ;"

Will Children yet unborn believe theſe words,

That F—x and D—d were our patriot Lords ?

That Pitt retir'd, that G———le took his place,

T—b—t appear'd at Court, and Bt———e ſaid grace ?

Won't friends, if friends they have, require belief,

Lo ! E—g—t expired in eating beef :

A lump of earth, a body mov'd by rule,

So much the Miniſter, ſo much the Tool,

So much the Patriot, that 'twas hard to prove,

Turtle or Country which engroſs'd his love :

A Ruffian's manners, and quite void of grace ;

Unfixt in principle, unfixt in place :

                         And

[11]

And yet at laſt through mighty dullneſs ſhone,

Amongſt the Tories foſter'd by the ——

How ſafe is Treaſon, when the blackeſt crimes

Are 'ras'd, are cancell'd, by ſeditious times:

When Fools, when Villains ſwarm in ev'ry place,

And riſe to power, tho' ſtudious of diſgrace:

Succeed in favours by affecting Fame,

Tho' damn'd by Truth to everlaſting ſhame.

H o w wiſe in counſel England art thou grown,

To move the very pillars of thy C——:

Like Jews to triumph in thy SAVIOUR's fall,

And tread on him, who trampl'd on the Gaul:

O! England! England let me wail thy Fame,

And with a WILKES record a TEMPLE's name:

What Engliſhman with ſpirit won't ſubmit,

To die with GRANBY, and *reſign* with PITT ?

N o w had the northern Loon with pains, with care

Attain'd the Hungerford, where Tars repair:

Where fir'd in heavy broad ſides oaths, and lies

Roll round the room, about ſome Spaniſh prize:

And

[12]

And yet it's hard the Room's fo very fmall,

To fight an *action* o'er 'tween wall and wall.

So m e vain of conqueft tell their various fcars,

And o'er two penn'orth fight two bloody wars :

Some weigh an anchor,—and fome *mend a reef*,

Some chaw tobacco, and fome eat hung beef :

True fons of Difcord all together roar,

Like heavy feas upon a rocky fhore :

From Mid to Captain built with equal parts,

Launch'd with the thickeft heads—the braveft hearts :

As empty drums make noife without defence,

So thefe are but the tympanies of fenfe.

N e x t Wills's came,——where Saunders ftood aloof

To fee fo long a room,—fo high a roof :

Such noble furniture, fo grand a bar ;

So fair a Dame amidft fuch pomp of war,

Struck Sawney dumb,—as Sawney did not ken

This heavy tribe of Neptune's Gentlemen.

Silent he bow'd with all a Scotfman's grace,

To the good Dame the Goddefs of the place :

A Goddefs,

[13]

A Goddeſs, if great merits merit fame ;

As tender Mother, and a gentle Dame :

In all a Woman, to all good inclin'd,

A loving heart, with an unſpotted mind.——

If I omit the Maſter,——" on my life"

(You'll cry) he's partial to the good man's wife,

It is not ſo ;——I bear him ſome eſteem,

But my *Ideas* are below the theme. ——

If I forget thee TOM, or more thy dues,

With boiling coffee ſcald my little Muſe :

Yet ſure the friend deſerves a better doom,

Who kindly gives thee *faithful* for thy Tomb.

By Tom's good counſel, Sawney went his gait,

Cloſe by that Fabric, where, in naval ſtate

Neptune's Vicegerents reign.——So ſhort their ſway,

'Tis hard to tell who blows the ſhell to-day ;

Should Neptune pay a viſit to this place,

Is there one Lord would know his Monarch's face ?

ANSON's it was who reign'd with credit long,

A voice long practis'd in the nautic ſong ;

Merit he had, for merit prov'd his care,

Tho' Nobles unprovided damn'd the Bear.

E   Rough

[14]

Rough were his manners, but his soul was brave,

How much an honest man, how much a Knave

I can't define.——Suffice it then to sing,

He serv'd his Country, and he lov'd his King.

Some favour'd few, have bask'd beneath his smiles,

Obtain'd more prizes, and acquir'd more spoils ;

Amongst that few, 'twas He alone could say,

He only rais'd one *Coward* to the Sea.

Run o'er the lifts, what MINISTER can boast ;

He only rais'd one Villain to a post ?

A fault this was ;——(for many NOBLES swore)

They knock'd, they call'd ;—they heard, they saw the door :

Yes, there he swerv'd from that most civil rule,

To pass a NOBLE whom he knew a TOOL :

Tho' oft in spite of reason, and the man,

High, very high connections broke his plan :

This we may say without offence or fear,

He liv'd to Sev'nty, and he died a PEER.

ESTRANG'D from KINDRED G—— next appears,

G—— adorn'd with honours and with years :

So blest, so perfect in the arts to please,

So full of eloquence, so full of ease,

So

[15]

So full of manners, and so well array'd,

A Prince he seems,——and for a *Levee* made :

Ask what you will no MINISTER so kind,

If bore by water, and if mov'd by wind :

He, in the HOUSE pass'd other Gentlemen ;

Barring the *gentle Shepherd*——" you know when."

From that he leap'd to favour, and to grace :

And holds, and shakes ; but shakes, and holds the place.

THE third was Cinque-port,—Cinque port took the helm,

Fitter to rule a Bagnio, than a realm :

Prime Prince of Pimps, of meretricious fame,

Callous alike to honour, and to shame :

Studious to have a friend, when fairly won,

Studious to have that very friend undone :

Studious, if any study yet he had,

To prove to pimps, to whores, how rash, how mad :

A very Statesman ever in disguise,

In all a Proteus,—but in forming lies :

Fond of sedition, without hopes of fame,

Strenuous to sink in credit, rise in shame ;

So deep in vice repentance cannot mend,

Alike prevaricates with God, and friend :

In

[16]

In words fo blafphemous the Drury race,

Have fcream'd for mercy and forfook the place ;

Impiety himfelf his converfe fled,

For fear the houfe fhould tumble on his head ;

A fad, bad Atheift, an Adulterer,

Blotted in every page of Character.

Flagitious more by half than what I've faid ;

Yet he was heard to curfe the Orlean * Maid,

To blufh pretended, trembled at fuch crimes,

And with a Bifhop rail'd at bawdy rhimes.

DULLNESS himfelf aftonifh'd, rofe, and fwore,

" He never heard the Devil preach before."

So Satan tempted Angels in difguife,

Fair was his form, within were fin, and lies.

Satan prevail'd,——triumphant Satan reigns,

O'er Freedom bound in honourable chains :

Great in his wounds the BRITISH Freedom lies,

Certain of refuge in his native fkies.

    'T I S E—g—t's now ;—a genius known, and great,

A ble to bear the pillars of a ftate !

---

          * Pucelle D'Orleans.

                                     Fitter

[17]

Fitter, if Minifters require a head,
To fteer a Kingdom, than to heave a lead.
Seamen we think fhould hold the reins, the whip,
Seamen muft know a windmill from a fhip :
'Tis not fuppos'd that men of rank and eafe,
Should be fit judges of unfettl'd feas:
How is it poffible, that they fhould tell,
How anchors ftart, how weftern winds compel.
How dangers yawn upon a hard *lee fhore*,
How tides deceive, and how the *Gaskets* * bore :
How foes efcape in fpite of ev'ry care,
Tho' Hawke was *here*,—and tho' the French were *there*.
It would be better if in one to find,
The Seaman's knowledge, to the Statefman's join'd ;
For note, I do not mean to make defence,
That ev'ry Seaman's bleft with common fenfe :
Eg—t would fhine, would grace a Council board,
HervEy would prove Tar, Minifter, and Lord.

My journey's done—and thank the happy hour,
See, Sawney enters at the BRITISH door :

---

* Rock in the Englifh Channel.
F   See

[18]

See where he ſtands amidſt a ſpaniel crowd
Of fawning Phariſees, as poor as proud :
Who true to inſtinct *ken* the leering Loon,
And all the Booby praiſe, in one dull tune.
Equally partial to the knave, and fool,
All take the Berwick oath, and keep the rule :
Partial alike from Beggars, up to Peers,
Tho' from the head the pill'ry tore the ears :
'Tis ſtrange theſe pilgrims of the frigid North,
Should prove as true to Knaves, as true to worth ;
Honour, or honeſty they ne'er prefer,
For in one word,——" A Scot's a character.

N o w ridicule thy HOGARTH's grin aſſume ;
Behold thy Champions ſpurn the ſanded room :
Champions on pride, and beggary begot,
" Living ridiculous, and dead forgot."

A M O N G S T the Legions for thy partial cauſe,
Could not one man be found whoſe Country's laws
Gave ſanction to his deeds ? Muſt Champions riſe
For hapleſs SCOTLAND under Gallic ſkies ?

Ignoble

[19]

Ignoble deed,——to drag a wretch, who ftood
In arms ;——in arms againft his Country's good :
A fool, a fugitive ;——without debate,
A bafe, fad out-caft both of Church and State.
Was he the man ?——the rebel fword to wield
O'er WILKES, o'er LIBERTY in Gallia's field ?
Prepofterous, low, ignoble, bafe-born plan,
Prefumptuous flave I to *dare* an ENGLISHMAN.

SEE how the pebble ftirs the peaceful rill,
Another circle, and another ftill.
So fpread the Champions in a rotten caufe,
To tread on Englifhmen, and Englifh laws.
TARTUB come forth,——thou Falftaff of thy age,
With Piftol too, thy antient, bully, page :
New, huge edition of Don Quixot flain,
And FORBES the Sancho Panza of thy train.

ENOUGH, enough,—ye wind-mill Heroes hence,
And in the fteady fcale of common fenfe
Weigh your opinions, conducts, follies, parts,
Your heads how heavy, and how light your hearts :

         Truth

[20]

Truth will unbiafs'd fhew—where error lies,
How much you've fwerv'd,—from all that's brave and wife.
How Scots afpiring againft Britain fell,
How you afpiring againft Sense rebel.

'Tis right the noble fhould the *bafe* controul :
Or Scots in time would tyrant o'er the whole :
Freedom, fuch Tyrants checks ;——refolv'd to bind
Unthinking beings, falfe, rebellious, blind.

Some few there are may call the Muse fevere,
Some name her cenfure juft,—her praife fincere :
Minds void of principle fhe will not fpare,
But blot the word where Virtue drops a tear :
She bears no prejudice to name, or fpot,
Scot, Spaniard, Pruffian, Dutch, or Hottentot :
Thro' partial zeal to no one fect a rod,
But pleas'd furveys the virtuous fent from God.

Sawney, altho' amidft his own dear race,
Could not conceive fo gay, fo grand a place
Should be a fit receptable for him,
So rude in manners, and fo rude in trim :

                                        Green

[21]

Green cloth to feat, what ruffet fod before,

In native luxury fupinely bore !

Upon the wall intent he fix'd his eye,

And gaz'd aftonifh'd at a brighter fky :

A form he faw :———and ftarted with furprife,

It ftarted too :———he fix'd,—it fix'd it's eyes :

He mov'd,—it mov'd,—he touch'd—it touch'd as foon ;

The fhining fubftance ftagger'd more the Clown :

He felt behind,———and ftill the myft'ry grew,

He ftruck the phantom, and the mirrour flew :

Then to the bar with bleeding fingers reel'd,

And told, elated, " how he'd *bang'd the Chield.*"

Poor Mrs. D———s, (for I love the Dame,

And if I fay ought hurtful endlefs fhame

Perch on my iron brow :)———gave fuch a fquall,

What flefh can ftand, if glafs, if china fall ?

What mighty fouls at times have women fhown :

Yet wept,———

A Monkey ftrangl'd, or a Parrot flown,

I fhould advife her in thefe *fragil* times,

To give attention to a poet's rhimes,

To move her glaffes, to reduce her bar,

For fear thefe Quixotes fhould repeat the war ;

G   As

[22]

As loaded waggons daily come from thence,
Repute with valour, modesty, and sense;
Nobly, and justly grateful, meek, and good,
They leave the carcass when they've fuck'd the blood.
In power imperious, servile out of place,
False at the bottom, and ignobly base !
Partial to Scots, whom honour can't approve,
And vile, sad rebels to the prince they love :
Of praise ambitious, without parts to steer,
Serenely dull, and stupidly severe :
Tell me, I'll give you leave, if you can find,
A place yet visited by light or wind
Without a Scot,——sad pilgrims of the earth,
Yet boast in GUINEA pedigree, and birth
Subsist like toads, in ev'ry foreign hole,
From East to West, from Java to the pole;
Morose in spirit, and depriv'd of ease,
Intent to ruin, and unknown to please.

HERE satire pause,——nor in the name of Scot,
Let honour, truth, and candour be forgot.
Some men there are as justly worthy praise,
As many censure in these *partial* days ;

Yet

[23]

Yet let not ſpleen deſtroy the Muſe's plan,
And with the Rebel wound the honeſt man :
Forbid it Heaven that one word ſhould flow,
And injure Grant *, among the common foe ;
And many more whom honour muſt proclaim,
The firſt in Virtue, and the firſt in Fame.

But yet forgive me, if I cannot place,
The vagrant Sawney with th' illuſtrious Race :
Now high advanc'd to dignity, and power,
Yet, ſhuns thy Coffee as he ſhuns the poor ;
Turns if his motto'd Chariot chance to paſs,
Conſcious dear Widow that he broke *thy glaſs*.
Tempers with honours, Fortunes change with days,
Virtue with gold, humility with praiſe :
Without one gift of genius, or of art,
And ſtrangely wanting in an honeſt heart ;
Curſt with inſatiate thirſt of public fame,
Yet daily bankrupts it by deeds of ſhame :
His ſtars are curſt, they never yield a ray,
His fog of dullneſs, dims his ſenſe of day ;

---

* Son to Sir Ludovic, Member for Elginſhire.

Studious

[24]

Studious, if any ftudy dwells within,

To prove by deeds polygamy no fin ,

Promifcuous takes, as paffions ftir his guft,

Wife, Widow, Concubine to eafe his luft.

What e'er he does makes fuch a public ftir,

In him alone 'tis natural to err.

The very Scots, who rais'd the thing to fame,

Now curfe their humours, and the *Calf* reclaim :

In contemplation fhrink at iron bars,

And wave remembrances of *rebel* wars.

Meet, daily weep, and weeping curfe the hour,

That brought the SAWNEY to the Britifh door ;

Numbers run o'er th' advertifement * with pain,

And vow to SCOTLAND they'll *gang back again* :

Others more refolute memorials buy,

And creep for wealth beneath a favage fky :

No more of ENGLAND ; crofs the briny feas,

And pick up principles from CHERROKEES.

---

* Alluding to two advertifements, one for goods and paffengers to Scotland, the other for memorials and petitions.

THE END.

*A Sunday Ramble; or, Modern Sabbath-Day Journey;
in and about the Cities of London and Westminster*, 2nd
edn (London, for the author by James Harrison, [1776]),
[11], 70pp.; 12°. BL: 10349.aaa.15. Extract, pp. 28–35.
Hünersdorff.

An extract from an anonymous prose satire on the manners and follies of
London and Westminster. The satire takes the form of 'a ramble', depicting the
protagonist's peripatetic travels around the city as a way of motivating a series of
loosely connected satiric characters and scenic descriptions. The ramble was an
established literary sub-genre as much as it was a mode of aimless ambulatory
travel. Ramble writings were clearly indebted to the spy-book pseudo-guides
made famous by Ned Ward's *London Spy* (1698–1700), which purported to
give a new insight into low life, but which were themselves complicated, allu-
sive and learned works of literature. *A Sunday Ramble*, as might be expected
from the title, takes the form of a survey of the city on Sunday – a day when
the city wore quite a different aspect from the rest of the week. The Sabbath
city is one devoted to piety and pleasure, both telling subjects for the satirist's
pen. Setting out early in the morning, the narrator and his interlocutor (an old
school-friend) undertake a perambulation around the city, visiting a range of
churches and chapels, a boxing match, various pleasure gardens, parks, taverns,
ordinaries, theatres and bagnios.

Of the author of *A Sunday Ramble* nothing is known. The book was published for the author by the bookseller John Bew of Warwick Lane, Paternoster
Row, and printed by James Harrison of Paternoster Row. The first edition was
undated: a copy at the John Rylands Library, University of Manchester, has a
manuscript date of 1774 that is probably contemporary. Internal references are
consistent with a composition date of 1774 (such as the reference to the Quebec
Bill, which received the Royal Assent on 22 June 1774). The first edition was
reviewed briefly but favourably in *The Critical Review*, 39 (January 1775), p. 80:
the reviewer thought that 'The several incidents which he relates are such as may
naturally be supposed to occur, the manners are justly described, and the charac-

ters in general strongly marked'. In the second edition, the preface states that the book had received a favorable reception and sold out the first edition, although the author's 'distance from the metropolis would not conveniently permit him to review the scenes'. The second edition was published around 1776, and further editions in *c.* 1778 and *c.* 1780. The British Library has an extra-illustrated copy of the second edition (578.i.10).

A
SUNDAY RAMBLE;

O R,

Modern Sabbath-Day Journey;

In and about the CITIES of

LONDON AND WESTMINSTER.

Defcribing, in an agreeable Manner, the various interefting
SCENES which are weekly to be met with at the

Mineral Wells,	Ordinaries,
Coffee-Houfes,	Publick Gardens,
Places of Publick	Parks,
Worfhip,	Sunday Routs,
Taverns,	Bagnios, &c.

OF THIS METROPOLIS AND IT'S ENVIRONS.

Exhibiting a true Account of the Manner in which that
Day is generally employed by all Ranks and Degrees of
People, from the common Beggar to the dignified Peer.

The Whole illuftrated with a great Variety of Original
CHARACTERS, ANECDOTES and MEMOIRS, of Perfons
in real Life; with pleafing Remarks thereupon. Intended to fhew, in their proper Light, the Follies of the
prefent Age; without the Severity of a CYNICK, or the
Indulgence of a SENSUALIST.

Perfons of ev'ry Rank, and ev'ry Age,
Who know the Scenes that occupy each Page,
Will, when they read my Book, with Pleafure fay—
" He's well defcrib'd our weekly Holiday."

THE SECOND EDITION.

LONDON;

Printed for the AUTHOR, by JAMES HARRISON,
No. 30, Giltfpur-Street:

And Sold by J. BEW, Paternofter-Row; W. DAVENHILL,
Cornhill, oppofite the Royal Exchange; and by all other
Bookfellers.

[Price *only* One Shilling.]

CHAP. III.

Coffee-houfe defcribed----Charaƈters there met with----Thoughts on the prefent State of Politicks.

THE place we judged moft convenient for our morning repaft, was one of the principal coffee-houfes near the Royal-Exchange; and, in our way thither, we could not but remark the great number of *frizeurs*, who were every where ftriding along the ftreets with the utmoft expedition.

When we arrived, we found the room tolerably full of various kinds of people. The fober citizen, the ftock-jobber, and the politician, were promifcuoufly feated together; fipping their coffee, reading the papers, and difplaying their feveral talents, (or want of talents) in curious arguments on their favourite topicks. Some were enquiring the price of ftocks, others the ftate of trade; while others, more ridiculous than either, were planning fchemes for paying the national debt *without any taxes at all*, and contriving methods to humble the Americans, and oblige them to fubmit to the decrees of a parliament which, fo far from reprefenting *them*, does not in reality reprefent *ourfelves*. Thefe were oppofed by thofe of contrary principles;

principles; and the noife of their arguments, together with the little reafon contained in them, gave neither fatisfaction nor information to any of the hearers.

In the midft of this confufion, I obferved a young man, very indifferently clad, whofe high cheek-bones prognofticated him to be a Caledonian, fitting in a box by himfelf, and writing with the greateft feeming compofure on feveral fmall pieces of paper which lay before him, figned pretty confpicuoufly with the letters T. S. When he had finifhed about half a fcore, he placed them carefully in an old letter-cafe; and fwallowing down the dregs of his liquor, hurried away, without appearing to take the leaft notice of any perfon prefent. When he was gone, my friend acquainted me, that he knew him well; and that he was a native of Scotland, who, having received a claffical education, was come to England in hopes of making a fortune, and eftablifhing his fame, by the literary merit he imagined himfelf to be poffeffed of. ‘ The London bookfellers, how-
‘ ever,’ continued my friend, ‘ not having
‘ difcernment enough to perceive the capacity
‘ of his extenfive genius, feldom employed
‘ him in any thing but elaborate tranflations,
‘ or fentimental novels; where he found
‘ himfelf obliged to write much more for
‘ money than an ordinary hackney-writer,
‘ without the leaft allowance for abilities.

D 3 ‘ Tired

30   A SUNDAY RAMBLE.

' Tired of such servile employ, he deter-
' mined to quit the service of the bookfellers,
' and woo the tragick muse.   For this pur-
' pose, he compleated a tragedy ; and doubt-
' ed not but it would gain him the appro-
' bation, as well as encouragement, of the
' publick : but, alas! the managers were too
' dull to obferve the beauties of this excellent
' performance ; and, after making him dance
' attendance above a dozen times, returned
' the piece, with the following laconick an-
' fwer---" *We have enough of* THIS *fort.*"
' Difappointed in an endeavour which he
' had flattered himfelf could not fail of fuc-
' cefs, he hardly knew what fcheme to de-
' vife, in order to gain a neceffary fubfiftence:
' at length he determined to advertife for a
' place; and, in confequence of fuch mode
' of application, has refpectively filled the
' feveral ftations of fhopman, boarding-fchool
' ufher, clerk, and out-rider ; moft of which
' employs were loft merely through inatten-
' tion to bufinefs, owing to the great defire
' he has to be confidered as an author, which
' engroffes the whole of his thoughts.   He
' is now commenced news-collector for the
' papers, and occafionally writes effays for
' and againft adminiftration, under different
' fignatures.   The fcraps you have juft feen
' him manufacture, are newfpaper para-
' graphs; which probably contain murders
' that were never committed, battles that
                                              ' were

‘ were never fought, rapes that were never
‘ attempted, or robberies that have never
‘ happened; notwithſtanding which, every
‘ one that appears in the papers of to-morrow,
‘ will intitle him to ſix-pence: and they are
‘ ſigned with the initials of the name he juſt-
‘ ly aſſumes, (viz. Tom Scribble) that it
‘ may be known by whom each was ſent;
‘ as there are many others who follow the
‘ ſame employ.’

The account my friend gave of this unfortunate young man, naturally ſuggeſted
that well-known aſſertion of Mr. Pope---

    " *A little learning is a dang’rous thing*;"

at the ſame time that it ſtrongly confirmed
an opinion I ever had, that education without genius is of little conſequence in the literary world, and that (though they appear
to be contradictory terms) it is even poſſible
to be a *learned blockhead*.

After theſe obſervations, my friend pointed
out a ſhabby old fellow with a dark com-
plection, ſtrongly expreſſive of the fraternity
to which he belonged; informing me that he
was a ſon of Iſrael, who had amaſſed a conſiderable fortune by the calamities of others.
‘ He lives,’ continued my friend, ‘ near St.
‘ Mary Axe, and daily advertiſes to lend
‘ money on annuities, places, commiſſions,
‘ and other valuable ſecurities; which he
‘ generally contrives to get entirely into his
                        ‘ own

' own hands for a trifle, and then difpofes of
' them at a very advanced price. Befides
' which he redeems goods out of pawn;
' procures bail for finking tradefmen; and
' buys off their whole ftock, previous to the
' fuing out a commiffion of bankruptcy by
' their creditors. In this manner he drags
' on his loathfome life; noxious to the pub-
' lick in general, detefted by every honeft
' man, and dreaded by all thofe whofe ne-
' ceffities or extravagance oblige them to
' have any concerns with him. And though
' he lives in the conftant commiffion of crimes
' of the moft alarming confequences, he fears
' not to be punifhed; as the legiflature can-
' not eafily reach his vices, was it even dif-
' pofed to make the attempt.'

The next that engroffed our attention was
a grave citizen, who fat liftening to the various debates without uttering a fingle word,
but now and then gave a contemptuous fmile
at their ridiculous arguments; not confidering, at the fame time, that himfelf was an
object of ridicule, from his unfocial behaviour, and the formal fingularity of his appearance.

During thefe remarks, an elderly gentleman walked into the room, and immediately
accofted my friend in the moft familiar manner, placing himfelf at the fame table with
us. After a few compliments, I ventured to
afk his opinion of the prefent ftate of politicks;

ticks; and what he thought would be the confequence of our prefent difpute with the Americans: to which he replied, that it was a topick fo differently handled, that it was almoft impoffible to get at the right-end of the ftory; but, from the little confideration he had beftowed on the fubject, he thought the Americans were indeed blamable, though much lefs fo than our parliament; who, according to his idea of the conftitution, could have no right to impofe laws on a people they do not reprefent, when thofe people are reprefented by others, who do not think fuch laws either juft, reafonable, or neceffary. With refpect to the confequences, he faid, there feemed to him but little doubt of their perfeverance in the refolutions they have formed, to hold no manner of commerce with this kingdom; the bad effects of which were already felt among fuch branches of our manufactures as have been accuftomed to trade to thofe parts. He then obferved upon the Quebeck-Bill; which, he faid, appeared to him of a much more alarming nature than the former; that being, at moft, but a temporal concern, this a fpiritual one. Nor could he conceive, as he faid, how it was poffible for both Houfes of Parliament to confent that Popery fhould be the eftablifhed religion of fo great a part of his majefty's dominions; when they know, that it cannot be eftablifhed in any part, according to the

exprefs

34   A   SUNDAY   RAMBLE.

exprefs words of the coronation-oath, without the moft flagrant breach of our invalu-
able rights and privileges.   He concluded,
with wifhing that thefe acts might be repealed: fince, if they are not liable to be attended with fuch bad confequences as is
too generally imagined, it would at leaft re-
ftore the publick tranquility, and revive the
languid ftate of our American trade.

I could not help admiring the extreme dif-
fidence that accompanied the old gentleman's
remarks; which contained, notwithftanding,
much more folid fenfe and reafon than all the
numerous arguments I had before heard on
the fubject.

As foon as he had drank his difh of chocolate, and fkimmed over the papers, he took
his leave, with the fame politenefs and freedom of behaviour he had ufed at his entrance.   My friend then began to inform me
who he was——' That gentleman,' faid he,
' is one of the principal merchants in this
' metropolis.   I have been acquainted with
' him many years; and though he is fuppo-
' fed to be worth upwards of a *plum*, has
' not half the pride and confequence of the
' meaneft of his clerks.   Though he poffeffes,
' as it is eafy to perceive, a very good fhare
' of underftanding, he does not think him-
' felf properly qualified to fill the high of-
' fices of this city; and has therefore care-
' fully avoided them, notwithftanding the
                                ' repeated

A SUNDAY RAMBLE. 35

' repeated solicitations of his friends. Un-
' ambitious of worldly splendour, he has
' trained his son to the same honourable em-
' ploy with himself; and only waits till he
' has sufficiently acquainted him with mer-
' cantile affairs, before he entirely quits the
' commercial world, and retires to a fine
' estate he has lately purchased in one of
' the most agreeable parts of the kingdom.'

By the time my friend had finished this
relation, we found our appetites sufficiently
satisfied ; and not perceiving any other characters worthy of notice, we thought proper
to quit this place : which we immediately
did, on paying for our breakfasts, and receiving an agreeable smile from the capti-
vating eyes of a very beautiful bar-maid.

Johann Wilhelm von Archenholz, *A Picture of England: containing a description of the laws, customs and manners of England*, 2 vols (London, Edward Jeffery, 1789), [10], iv, 210, [8], iv, 223pp.; 12°. BL: 1486.dd.1. ESTCT68455. Extract, vol. II, pp. 104–12.

A foreigner's account of the role of the coffee-house in English (or more specifically, London) life. Travel writing about England by foreign writers was popular in England, perhaps because the travel-writer's technique of defamiliarisation allowed English readers to gain a new view of themselves. In Archenholz they found a very flattering portrait of the nation, whose prosperity and liberty he declared to be the envy of Europe: even the women he found to be the most beautiful. In his account the coffee-house is primarily associated with sociability, newspapers and commerce: its relation to food and beverage retailing is not worth notice. Archenholz's *Picture of England* was first translated into English in 1789, by an unknown translator, from the French edition, *Tableau de l'Angleterre, contenant des anecdotes curieuses et intéressantes. Traduit de l'allemand*, translated by Ludwig Benedict Franz von Bilderbeck (published in Brussels in 1788). The first German edition comprised the first three volumes of *England und Italien*, 5 vols (Heidelberg, Winter, 1785), and this was used for a new English translation published in 1797, taken from the original German by Joseph Trapp, who had also translated his *Picture of Italy* in 1791. The second translation is substantially different from the first: major differences are noted in the explanatory notes at the end of this volume. The second translation was reprinted in 1797.

Johann Wilhelm von Archenholz (1741–1812) was born in the Hanseatic city of Danzig (now Gdansk) in the Kingdom of Poland, and served in the Seven Years' War in the army of the King of Prussia, Frederick II, attaining the rank of captain. He travelled in England in the 1770s, and may have stayed several years, perhaps supported by clandestine work for Frederick II. He was living in Dresden by 1780. In addition to his travel accounts, he wrote in German several well-received histories concerning the Seven Years' War, Gustavus Vasa and Elizabeth I, and edited several periodicals, including *The British Mercury*, an

English-language weekly periodical published in Hamburg between 1787 and 1791. As his publications suggest, Archenholz was both an anglophile and a defender of the Protestant faith. Edward Jeffery, the publisher, was a bookseller in Pall Mall.

CHAPTER IV.

The Manner of Living in England—Coffee-Houses—
Lloyd's — Affurance Offices—Domeftic Cuftoms—
The Contraft between French and Englifh Dinners
—Cookery—Liquors — Drefs — Singular Requeft
to the King—Servants—Sunday—Good-nature of
the People—Boxing—Marfhal Saxe's Difpute with
a Scavenger—The King of Bath.

THE Englifh live in a very remarkable manner. They rife late, and fpend moft of
the morning, either in walking about town or
fitting in the coffee-houfes. There they not
only read the newfpapers, but tranfact bufinefs. Affociations, infurances, bets, the trade
in foreign bills ; all thefe things are not only
talked of, but executed in thefe public places.
They there form connections, conclude bargains,
talk of the intrigues and the cabals of the
court, criticife works of genius and art, and

F 5   enter

[106]

enter into patriotic refolutions concerning the good
of the ftate.

Each profeffion has its own particular coffee-
houfe; fuch as lawyers, the military men, the
learned and men of wit.

There are feveral dozens of thefe around the
Royal Exchange, where more bufinefs is tranfacted than in the Exchange itfelf.   That of
Lloyd's in a particular manner deferves to be
noticed ; I do not think that there is another
equal to it in all the world.   Thofe merchants
who fpeculate in infurances, and who in 1778
amounted to fix hundred, affemble there.   They
fubfcribe ten guineas a piece per annum, and,
by means of that fum, carry on an immenfe
foreign correfpondence with all the countries in
Europe.

This fociety accordingly receives the earlieft
and moft authentic intelligence, refpecting the
politics or the commerce of all the nations
inhabiting the four quarters of the globe.   They
often inform government of circumftances that
they would not know till long after from
their minifters and their agents; and which,
perhaps, they would never otherwife hear of.
The

[107]

The fpirit of order and exactnefs, introduced introduced into their interefting regulations, is fo perfect, that the moft extraordinary news receives a certain degree of authenticity by coming from that place.

As thefe gentlemen, in common with the reft of the nation, are famous for their *public fpirit*, they are not barely contented with informing their particular friends, but tranfcribe their intelligence into a book, for the infpection of the nation at large. They alfo publifh the arrival of all veffels, whether Englifh or foreign, that come into any of the ports of England. There is not one of thefe, whofe good or bad properties they are unacquainted with. They alfo know their age, the character of the captain, &c. &c. Being compofed almoft entirely of rich merchants, there is no danger of lofing the fum affured, but in cafe of a *general bankruptcy*; and fuch is their known probity, and reputation, that they are often, in doubtful cafes, appointed umpires by foreign ftates.

An Englifh coffee-houfe has no refemblance to a French or German one. You neither fee billiards nor backgammon tables; you do not

F 6   even

[108]

even hear the leaft noife; every body fpeaks in
a low tone, for fear of difturbing the company.
They frequent them principally to read the
PAPERS, a tafk that is abfolutely neceffary in
that country.

The dinners of the Englifh, like all their
domeftic cuftoms, have fomething peculiar to
themfelves. By fuppofing every thing to be
entirely oppofite to what it is in Paris, one
may form a juft idea of thefe houfes in London, where the old fafhions are ftill kept up.
The number of people who live in the Anglo-
Gallic ftyle is very fmall.

Soup, which is the firft difh in France, never
appears on any table in London. The French
eat a great deal of bread, and very little meat;
the Englifh much meat, and little bread. Joints,
in France, are either roafted or boiled to rags;
they eat them almoft raw in England. Ragouts,
fauces, and *made difhes*, are the delicacies of
the French; the Englifh are for what is fimple
and natural; they even pufh this tafte too far.
The tables of the former are often too fmall
for the difhes; the entertainments of the latter
confift of two or three large pieces of meat,

or

or of prodigious pies, in which some hundreds of birds are entombed.

The deffert, in France, is compofed of fruits and confectionary; in England, of large cheefes. Among one nation, they eat more than they drink; among the other, they drink more than they eat, and regard their liquors as the chief article in a repaft.

The Englifh are in a hurry during their meals, that they may fooner indulge this paffion. The ladies then leave them to enjoy themfelves with greater freedom. Politics immediately commence, and *healths* continually go round; each gueft propofes a toaft in his turn, the mafter of the houfe having firft given his. They then fill their glaffes, and, naming either a minifter or a beauty, empty them in a moment.

Napkins, which have been difufed for twenty years, are now beginning to be introduced. Thofe who are attached to the old cuftoms, ridicule the ufe of them. This precaution, they fay, is only neceffary for children; grown perfons have no occafion for them, as they can cover themfelves with the table cloth, which is of an extraordinary length. They

chnage

[110]

change the knife and fork with every plate. They
do not ufe thefe inftruments indifferently in either
hand, as in all the other nations of Europe; the
fork is always in the left, and the knife in the right
hand. It is by this method, which is infinitely
more commodious than ours, that you may immediately know an Englifhman before he has fpoken
a fingle word.

The difcredit into which Englifh cookery has
fallen among foreigners, proceeds entirely from the
prejudices entertained againft their manner of
dreffing victuals. But who, in the whole world,
would not prefer flefh full of fucculent and
nourifhing juices, to thofe roafted meats which
are infipid to the tafte, if not eaten with
an unwholefome fauce? I have known ladies
brought up very delicately, and ufed to all the
elegancies of foreign tables, who, on their firft
arrival in London, have been difgufted with the
victuals; but they foon changed their minds, and
found them very agreeable afterwards. It is the
fimplicity in the dreffing, that alone generates
fuch prejudices in the breafts of ftrangers.

Their drinks alfo are remarkable, on account
of the fingular mixtures of which they are compofed. Sillabub, for example, is a compofition

I   of

[111]

of red wine, milk and fugar. The common people enjoy themfelves, during the winter, with warm * beer mixt with bitter effences, and with ale in which gin, fugar, and eggs have been boiled together. It is their attachment to ftrong liquors, that makes them fo very fond of port-wine, which is fold at a high price. Burgundy and champaign, are exceedingly dear, on account of the duties: notwithftanding this, the confumption of thefe wines is very great in London, where they like every thing that is *powerful* and *heady*. Although cyder is allowed to be equally agreeable, yet it is drunk only in the diftant counties.

They are peculiarly attached to porter: on this account, there are no lefs than eight thoufand ale-houfes in the metropolis and its neighbourhood. In thefe, all ranks are mixed and confounded together: it is not uncommon to meet with even perfons of quality there.—It is well known that Swift and Sterne frequented them, to ftudy the human heart.

The impoft on coffee is fo great, that it pays a duty of more than feven pence a pound.

* Pud,

This

[112]

This does not, indeed, leſſen the conſumption; the exorbitant price, however, occaſions it to be drunk very weak. This cuſtom is ſo prevalent, that even the richeſt people will not uſe it when ſtrong; the moſt contemptible tradeſman in all Germany drinks better coffee than they do. In reſpect to tea, the Engliſh are, on the other hand, uncommonly nice; and it is calculated, that they conſume more of this commodity than all the reſt of Europe. Thouſands of poor people live on this beverage, and bread and butter, which is ſaid to correct its bad qualities; but they take care that the one is good, and the other ſtrong. Our manner of drinking it, would not in the leaſt agree with them; for, that they may the better enjoy the flavour of the herb, they colour it with only two or three drops of milk.

EXPLANATORY NOTES

Coffee: a tale

p. 6, l. 1: Whifflers: a trifler, an insignificant or contemptible fellow (*OED*).

p. 6, l. 2: *rumple my* Bayes: to disturb my verses, that is, to make critical remarks.

p. 6, l. 6: plerúmque: Latin, 'frequently, commonly'.

p. 6, l. 8: Crimen Clerumque: Latin, 'clerical offence, a crime of the clergy'.

p. 7, ll. 7–8: Puritan-Tiff, / *Before* CALVIN *and* LUTHER: Protestant theologians: John Calvin (1509–64) and Martin Luther (1483–1546).

p. 7, l. 16: *a* Punk: a prostitute, strumpet, harlot (*OED*).

p. 8, l. 12: HENLEY: John 'Orator' Henley (1692–1756), a Church of England minister who left the church in 1725 to found his own chapel, The Oratory, in a large room above the Newport Meat Market in London. His hack writings, some in support of Robert Walpole's ministry, were published by Edmund Curll.

p. 8, l. 15: *pull'd down their* Bush: a bunch of ivy hung up as a vintner's sign, perhaps because the plant was sacred to Bacchus; hence, the sign-board of a tavern (*OED*).

p. 9, l. 5: PAUL'S: St Paul's Cathedral and the alleys and yards surrounding it were home to numerous coffee-houses.

p. 9, l. 12: Protestant-*POPE*: an oxymoron, and commonplace of religious controversy of the eighteenth century.

p. 10, l. 8: Arcanums *of* State: the profound secrets of the government and its ministers.

p. 10, ll. 15–16: Human-Proroguing / Divine-Convocation: the ongoing and complicated conflict within the Church of England of the precedence between the episcopate and the Convocation, the parliament of the clergy of the Church. The great Whig bishops argued that only they could call or prorogue a convocation, as directed by God, while the Convocation, dominated by High-Church clergy, argued that it was an earthly and political decision that should be made by the clergymen themselves.

p. 10, l. 19: D—rs-C—ns: Doctors Commons, a colloquial name for the College of Advocates and Doctors of Law in St Bennet's Hill off St Paul's Church Yard. In it were based the Ecclesiastical and Admiralty Courts, together with the advocates who practised these branches of law.

p. 11, l. 5: Council o'Trent: an ecumenical council called between 1545 and 1563 which defined the beliefs and rituals of the Roman Catholic Church as distinctive from those of the Protestant Reformation.

p. 11, l. 16: Isosceles: a triangle with two equal sides.

p. 11, l. 20: Theometry: measurement or estimation of God (*OED*).

p. 12, ll. 11–12: *Innuendo* — Darius / *Or else* Alexander: Alexander III (356–23 BC), known as 'the Great', king of Macedon, who defeated Darius III Codomannus at the Battle of Issus in 333 BC. After the battle, Darius fled the scene, leaving behind his mother, wife, children and treasure.

p. 13, l. 13: Passive-Obedience: the willing, uncomplaining, unresisting submission to the will of God: specifically the doctrine espoused by Tory High-Church divines to give biblical weight to the authority of the episcopate and crown. (*OED*)

p. 15, l. 9: Indeleble-Stamp: the spiritual character which is held to be impressed or conferred by some of the sacraments, such as baptism.

p. 15, l. 11: Sanctify'd-Sinner: a Christian who has achieved the state of grace, and can do no sin.

p. 15, l. 13: MOHOCK: a member of a band of aristocratic ruffians who allegedly roamed the streets of London at night perpetrating arbitrary acts of violence for fun.

p. 16, ll. 11–12: Nemo nos / Impunè lacesset: Latin, 'no one molests us with impunity'.

p. 19, l. 1: Jus-divinum's *evinc'd* / Common Tenure *to all*: 'Jus divinum' is the divine law (the law of God). 'Common tenure' is a legal term describing a form of feudal land-holding also known as 'meer copyhold', by which the land reverts to the Lord of the Manor if the tenant commits a felony. Here the term is used to describe a Christian's mortal life.

p. 19, l. 3: *Cr—n or to Mi—re*: crown or mitre, king and bishops.

p. 19, l. 20: *Sir* Fopling-flutter: the hero of Sir George Etherege's play *The Man of Mode, or, Sir Fopling Flutter* (1676); by extension, a fop or man of fashion.

p. 20, l. 11: *Great* GEORGE: George I (1660–1727) or George II (1683–1760), kings of Great Britain and Ireland. George I died on 11 June 1727, in the month that *Coffee, a tale*, was published.

p. 21, l. 4: Deodand: a thing forfeited or to be given to God: specifically, in English law, a personal chattel which, having been the cause of the death of a human being, was forfeited to the Crown to be distributed in alms (*OED*).

p. 21, l. 5: ERASMUS: Desiderius Erasmus of Rotterdam (1466–1536), Dutch humanist and theologian.

p. 21, ll. 11–12: COLBERT ... RICHELIEU: French ministers under Louis XIV: Jean-Baptiste Colbert (1619–83) and Armand Jean du Plessis, Duc de Richelieu (1585–1642).

p. 21, l. 13: BERMUDA: an island in the North Atlantic, settled in 1609 by English colonists of the Virginia Company.

p. 21, l. 20: THOMAS-a-BECKET: Thomas Becket (1115–70), Archbishop of Canterbury 1162–70, assassinated on the order of Henry II.

p. 22, l. 4: *No B—PS, no K—GS*: 'No Bishops, no Kings', a political maxim associated with Puritan republicans.

p. 22, l. 20: JACK-GENTLEMAN'S Hat: an upstart, a man of low birth or manners making pretensions to be a gentleman (*OED*)

p. 24, ll. 1–4: LANE ... AVE MARIA: Ave-Maria Lane, a lane leading to Pater-Noster Row in the centre of the London book-trade, and home to the Stationer's Company.

p. 24, l. 5: WILKINS and WOLLASTON: John Wilkins (1614–72), theologian and natural philosopher, who posthumously published in 1675 *Of the Principles and Duties of Natural Religion*; and William Wollaston (1660–1724), moral philosopher, who published *The Religion of Nature Delineated* in 1722 (*ODNB*); influential works that variously argued that the existence of God and Christian principles could be derived using reason.

p. 24, l. 9: Succedaneums: a thing which replaces or stands in for another, a substitute (*OED*).

p. 25, l. 9: scarlet-dye CRIMES: a crime which would make the perpetrator red with embarrassment, after Isaiah 1:18: 'Come now, and let us reason together, saith the Lord: through your sins be as scarlet, they shall be as white as snow'.

p. 25, l. 12: NUPTIALS-CLANDESTINE: an illegal marriage that has not been conducted accordingly to the letter of the law, or not by a legitimate clergyman.

p. 26, l. 13: CANONOCLAST: a nonce-word meaning someone who is destructive of the canons or ecclesiastical laws of the church.

p. 26, l. 19: JERRY-WHITE'S Sneer: Jeremiah White (1629–1707), chaplain in the family of Oliver Cromwell, and subsequently, chaplain to the Calves-Head Club, a republican secret society which supposedly met yearly on the anniversary of the execution of Charles I.

p. 27, l. 3: *P—rs-Bills*: not traced.

p. 27, ll. 11–12: NON-ADHERENCE, and latent / SKREENS: non-adherence was a term used to describe those who did not adhere to the 39 Articles of the Church of England.

p. 27, ll. 13–16: *The* traytor'd *Case, / Of M—R P—N; /* Contra. *The reverend / JOINER, Rabbi B—N*: not traced.

p. 28, l. 17: Advertisements: the footnote directs the reader to *Mist's Weekly-Journal* and the *Post-Boy*, November 1726. On 26 November 1726, these papers carried news of Mary Toft of Guildford, who claimed to have given birth to nine rabbits.

p. 30, l. 9: Non-obstante: Latin, 'notwithstanding': in law, a dispensation, usually from the King, authorising the violation of the law.

p. 31, l. 9: *BEN JOHNSON*: Ben Jonson (1572–1637), dramatist and poet, who was at the centre of a convivial literary drinking circle who met at the Devil Tavern in Fleet Street, known as the Sons of Ben.

p. 32, l. 13: *DIANA*: in Roman mythology, the goddess of chastity.

p. 33, l. 16: *COMPREHENSION in* Twist: Twist, a combination of coffee and tea, is made a metaphor for Comprehension, the inclusion of the Nonconformists within the Church of England by enlarging the terms of ecclesiastical communion (*OED*).

p. 33, l. 20: Jugulare Falernum: Latin, 'to murder Falernian wine'.

p. 36, l. 4: In tutamen Authoris: Latin, 'to protect the writer'.

p. 37, l. 11: Exegi-Monumentum: Latin, 'finished book'.

p. 37, l. 14: Corinthian-Brass: an alloy of gold, silver and copper produced at Corinth, much prized for use in ornaments (*OED*).

p. 37, l. 18: *POETA DIVINUS*: the sacred poet, that is to say, God.

p. 37: ll. 19–20: *Si propiús stes, / Te capiet MINUS*: a quotation from Vincent Bourne, English Latin poet, and a schoolmaster at Westminster College, London. The line is a revision of 'Si propius stes, / Te capiet Magis', the epigraph to Dryden's *Absalom and Achitophel*, from Horace, *Ars Poetica*, ll. 361–2. Minus means small, unimportant.

The Velvet Coffee-woman

p. 43, ll. 1–2: *A Funeral Oration, &c.*: supposedly written by a female writer in praise of Anne Rochford. The entire oration, excepting the final two paragraphs and minor changes, is taken from the 'Epistle Dedicatory' of Capt. Charles Walker's *Authentick Memoirs of the Life, Intrigues and Adventures of the Celebrated Sally Salisbury* (London, 1723), pp. 2–30.

p. 44, ll. 4–6: *a* Jilt ... *a* kept Mistress ... *a* common Runner: forms of prostitution: a 'Gilt or Jilt: a Cheat, a Woman who has defeated her Gallant in his Amours' (Thomas Blount, *Glossographia*, 4th edn (London, 1674)); a kept mistress, a woman supported by a man for the purposes of a sexual relationship; a common runner, a prostitute who works the street.

p. 44, l. 10: *Prolocutors*: spokesmen or advocates (*OED*).

p. 44, l. 12: *QUIXOT*: an enthusiastic visionary, inspired by lofty and chivalrous, but false and unrealisable, goals (*OED*), like the eponymous character of Cervantes's *Don Quixote* (1605–15).

p. 44, l. 15: *BESSUS*: Bessus (d. 329 BC) was the Satrap of Bactria and Sogdiana in Persia. After the defeat of Darius III, King of Persia, by Alexander the Great in 331 BC, Bessus arrested then executed his king. Here his name is a term for a military traitor.

p. 46, ll. 11–18: *BELLE ... PRUDE*: a belle, a handsome woman, the reigning 'beauty' of the place; a prude, a woman who maintains or affects excessive modesty or propriety in conduct or speech (*OED*).

p. 50, l. 14: *PHRYNE, of* Bæotia: a celebrated hetaera or courtesan of the fourth century BC, who charged customers according to her whim: Diogenes the philosopher was not charged, but the King of Lydia was charged an extraordinarily high sum, and paid. When she was tried for her life, she was acquitted chiefly by the effect that a display of her naked beauty had on the court.

p. 51, l. 3: *LAMIA of* Athens: a lamia is a Latin term for a witch who murders children by sucking their blood, and appears in the form of a woman's head and torso conjoined with a serpent's tail. In Roman mythology, she was the daughter of Poseidon and Lybie, and was loved by Zeus.

p. 51, l. 16: *LAIS of* Corinth: a courtesan born in Hyccara in Sicily, and brought as a prisoner to Corinth as a child. She charged a very high fee (Demosthenes reported it to be ten thousand drachmas), but she was equally known for her wit and conversation.

p. 52, l. 6: *THAIS*: celebrated Athenian courtesan who accompanied Alexander the Great on his expedition to Persia, notorious for having driven Alexander to such a passion that he set fire to the palace of the Persian king (Smith).

p. 52, ll. 18–19: *ARIADNE ... THESEUS ... BACCHUS*: In Greek mythology, Ariadne is the daughter of King Minos of Crete, who fell in love with Theseus, and aided him in his fight with the Minotaur. Bacchus is the god of wine.

p. 52, l. 22–p. 11, l. 1: *CELIAS ... MANILLAS ... JULIAS*: untraced, probably intended as common Roman women's names.

p. 53, l. 7: *LYCORIS of GALLUS*: Cytheris, a celebrated courtesan, the mistress of Anthony, and then the Roman governor of Egypt, Gaius Cornelius Gallus (69–26 BC), who made her the subject of his elegiac poems under the name Lycoris (Smith).

p. 53, l. 14: *CORINNA, the Mistress of OVID*: Publius Ovidus Naso (43 BC–AD 17), Roman poet known in English as Ovid, whose love poetry, *Amores* (*The Art of Love*), written in 10 BC, was addressed to Corinna. The name was perhaps meant to recall the Ancient Greek poet Corinna, probably sixth century BC, teacher of Pindar.

p. 54, ll. 1–2: *LELAGE of HORACE*: a laughing, chattering woman who is the object of the poet's desire in Horace's *Odes* (I:22 and II.5).

p. 54, ll. 3–4: *Hoyden*: a rude, ill-bred or boisterous girl (*OED*).

p. 54, l. 5: *LESBIA of CATULLUS*: the Roman poet Gaius Valerius Catullus (84–54 BC), who addressed about half of his surviving erotic poems to a woman he calls Lesbia, perhaps after Sappho of Lesbos.

p. 54, ll. 15–18: *the PINE-APPLE of* Great Britain, *which includes the several Flavours of all the delicious Fruits in the World*: the pineapple (the juicy edible fruit of *Ananassa sativa*) was first introduced into Britain in 1664, and was the toast of Restoration gardening. The taste was thought to be very complex: John Locke observed in *An Essay Concerning Human Understanding* (London, Thomas Basset, 1690) that 'He that thinks otherwise, let him try if any Words can give him the taste of a Pineapple, and make him have the true *Idea* of the Relish of that celebrated delicious fruit', p. 28.

p. 55, ll. 8–9: *Parent of* Gods *and* Men / *Began the Sportive-Dance*: verses original to Walker's *Sally Salisbury*.

p. 56, l. 19: *St. AUSTIN*: Aurelius Augustine (AD 354–430), known as Saint Augustine of Hippo or St Austin.

p. 57, l. 5: *ADEODATUS*: Latin, 'gift of god'. When he was seventeen, St Augustine, who was not converted to Christianity until he was thirty-two years of age, fathered an illegitimate boy who he named Adeodatus.

p. 57, footnote: *1. A Modest Defence of Publick Stews. 2. Its counterpart,* A Modest Defence of Chastity: works on prostitution. Phil-porney [Bernard Mandeville or George Ogle], *A Modest Defence of Publick Stews: or, an essay upon whoring* (London, A. Moore, 1724) and an anonymous reply to it, *A modest defence of chastity* (London, A. Bettesworth, 1726).

p. 58, ll. 1–3: *At* Rome *every pleasurable Female pays a JULIO* per *Week to the* CHURCH: a julio was a silver coin struck by Pope Julius II (1503–13), current in Italy and worth about sixpence. A reference to prostitutes in Rome buying indulgences to exculpate the sin of their trade, perhaps apocryphal.

p. 58, l. 10: *Pope SIXTUS erected a noble* Brothel-House: Pope Sixtus IV (1471–84) was commonly accused – especially in Protestant tracts – of having fathered illegitimate children with his sister, and licensed the brothels of Rome so as to raise a tax on them.

p. 59, l. 1: *RHODOPE*: in Greek mythology, Queen Rhodope of Thrace compared herself favourably to Zeus and Hera, and was changed into a mountain in punishment.

p. 59, l. 4: *FLORA*: in the Roman mythology, the goddess of flowers and spring.

p. 59, l. 13: Cyprian Girls: literally girls from Cyprus, an island in the eastern Mediterranean, but also another name for prostitutes.

p. 60, ll. 7–8: *when* Xerxes *invaded the* Pelopenesus: a Persian king (reigned 485–65 BC) who invaded Greece in 480 BC and was defeated at the Battle of Salamis (28 September 480 BC).

p. 60, l. 11: *SOLON*: an Athenian lawmaker (638–558 BC).

p. 60, ll. 17–18: *a CHAPEL of* Ease *in* Russel-Court, Covent-Garden: a brothel. Russell Court was a narrow alley running between Drury Lane and Bridges Street, and ironically it did contain a chapel, in the burying ground of St Mary's Le Strand.

p. 61, l. 2: Amorosa's: a female lover, a wanton, a courtesan (*OED*).

p. 62, l. 11: Royal Japanners: court sycophants, those who polish the shoes of the King. Daniel Defoe, *Every-Body's Business, is No-Body's Business* (London, W. Meadows, 1725): 'These are call'd the black-guard, who black your honour's shoes, and incorporate themselves under the title of the Worshipful Company of Japanners'.

p. 62, ll. 15–17: *that famous* College *of the celebrated Mrs.* Weybourn: Mother Wisebourn, Wyburn or Weyborn was a celebrated bawd and brothel keeper in Drury Lane (see Anodyne Tanner, *The Life of the Late Celebrated Mrs. Elizabeth Wisebourn, Vulgarly Call'd Mother Wybourn* (London, A. Moon, [*c.* 1721]); reprinted in Julie Peakman (ed.), *Whore Biographies, 1700–1825, Part I*, 4 vols (London, Pickering & Chatto, 2006), vol. 1). In Walker's *Sally Salisbury*, this reference is to 'that famous *College* of *Sherard-Street*, under the celbrated [sic] Mrs. *N—d—am*', which is to say Mother Needham's brothel in Gerrard ('Sherard') St.

p. 64, l. 6: *ASPASIA*: Aspasia (*c.* 469–406 BC), a hetaera or courtesan, she was the mistress of Pericles (495–29 BC), Greek statesman. Their house was a centre for cultural and intellectual life in Athens. Aspasia's political influence was unpopular, however, and she was blamed by some for causing the Peloponnesian war with Sparta (431 BC).

p. 65, l. 9–p. 66, l. 5: the final two paragraphs are the only original additions to the 'Funeral Oration'.

p. 65, l. 17: South-Sea-Tempests: the financial crash that accompanied the end of the South Sea Bubble, 1720–1.

p. 65, ll. 18–19: *the* Gully-Hole *of the* Meuse: a gully hole was 'a Place at the Grate or Entrance of the Street-Canals [drains] for a Passage into the Common-Shore [sewers]', John Kersey, *Dictionarium Anglo-Brittanicum* (London, 1726). Rochford's coffee-house was in, or backed on to, the Royal Mews, an open court opening onto Charing Cross, once used as stabling for the King's falcons (a mew is a cage for falcons), and later horses. In 1734 the main stable block fronting onto Charing Cross was rebuilt by William Kent, and in the 1830s this building, and Charing Cross, were incorporated in to John Nash's Charing Cross development, which saw the construction of Trafalgar Square and the National Gallery (the latter on the site where Rochford's Coffee-house was located) (*LE*).

p. 66, ll. 1–3: *SHAKESPEARE says, that,* with all her Imperfections on her Head, she is called to her Account: The Ghost to Hamlet, in Shakespeare, *Hamlet*

(1623), I.v.297–8: 'Sent to my account / with all my imperfections on my head'.

p. 67, ll. 6–8: *our Female Triumvirate,* (Sally Salisbury, *the* Royal Sovereign, *and Mrs.* Rochford,*)*: three recently-dead women: Sarah (Sally) Salisbury, née Pridden (1690–1724), courtesan; Princess Sophia Dorothea of Celle (1666–1726), electoral princess of Hanover and divorced wife of George I; and Anne Rochford (d. 1727), coffee-woman. Sophia Dorothea's appearance on this list reflects her scandalous status: after her affair with Count von Konigsmark in 1692–4, she consented to divorce from Georg Ludwig, and was imprisoned in a castle at Ahldern in Celle in 1695, where she remained for the rest of her life. George I attempted to keep this narrative secret, but opponents of the Hanoverian succession made sure her life-story was circulated widely, as a measure of the dynasty's immorality (*ODNB*).

p. 67, l. 11: Manes: Latin, 'shades or ghosts of the dead'.

p. 68, l. 21: Francis Woase, *Waterman*: watermen carried passengers on the Thames, one of the principal thoroughfares of London in the eighteenth century. Watermen and lightermen were regulated by the Waterman's Company, under the control of the City Corporation, although watermen were not free of the City.

p. 68, l. 22: *Earl of* Torrington: Arthur Herbert, Earl of Torrington (1648–1716), naval officer and politician. Torrington, a popular naval hero in the Stuart navy, rose to commander-in-chief after serving as the admiral of William of Orange's invasion force in 1688. After the disastrous Battle of Beachy Head in 1690 he was court-martialled, after which he retired to his house Oatlands, at Walton-on-Thames, near Weybridge (*ODNB*).

p. 69, l. 26: Deal: a town in Kent on the Channel, eight miles north-east of Dover, one of the Cinque Ports.

p. 69, ll. 26–7: Stangate, *in the Parish of* Lambeth: a riverside street and wharf in Lambeth, across the river from the Houses of Parliament. Stangate was the location of the Roman ford or ferry across the Thames. Edward Hatton says Lambeth 'is a Parish over against Market Street (the most Sly part of Westminster) being in the County of Surrey' (*A New View of London*, 2 vols (London, 1708), vol. I, p. 45).

p. 69, ll. 29–30: Mitre *Alehouse near those Stairs*: Stangate Stairs (a wharf for watermen and ferries), directly across the river from Parliament Stairs, leading to Old Palace Yard.

p. 70, ll. 30–1: *Old Swan Stairs*: a wharf or quay, on the river just above London Bridge, at Ebbgate Lane off Thames Street.

p. 71, l. 8: *Memoirs of the* Comte de *ROCHEFORT*: a 'merry adventure' mixing gossip, scandal and fiction, written by Gatien de Courtilz de Sandras (1644–1712), and first published in French in 1687. The English translation, from which the quotation is taken, was published in 1696 as *The memoirs of the*

Count de Rochefort containing an account of what past most memorable, under the ministry of Cardinal Richelieu and Cardinal Mazarin, with many particular passages of the reign of Lewis the Great. Made English from the French (London, James Knapton, Richard Parker, and Tho. Nott, 1696).

p. 71, l. 13: Utrum harum mavis accipe: Latin commonplace, 'Utrum horum mavis accipe': 'Take whichever of those you prefer'. David Macdonnel, *A Dictionary of Quotations* (London, 1797).

p. 71, l. 21–p. 73, l. 31: *"The Count* de Rochefort *one Day ... for a considerable Time*: The footnote correctly identifies the quotation from the English translation of Courtilz de Sandras, *Memoirs of the Count De Rocheforte*, 3rd edn (London, 1705), pp. 208–9.

p. 72, l. 3: Pomatum: pomade or pomatum, a scented ointment for application to the skin and hair. The joke turns on a misrecognition: instead of pomade, Rochefort rubbed a vesicant unguent (such as cantharides) on his lips.

p. 72, ll. 25–6: *Duke* de Roquelaire: untraced.

p. 74, l. 10: *two Houses at* Stangate: Anne Rochford persuaded her mother-in-law Mrs Weston to give her title to two houses in return for renewing the leases and repairing them. She additionally built two further houses, suggesting considerable financial acumen.

p. 75, ll. 7–8: *introduced at Court in* Velvet: velvet is a type of tufted fabric with dense, even-cut threads with a short dense pile, giving a soft feel and lustrous colour. Velvet was very expensive to produce, and was a luxury closely associated with the clothes and vestments of the Court and Church. By being presented to the King wearing a velvet dress, the coffee-women are claiming or dissimulating a high status they do not have.

p. 75, l. 20: *Mr.* Congreve'*s Song* — Ye Commons and Peers: One of the most popular ballad songs of the eighteenth century, commonly attributed to Congreve, but more likely by Swift.

p. 75, l. 26: Jenny, Fenwick, *and* Nanny: the three coffee-women: Jenny Man, proprietor of one of the three Man's Coffee-houses in Charing Cross; Mrs Ann Fenwick, proprietor of the British Coffee-house in Charing Cross (*Daily Post*, 6 July 1728, 'the famous Mrs Anne Fenwick, Mistress of the British Coffee-house near Charing Cross interred at St Martin's in the Field'); and Anne 'Nanny' Rochford, of Rochford's Coffee-house Charing Cross.

p. 76, l. 4: *a Star*: the insignia of the higher chivalric honours, denoting aristocratic status. The footnote adds that the star was worn by 'the Duke of ——— who introduced them'. The identity of this duke has not been traced.

p. 76, ll. 13–16: Jenny Man, *pleaded her* Interest *with the* Officers, *Mrs.* Fenwick *her Influence over the* Highland-Clans *in* Scotland: Jenny Man's Coffee-house was noted for its military clientele, especially officers on half-pay; Anne Fenwick's British Coffee-house was noted as a place of resort for Scotsmen and others concerned in Scottish affairs.

p. 77, ll. 1–2: *two Sisters of the* Coffee-Pot *and* C—y-Burrough: coney-burrough is presumably obscene: coney, a rabbit, an indecent term for a woman, and burrow, a rabbit hole, or rabbit warren, hence either the female genitalia, or a brothel.

p. 77, ll. 5–6: *obtain Leave to build a house in the* Meuse: the Royal Mews was within the Verge of the Court, where licensing for taverns was controlled by the office of the Lord Steward.

p. 77, ll. 11–12: Arrack Punch, *and* L'Eau de Barbadé: arrack is a spirituous liquor made of any native ingredient, such as rice or dates; punch is a drink made of wine and spirits mixed with water, sugar, lemon and spices; and *l'eau de Barbadé* is rum from Barbados.

p. 77, l. 13: *polite* Caberet: a drinking house, a pot-house (*OED*). The word now refers to something French, denoting a place where entertainment is offered alongside meals, but in the seventeenth century, the term was 'somewhat naturalized' (*OED*).

p. 77, l. 15: *that noted* Irish-*man* Mac Dermot: see below, note to p. 78, l. 2. A ballad supposedly by him was published in 1727: Shane-Baune Mac-Dermot, *Monster Juggy preferr'd or an Answer to Molly Mogg of the Rose* (London, J. Gowan, 1727).

p. 77, ll. 24–5: *play the Sosia*: the living double of another. Sosia is the servant of Amphitryon in Plautus's comedy *Amphitryon*, adapted by Dryden in 1690 as *Amphitryon or the Two Sosia's*.

p. 78, ll. 2–4: Mac Dermot: *Or,* The Irish-Fortune Hunter, *a Mock-Heroic Poem, in six Cantoes*: John Durant Breval (*c.* 1680–1738), *Mac Dermot: or, the Irish fortune-hunter. A Poem. In six canto's* (London, E. Curll, 1717), an extended 48-page mock-heroic amorous biography of a young and attractive Irish man who seduces a series of wealthy London heiresses and widows.

p. 78, ll. 5–6: *a Bookseller in the* Strand, Tota notus in Urbe: the shop of Edmund Curll, 'only too well known all over town' (Latin phrase).

p. 78, ll. 7–13: *Mrs.* Rochford*'s* Library ... *or the* Altar of Love *it self*: Rochford's library of supposedly lubricious books, all published by Curll.

p. 78, ll. 22–3: *Descent from the* Kings *of* Munster ... *a* Noroy: the Norroy is the third Kings of Arms in the College of Arms (which grants heraldic arms), with jurisdiction over the north of England. These lines are closely adapted from the 'Dedication' to the poem *Mac Dermot*, pp. iv–vi.

p. 80, ll. 7–8: *middle Isle of* Lambeth Church, *on the 29th Day of* August *1727*: St Mary-at-Lambeth, the parish church of Lambeth, next to Lambeth Palace, and now the Museum of Garden History.

p. 80, ll. 31–2: *Count Brandenburg*: another imposter at court, later named Florentius Van Brandenburg of Namur. His name recalls that of Queen Caroline, the consort of the George II, who was a princess of Brandenburg-Anspach.

p. 80, l. 32–p. 81, l. 1: *Monsieur Constantine de Renneville*: author of *The French Inquisition, or, the history of the Bastille in Paris* (London, A. Bell, 1715), a collection of scandalous, obscene and mysterious anecdotes, from which this series has been extracted (e.g. pp. 320–2). As they have no relation to the life of Anne Rochford, this material has presumably been used to bulk out the book.

Coffee-man, *The Case of the Coffee-men of London and Westminter [sic]*

p. 93, ll. 5–6: Necessity is the Mother of Invention: commonplace reworking of 'Necessity, who is the mother of our invention': Plato, *The Republic*, II.369C (Oxford, Oxford University Press, 1983).

p. 96, ll. 9–10: *Sons of* Mercury: journalists (after Mercury, the messenger god), specifically those who haunt coffee-houses to pick up the latest news. In this case they are deliberately fed old or fraudulent news to expose their credulity.

p. 96, ll. 19–20: *The* Conde de las Torres, *at the Siege of* Gibraltar: British forces occupied Gibraltar from the first Siege of Gibraltar in July 1704. In 1726, Spanish forces under the Count de Las Torres again laid siege to the fortress, which was defended by British forces under General Jasper Clayton, Brigadier Richard Kane and David Colyear, the Earl of Portmore.

p. 98, ll. 1–2: *Lords of the Admiralty*: the office that oversaw the Royal Navy, exercised since 1689 by a Board of Commissioners comprising seven naval and civil commissioners.

p. 98, ll. 22–3: Bartlet's *Buildings*: Bartlett's Buildings, a pleasant square court near Holborn Circus against Hatton Street, in Farringdon Ward Without.

p. 100, ll. 26–7: *old* Stow: John Stow (1524–1605), historian whose *A Survey of London* (1598) offered a topographical survey of the city together with historical records. Frequently reprinted, the book was comprehensively updated by John Strype (1643–1737) in 1720.

p. 100, l. 29: *Lies of* Geoffery *of* Monmouth: Geoffrey of Monmouth (d. 1154/5), bishop of St Asaph, author of the *Historia regum Britanniae*, an account of the early history of Britain.

p. 101, l. 2: *Mr.* Eachard: Laurence Eachard or Echard (1672–1730), a historian who completed several extensive histories, including his *History of England* (1707–18) from the entrance of Julius Caesar to William and Mary.

p. 101, ll. 5–6: Luther's Table Talk: Martin Luther (1483–1546), *Dris Martini Lutheri colloquia mensalia: or, Dr Martin Luther's divine discourses at his table, &c. ... Collected first together by Dr Antonius Lauterbach*, trans. by Henrie Bell (London, William Du-Gard, 1652), ch. XLV, 'Of Lawyers'. A miller's ass went into a fisher's boat that stood in a river, and both were carried away by the current. The miller complained that the fisher has stolen his ass; the fisher that the miller had stolen his boat.

p. 101, ll. 9–10: Post-Boy: newspaper established by Abel Boyer, published 1695–1735.

p. 101, l. 15: *Sir* Richard Steele: Sir Richard Steele (1672–1729), writer and politician. The anecdote is related in *The Theatre*, No. 5, Saturday 16 January 1719–20.

p. 101, l. 21: Upholders: a dealer in small wares or second-hand articles (*OED*).

p. 104, l. 29: Coup de Maitre: French, 'masterstroke'.

p. 108, l. 25: *Circular Lerter*: the Circular Letter of 6 November 1728, printed by the coffee-men committee to promote their proposal. There are no known extant copies.

p. 115, ll. 7–17: *JAMES ASHLEY* ... Lombard-Street: The projectors of the undertaking are proprietors of eleven coffee-houses, with a pronounced geographical focus on the City of London and the Inns of Court. Kent's Coffee-House, Chancery-Lane (not in Lillywhite); Baker's, Exchange Alley (Lillywhite 65); Robin's, Old Jewry (Lillywhite 1080); Elford's, George Yard (Lillywhite 374); Anderton's, Fleet Street (Lillywhite 34); Tom's, Wood Street (Lillywhite 1363); Will's, Lincoln's Inn Back Gate (Lillywhite 1547); Abington's, Holborn, near Gray's Inn Gate (Lillywhite 2); Garraway's, Exchange Alley (Lillywhite 433); John's, Sheer Lane (Lillywhite 645); and Lloyd's, Lombard Street (Lillywhite 736).

p. 117, ll. 8–9: *Mr. FIELDER*: John Fielder, proprietor of John's Coffee-House, Sheer Lane, near Temple Bar (Lillywhite 645). Lillywhite describes Fielder as the leader of the subscribing coffee-men, a view perhaps confirmed by *The case between the proprietors of news-papers, and the subscribing coffee-men, fairly stated*, below, p. 138.

p. 121, l. 16: *Canals*: channels

p. 121, ll. 26–7: *Two small* Slate *or* Ivory *Books, with* Slate *or* Brass *Pencils*: erasable notebooks, either of slate or ivory, written on with slate or brass pencils, to be used to record the news and gossip of each coffee-house. As the notebooks were erasable, the reported news would not be able to be traced: such anonymous and unattributed news, the coffee-men argue, would be more accurate.

The case between the proprietors of news-papers, and the subscribing coffee-men, fairly stated

p. 133, l. 19: Ne Sutor ultra Crepidam: Latin proverb, 'Cobbler, stick to thy last', meaning 'do not presume to address matters beyond your competence'. The saying is attributed to Apelles, who said it to a shoemaker who pointed out some errors in the depiction of a slipper in one of the artist's works, and then began to criticize other aspects of the picture.

p. 135, l. 3: *the* Subscribing Coffee-Men: those coffee-men subscribing to the proposal outlined in *The Case of the Coffee-men* (1728) to publish their own newspapers.

p. 136, l. 9: Staples of News: a staple is a factory or authorized place of trade for merchants of a foreign country, and hence, a warehouse or storehouse for provisions (*OED*).

p. 138, l. 3: Sheer-Lane Chairman: John Fielder, proprietor of John's Coffee-House, Sheer Lane, near Temple Bar (Lillywhite 645), the leader of the Subscribing Coffee-Men.

p. 138, l. 27: *Bastinado*: a blow with a stick or cudgel (*OED*).

p. 140, l. 36: *Japanners, and Vagabonds*: a japanner is a humorous term for a shoe-black, see above, note to p. 62, l. 11.

p. 140, ll. 37–8: *the Dignity of Waiters*: though practicing an ancient and dishonourable trade, the waiter has no dignity.

p. 140, l. 39: *Vails*: tips, money given to servants.

p. 141, ll. 3–4: *Remnants of Composition-Money*: composition-money is a sum paid in settlement of some claim of liability; for example, the proportion of a debt paid, according to agreement, by an insolvent debtor (*OED*). The remnants of composition-money is presumably the money left to the debtor after he has declared bankruptcy.

p. 143, l. 35: Home Collectors: news-writers who collect domestic or home news, typically described as frequenters of coffee-houses.

p. 144, l. 18: Gothamites: residents of Gotham, the name of a village proverbial for the folly of its inhabitants, a simpleton (*OED*). The transferential application to New York dates from the mid nineteenth century.

p. 144, l. 29: Wiseacres: those who think themselves wise, pretenders to wisdom (*OED*).

p. 146, l. 28: Reversionary Prospect: a reversion is the return of an estate to the donor or grantor, or his heirs, after the expiry of a grant: here the wife's coffee-house is a kind of insurance against the death or bankruptcy of her husband.

The case between the proprietors of news-papers, and the coffee-men of London and Westminster, fairly stated

p. 157, ll. 30–1: A Compound of Madness ... you are bit: original verses.

p. 161, l. 13: Athenians: Acts 17:21: 'For all the Athenians and strangers which were there spent their time in nothing else, but either to tell, or to hear some new thing'.

p. 162, l. 3: *Cutler*: one who deals in or repairs knives (*OED*).

p. 162, ll.12–13: With dismal Coffee ... sleepy God: Richard Burridge, *Hell in an uproar: occasion'd by a scuffle that happen'd between the lawyers and the physicians, for superiority. A satyr* ([Dublin], n.p., 1725), p. 4.

p.163, l. 3: *grand Magazines of Intelligence*: see *Case of the Coffee-men*, above, p. 113.

p. 165, l. 8: *Surloin of Beef*: a prime cut of beef steak cut from the lower portion of the ribs: as a substantial cut of meat, it would not be cooked by the heat of the sun in winter.

p. 167, ll. 10–11: *Ratifee, or Dr.* Stephens's *Water*: a distilled wine flavoured with ginger, galangal, cinnamon and other spices, thought to have medicinal properties.

James Salter, *A catalogue of the rarities to be seen at Don Saltero's Coffee-house in Chelsea*

p. 173, l. 5: Curiosities: a curiosity is an object of interest, valued as curious, rare, or strange.

p. 174, l. 5: Sir *John Cope*, Bart.: Sir John Cope, 5th Baronet of Hanwell (1634–1721), MP for Oxfordshire and Banwell in several parliaments in the Whig interest, resided at Little Chelsea. His son, also Sir John Cope, represented various constituencies in Devon and Hampshire during Walpole's ministry.

p. 175, l.1: Compleat *LIST* of the Benefactors: the list of the benefactors (those who have given specimens to the museum) is a conspicuous list of Chelsea nobility, gentlemen and military men. In scientific terms, the foremost among them was Sir Hans Sloane (1660–1753), president of the Royal Society.

p. 177, ll. 1–4: *A Catalogue of the Rarities, &c.*: the catalogue entries detail 249 items. They are not arranged according to any obvious typology, although evidence from later catalogues suggests that the list corresponds to a circuit around the coffee-room. Subsequent editions show that the collection was slowly evolving, both by addition and deletion: the twelfth edition (1741) has 420 items listed on the same sixteen pages. The 36th edition (*c.* 1785) suggests that the collection was by then installed in glass cases. The notes below do not attempt to identify to what the items refer, although obscure terms are explained.

p. 178, l. 5: *16 Serratura Italiana*: literally, an Italian lock. This may be a trick contrivance or lock puzzle: Steele, in *The Tatler* (No. 34, 28 June 1709), notes that Don Saltero's had an '*Italian* engine for the Imprisonment of those who go abroad with it' (ed. by Donald F. Bond, 3 vols (Oxford, Clarendon Press, 1987), vol. I, p. 254).

p. 179, ll. 15–16: *56 Pontius Pilate's Wive's Chambermaid's Sister's Sister's Hat*: Steele, in *The Tatler* (No. 34, 28 June 1709) says of this item that it is a

'Straw-Hat, which I know to be made by *Madge Peskad*, within three miles of *Bedford* ... To my knowledge of this very Hat, it may be added, that the Covering of Straw was never us'd among the *Jews*, since it was demanded of 'em to make Bricks without it. Therefore this is really nothing, but under the specious Pretence of Learning and Antiquity, to impose upon the World' (*New Letters to the Tatler and the Spectator*, ed. by Richmond Bond (Austin, TX, University of Texas Press, 1959), p. 254).

p. 180, l. 17: *88 A Chinese Dodgin*: a dotchin, the name in the south of China for a kind of small hand-steelyard or weighing machine (derived from the Cantonese word *toh-ch'ing*) (*OED*).

p. 181, l. 25: *124 The Horns of a Shamway*: the horns of a chamois, the capriform antelope (*Rupicapra tragus*) found in the high mountains of Europe and Asia.

p. 184, l. 31: *214 Quick a Hatch*: a wolverine, a carnivorous quadruped (*Gulo luscus*), found in North America: an adaptation of the Cree (Indian) name, given by J. Richardson (in *Fauna Boreali-Americana*, 4 vols (London and Norwich, 1829–37), vol. I, p. 42) as *okeecoohagees*; from other Algonquin dialects, the name *carcajou* is derived.

p. 185, ll. 31–2: *242 Robinson Crusoe's, and his Man Friday's Shirt*: Daniel Defoe's *The Life and Strange Surprising Adventures of Robinson Crusoe, of York, mariner* was published in 1719. This work of fiction, often described as the first English novel, describes how after several years on the island, Crusoe fashioned from goat-skin 'a great Cap for my Head', and 'a Suit of Cloaths wholly of these Skins, that is to say, a Wastcoat, and Breeches open at the Knees, and both loose' (p. 159).

Anthony Hilliar, *A Brief and Merry History of Great Britain*

p. 189, ll. 11–13: *his Excellency COSSEM HOJAH, late Envoy from the Government of* Tripoli, *in* South-Barbary: Cossum Hojah, 'Envoy Extraordinary from the Bey, Divan and Regency of *Tripoli* in *Barbary*' had his first ceremonial public audience with George II on 12 September 1728 (*Historical Register*, XIII (1728), p. 50), and a leave-taking ceremony on 15 May 1729 (*Historical Register*, XIV (1729), p. 35). 'Barbary' was an inexact description used by the British in the eighteenth century for the coastal regions of North Africa from what is now Libya to Morocco. 'South-Barbary' is obscure, and perhaps deliberately so. Tripoli, a city in modern-day Libya, was then often recognised as the capital of the region, which was officially a province of the Ottoman Empire, but was actually ruled by a *bey* who operated with a high degree of autonomy, and was notorious for engaging in piracy.

p. 192, l. 27: White's, St James's, Williams's: three coffee-houses in St James's Street, associated with court politics and manners, due to their proximity to the main entrance to St James's Palace: White's Coffee-house, No. 69 St James's Street (Lillywhite 1511); St James's Coffee-house, No. 87 St James's Street (Lillywhite 1131); Williams' Coffee-house, No. 86 St James's Street (Lillywhite 1552).

p. 192, l. 28: *Equipages, Essence, Horse-Matches, Tupees, Modes, Mortgages and* Maidenhead*s*: topics associated with high society discussed in the Court coffee-houses of St James's: equipages (the appurtenances of rank, such as Court dress or a carriage and horses), essence (an essential oil or perfume), horse-matches (racing), tupees (an artificial lock of hair worn as the crowning feature of a periwig, combed up over a pad into a top-knot, worn by both sexes), modes (fashionable dress), mortgages (debts) and maidenheads (the marriage market) (*OED*).

p. 192, l. 30: *the* Cocoa-Tree *upon* Bribery *and* Corruption, Evil-Ministers, Errors *and* Mistakes in Government: the Cocoa Tree Chocolate House, Pall Mall (Lillywhite 262), a coffee-house associated with Tory politicians. The topics discussed suggest the clientele's opposition to the Whig ministry of Sir Robert Walpole.

p. 192, ll. 32–3: *the* Scotch *Coffee-Houses, towards* Charing-Cross, *on* Places and Pensions: the British Coffee-house in Cockspur Street opposite Suffolk Street, Charing Cross (Lillywhite 179), a house notable for attracting Scottish gentlemen and army officers. The union of England and Scotland in 1707 meant that Scotsmen seeking to advance themselves in the army or government had to come to London to seek their fortune, hence the discussion of places (an office in the service of the crown) and pensions (a regular payment to persons of rank, royal favourites, or one who is not a professed servant, to enable them to maintain their state, or to retain their alliance, good will or secret service) (*OED*).

p. 192, ll. 34–5: *the* Tilt-yard *and* Young-Man*'s on* Affronts, Honour, Satisfaction, Duels and Rencounters: the Tilt-Yard Coffee-house, Whitehall (Lillywhite 1353) and Young Man's Coffee-House, Charing Cross (Lillywhite 1579), two coffee-houses where army officers assembled. Their discussion, according to Hilliar, was on matters of honour and chivalry: such as those affronts to honour that end in duels and rencounters (a hostile meeting between two adversaries distinguished from a regular duel by being not premeditated) (*OED*).

p. 193, ll. 5–6: *Verdict of* Se Defendendo *or* Manslaughter: Legal terms: 'se defendendo' means 'in self defence', removing legal guilt from a homicide; or manslaughter, a type of criminal homicide of a lower degree of criminality than murder (as when one causes the death of another by culpable negligence or as a consequence of some unlawful act) (*OED*).

p. 193, ll. 6–9: *Coffee-Houses about the* Temple ... Exception*s*: Many coffee-houses around the Temple Bar were renowned for their legal clientele from the Inns of Court, where one might hear of causes (the case of one party in a suit), costs (the expenses of litigation, prosecution, or other legal transaction), claps (a bill or poster stuck on a wall), demurrers (a pleading which admits for the moment the alleged facts but denies that the opponent is entitled to relief), rejoinders (the defendant's answer to the plaintiff's replication), salivations (unclear, perhaps to display relish at some anticipated verdict), and exceptions (a plea made by a defendant in bar of the plaintiff's action) (*OED*). Examples of such places are George's, Devereux Court (Lillywhite 445); Tom's, Devereux Court (Lillywhite 1369); the Grecian, Devereux Court (Lillywhite 494); and Nando's, Inner Temple Gate, Fleet Street (Lillywhite 857).

p. 193, ll. 9–10: Daniel*'s, the* Welch *Coffee-House in* Fleet-street, *on* Births, Pedigrees *and* Descents: Daniel's Coffee-house, near Temple Bar, Fleet Street (Lillywhite 331), was a house where Welshmen assembled. Hilliar describes their conversation as being dominated by genealogy: the coffee-house was also used by Freemasons in this period.

p. 193, ll. 11–13: Child*'s and the* Chapter *upon* Glebes, Tythes, Advowsons, Rectories, *and* Lectureships: Child's Coffee-House, St Paul's Churchyard (Lillywhite 241) and the Chapter Coffee-house, Paternoster Row, off St Paul's Churchyard (Lillywhite 234). Hilliar describes the clientele as being dominated by clergy and the discussion of glebes (a portion of land assigned to a clergyman as part of his benefice), tythes (the tenth part of the annual produce of agriculture being a due or payment for the support of the clergy), advowsons (the right of presentation to a benefice or living), rectories (a benefice held by a rector) and lectureships (the office of a lecturer in a church) (*OED*). Other authorities noted the number of physicians and writers at Child's, and the booksellers, printers, writers and hacks at the Chapter.

p. 193, ll. 13–14: North*'s,* Undue Elections, False-Polling, Scrutinies, *&c.*: North's Coffee-house, King Street, Cheapside (Lillywhite 411), was close to Guildhall, and attracted men interested in the tumultuous politics of the City. An undue election was one which was in some way illegal, through voter fraud (or false-polling), detected by scrutiny (a formal taking of individual votes when the result of a show of hands or acclamation was not accepted) (*OED*).

p. 193, ll. 14–16: Hamlin*'s,* Infant-Baptism, Lay-Ordination, Free-will, Election, *and* Reprobation: Hamlin's Coffee-house, Sweeting's Alley, near the Royal Exchange (Lillywhite 532). Hillier suggests that Dissenters and Nonconformists congregated there, where they discussed key Protestant theological controversies, such as those on infant-baptism (rather than baptism of consenting adults), lay-ordination (the action of appointment or admission to the ministry without the episcopate, as used by the Presbyterians), free-will (the power of directing our own actions without constraint by necessity or fate), election (eternal salvation by predestination rather than by conduct or disposition), and reprobation (rejection by God in the Calvinist doctrine of predestination).

p. 193, l. 16: Batson's *the Prices of* Pepper, Indigo, *and* Salt-Petre: Batson's Coffee-House, Cornhill (Lillywhite 90) used its location near the Royal Exchange to draw customers involved in commerce and finance, especially insurance and the merchants from the Levant Company and the Russia Company.

p. 194, l. 11: Westminster-Hall: Westminster Hall, in New Palace Yard, a large and crowded hall of medieval origin in which sat certain higher law courts, alongside other stalls selling books and trinkets.

The Life and Character of Moll King, late mistress of King's Coffee-house in Covent-garden

p. 199, l. 13: Vine-street: a lane running between St Giles's High Street and Russell Street, an area generally known as a slum.

p. 200, ll. 4–5: *Nymphs of either* Billingsgate *or* Covent-Garden *Market*: markets for fish and vegetables respectively, where the market workers were renowned for the spectacular vulgarity of their language.

p. 200, ll. 14–15: *Mrs.* Atwood, *then of* Charles-Court *in the* Strand: untraced.

p. 200, l. 27: Thomas King: Tom King (d. 1737), known as 'Smooth'd-Fac'd-Tom' (below, p. 201), married Moll when she was fourteen years old. Tom King, born at West Ashton in Wiltshire, had been a scholar at Eton and at King's College, Cambridge, but in 1715 'went away in apprehension that his fellowship would be denied him' (Thomas Harwood, *Alumni Etonenses: or, a catalogue of the provosts and fellows of Eton College and King's College, Cambridge* (Birmingham, 1797), p. 293). Thomas King 'from Hampstead' was buried on 11 October 1737 (*Registers of St Paul's Church, Covent Garden*, ed. by William Hunt, Harleian Society Register Section, No. 36 (London, Harleian Society, 1908), p. 359).

p. 201, ll. 2–4: *to the* Fleet, *and were tack'd together by one of the* Couple-Beggars: the liberties of the Fleet Prison were home to numerous fraudulent, defrocked or imprisoned clergymen who were prepared to perform clandestine marriages for a fee. A couple-beggar was a disreputable priest who made it his business to 'couple' beggars, or perform irregular marriages (*OED*).

p. 201, l. 12: M—r—y: manuscript additions identify Moll's seducer as Murray, otherwise untraced.

p. 201, l. 27: Nanny Cotton: a noted courtesan.

p. 201, l. 28: Sally Salisbury: Sarah Pridden, known as Sally Salisbury (1690–1724), noted courtesan. See Capt. Charles Walker's *Authentick Memoirs of the Life, Intrigues and Adventures of the Celebrated Sally Salisbury* (London: 1723).

p. 203, ll. 12–13: *a little House, or rather Hovel, in* Covent Garden *Market*: Tom and Moll King first opened a coffee stall (date unclear, *c.* 1728) in the market place in Covent Garden, on the south side of the market close to the portico of St Paul's Church (Lillywhite 1370). As their business grew they incorporated two more of the market stalls into the coffee-house. In Hogarth's *Four Times of Day* (25 March 1738), the entrance to Tom King's Coffee-house can be seen in the background of the plate entitled 'Morning': inside some sort of altercation seems to be underway, perhaps led by the constables, whose staves can be seen. King's Coffee-house originally kept night hours as a service to the workers of the fruit and vegetable market, who arrived early in the morning. Covent Garden market for fruit and vegetables began in 1656 as a thrice-weekly market. By the 1730s it was the most important such market in the city, especially after the closure of Stocks Market in 1737. The simple sheds housing the market stalls were frequently rebuilt, making them progressively more permanent, adding upper stories after 1748. The present market buildings, designed by Charles Fowler, were built in 1828.

p. 204, ll. 6–7: *from the Star and Garter to the Coffee-House Boy*: from one end of the social scale to the other: stars and garters refers to the insignia of the chivalric orders worn by the nobility; a coffee-house boy was the lowest level of servant in the coffee-house.

p. 204, l. 21: deceitful Water-Wag-Tails: a wag-tail is a contemptuous term for a profligate or inconstant woman, hence a harlot, courtesan (*OED*).

p. 206, ll. 24–5: *King's College*: that is, the place of learning belonging to Tom and Moll King, but also a reference to King's College, Cambridge. This was a witty remark, not least because the latter was notorious for the indolence and stupidity of its fellows and students: Horace Walpole quipped that it was 'a cenotaph to learning'.

p. 206, l. 25: a Dish of *Flash*: as the text explains it, 'This *Flash* ... is talking *in Cant Terms*; very much us'd among Rakes and Town ladies. Note that although flash is associated with the criminal under-class, it is actually spoken by a wide social range, including high status rakes.

p. 207, l. 1: Lingua: a language or lingo (*OED*).

p. 207, ll. 6–7: The Humours of the Flashy Boys at Moll King's: untraced, supposedly published *c.* 1731. The dialogue was published below the engraved plate 'Moll King' (London: Sold at ye picture shop in Mary's Buildings Covent Garden, 1738), The Lewis Walpole Library, Yale University, 738.0.3.

p. 207, ll. 15–16: Moythen, *who was stabb'd some Time ago by* Dick Hodges, *the Distiller*: Henry Moythen of Drury Lane was called as a witness in the trial of John Smith on 16 January 1735 at the Old Bailey for theft of a bag of money from Nicholas Pollamounter in the Angel and Crown Tavern by Temple Bar, kept by Mary Glascock (*The Proceedings at the Sessions of the Peace, and Oyer and Terminer, for the City of London, and County of Middlesex, on*

Thursday the 16th, Friday the 17th, Saturday the 18th, and Monday the 20th
of January, 1734–5 (London, J. Roberts, 1735), vol. II, p. 40).

p. 207, l. 17–p. 208, l. 30: Harry. *To pay,* Moll ... *see you in the morning*: the obscure terminology of the flash dialogue is clarified by the key appended to *The Life and Character of Moll King* (above, pp. 219–20), and will not be further referenced.

p. 209, l. 12: *Money-Droppers*: 'Cheats who drop money, which they pretend to find just before some country lad; and by way of giving him a share of their good luck, entice him into a public house, where they and their confederates cheat or rob him of what money he has about him'. Grose, *Dictionary of the Vulgar Tongue* (London, C. Chappel, 1811).

p. 209, ll. 22–3: *Tavistock-Hill*: Haverstock Hill, a road running between Chalk Farm and Hampstead. In 1779 it was reported that Moll King 'built a row of houses on the road near Hampstead, where she resided till her death' (*Nocturnal Revels: or, The History of King's Place and all the Modern Nunneries* (London, M. Goadby, 1779), p. 12. Moll King's substantial four-story terrace is depicted in the background of Hogarth's *March to Finchley* (1745): see Thomas Barratt, *Annals of Hampstead*, 3 vols (London, A. and C. Black, 1912), vol. I, p. 266. The house is also depicted in Jean Baptiste Claude Chatelain's 'A View of Hampstead Road near Tom's King's House' in Daniel Lysons, *Environs of London*, 2nd edn, 5 vols (London, T. Cadell and W. Davies, 1800–11), vol. II, iii, p. 528.

p. 210, l. 15: Jack-an-Apes: a jackanapes, a man using the tricks, or displaying the qualities, of an ape (*OED*).

p. 210, l. 31–p. 211, l. 1: *which Indictment she removed from* Hick's Hall *into the Court of* King's-Bench *by* Certiorari: Hick's Hall, St John's Street, Clerkenwell, was the courthouse for the Middlesex Quarter Sessions. The Court of King's Bench was the highest criminal court in England, and met in Westminster Hall. *Certiorari* is a legal term defining a prerogative writ used to direct a lower court to certify for review the record in the case. Moll King successfully moved to have her case reviewed by the higher court, hoping that its expense would persuade the plaintiffs to abandon their indictments.

p. 211, l. 21: *the Prison of the* King's Bench: as Moll refused to pay the enormous fine of £200, she was committed to the King's Bench, a large jail in Borough High Street, Southwark, used to imprison debtors.

p. 212, l. 2: *High Bailiff*: a bailiff is one changed with public authority in a certain district. The High Bailiff of Westminster was the chief magistrate within the City of Westminster.

p. 212, ll. 8–9: *compounded with her for less than Half the Sum she was mulcted*: The High Bailiff received the money paid in fines in Westminster: after some time in prison refusing to pay, Moll was able to bargain her fine down to £100. To be mulcted is to be robbed or fined.

p. 213, ll. 1–2: *Sir John G—ns—n*: Gonson, name identified in manuscript. Sir John Gonson (d. 1765) was a magistrate (a Justice of the Peace for the county of Middlesex) involved in the suppression of bawdy-houses: see Robert Shoemaker, *Prosecution and Punishment: petty crime and the law in London and rural Middlesex, c. 1660–1725* (Cambridge, Cambridge University Press, 1991), pp. 86, 249. He is often described as being depicted as the magistrate arresting a prostitute in plate three of Hogarth's *The Harlot's Progress* (1732).

p. 213, ll. 6–7: *the Bench of Justices, sitting at* Covent Garden *Vestry*: in July 1730, local tradesmen petitioned the Westminster magistrates to act against the disorderly 'night-houses' of Covent Garden (brothels, bagnios, taverns and coffee-houses). The justices met in committee in the vestry of St Paul's Covent Garden 'on purpose to suppress those disorders' on 18 July 1730, issuing warrants against ten disorderly houses (*London Journal*, 18 July 1730).

p. 214, ll. 4–5: *Mother Haywood*: a bawdy-house keeper of Covent Garden.

p. 214, ll. 9–10: a Regale: a choice repast, feast or banquet (*OED*)

p. 215, l. 29: *One H—k [Haddock], a noted Bagnio-Keeper*: Haddock's Bagnio was a bathhouse and brothel in Charing Cross, operating from at least 1747 to 1800.

p. 216, l. 7: *the* Marshalsea *Prison*: in Southwark, the Marshalsea was a prison mainly used to hold debtors, but also for the incarceration of anyone thought to defy or ridicule authority (*LE*).

p. 216, ll. 19–21: Drury-Lane Populus, *(or by some better known by the name of the* Covent-Garden Porpus*) an odd Creature of the* Bum *Order*: obscure. A porpus is defined below as an 'ignorant, swaggering Fellow' (p. 220).

p. 217, l. 1: wagging Nod: a nod or noddy is a fool or simpleton (*OED*).

p. 217, ll. 2–3: *die of a Suffocation in the Road to* Paddington: a circumlocution for being hanged at Tyburn.

p. 217, ll. 13–14: *Skill in Rapping*: rapping was false utterance of an oath, or perjury, defined in Fielding's *Jonathan Wild* (London, 1754): '*Rapping*, is a Cant Term for Perjury' (p. 54).

p. 217, ll. 15–16: *Overseer of the Mob in* Kingston *Market Place*: Kingston, in Surrey, held a market three times a week. The title of Overseer of the Mob is not one of the numerous official market offices; as the mob refers to the common people, the notion of their overseer is contemptuous.

p. 217, l. 29: Tothil-Fields *to* Limehouse-Hole: from one end of the city to the other: Tothill Fields lay between Westminster Abbey and Millbank, and Limehouse was a riverside hamlet east of the City, next to Stepney.

p. 218, l. 4: *Mr.* Hoff: also spelled Huff. Moll kept using the surname King after her second marriage.

p. 218, ll. 15–16: Thursday *the 17ᵗʰ of* September: 'Mary Hoff Widow, from Hampstead in Middx' was buried on 27 September 1747 (Hunt (ed.), *Registers of St Paul's Church, Covent Garden*, p. 429).

p. 219, l. 25: *A KEY to the* Flash Dialogue: a key is an explanatory scheme for the interpretation of a cipher or code. The key explains the 'flash dialogue' on pp. 207–8.

p. 220, l. 10: *Affidavit-Men*: men prepared to swear affidavits for money (an affidavit is a statement in writing, confirmed by the maker's oath, and intended to be used as judicial proof).

Arthur Murphy, '[Account of Jonathan's Coffee-House]'; '[Proposal for a Female Coffee-House]'

p. 223, l. 6: *Gray's Inn*: one of the Inns of Court, in Holborn, and the fictional home of Charles Ranger, the persona adopted by Murphy to conduct the journal.

p. 223, l. 7: Ecce iterum Crispinus *Juv.*: Latin, 'Here's Crispinus again', from the opening line of Juvenal, *Satires*, IV.1, trans. by Susanna Morton Braund (Cambridge, Cambridge University Press, 1996), p. 197, referring to a decadent Egyptian courtier under Domitian.

p. 223, l. 10: *TEMPLE of LAVERNA*: As described in Murphy's first essay on the stock-brokers at Jonathan's Coffee-house, *Craftsman*, 10 March 1750.

p. 223, l. 16: *JEWS* circumcised and uncircumcised: stockbrokers. The securities market had several hundred stockbrokers and stockjobbers, of which twelve were permitted to be Jewish. Both stockbrokers and stockjobbers were subject to considerable public criticism: here, by invoking historically enduring anti-Semitic sentiment, Murphy pejoratively equates them to Jews. See P. G. M. Dickson, *The Financial Revolution in England: a study in the development of public credit 1688–1756* (London, Macmillan, 1967); and Ranald Michie, *The London Stock Exchange: A History* (Oxford, Oxford University Press, 1999), pp. 15–20.

p. 223, l. 17: the Temple: a reference to the Temple, or 'House of the Lord', in Jerusalem, from which Jesus cast out the moneychangers (Matthew 21:12). Specifically, here, a reference to the securities market for stocks conducted at Jonathan's Coffee-house, Exchange Alley (Lillywhite 656).

p. 223, l. 19: *TICKETS – Tickets – Lottery-Tickets*: lottery tickets were a form of stock. Lotteries were an important source of government finance, taking the form of long-term loans to the government, where the contributors received annuities to be paid by future revenue from excise duties. The 'fortunate tickets' (one in forty) received much higher rates of interest. Complex financial instruments were developed to trade such tickets, including 'hiring' and 'insuring' them. See Richard Richards, 'The Lottery in the History of English Government Finance', *Economic History*, III:9 (January 1934), pp. 57–76; especially pp. 58–59.

p. 224, l. 9: *Woons*: a euphemistic abbreviation of 'by God's wounds', used in oaths and asseverations (*OED*).

p. 224, ll. 13–14: the Waiter comes up and demands Sixpence: entry to the coffee-room at Jonathan's cost six-pence, for which, as Thomas Mortimer explained in *Every Man his Own Broker* (London, 1761), anyone might walk in 'to do business there', and be entitled to 'pen, ink, paper and a small cup of chocolate', and 'if he understands the business' be his own 'Broker for that day' (p. 72n.).

p. 224, l. 34: Caiphas: the figure of the wealthy Jewish financier could be based on any of the twelve Jewish brokers permitted in 1729 to trade on the Royal Exchange. Nonetheless, the portrait of Caiphas resembles the most famous of these men, Samson Gideon (1699–1762). Born at London Wall, he was the son of a West India merchant, and the grandson of Jewish immigrants from Portugal. His fortune was reckoned at £25,000 in 1729, made in underwriting, bottomry (marine insurance), respondentia loans (paid on safe arrival of a cargo), and as a subscriber to Treasury stock. He married an Anglican in the early 1740s, and raised his children as Anglicans, although he never changed his own religion. He was close to the Walpole and Pelham administrations, and made significant loans to the Treasury on several occasions. In 1753, following the Jewish Naturalisation Act (see below, note to p. 224, ll. 11–12), he was made the subject of much satirical notice: numerous references to him are made in *The Gray's Inn Journal*. The Biblical Caiphas was a Jewish high priest (AD 18–36), head of the Sanhedrin, who persecuted the followers of Christ after his crucifixion.

p. 224, l. 40: *Tickets – India-Bonds – Rescounters – Consolidate*: the names of several of the different stocks and financial instruments: lottery tickets (see above, note to p. 223, l. 19); East India Company Bonds, rescounters (a rescounter is a balancing of contra-accounts, the delayed settlement of which were used as a form of futures trading) and consolidated annuities (Government securities of Great Britain, consisting originally of a great variety of public securities, which were consolidated in 1751 (25 Geo. II, c. 27) into a single stock bearing interest at 3 per cent.). As the Country Gentleman says, the arcane jargon of the open outcry market was like a 'perfect Babel', as was intended, as market traders used the confusion of languages as a way to exclude day traders.

p. 224, ll. 11–12: *we shall soon have them swarm in all Parts of the Kingdom now, that they are naturalized*: The Jewish Naturalisation Act, often known as 'The Jew Bill', was passed in May 1753 (26 Geo. II, c. 26). It conferred on a very small number of very wealthy Jews resident in England the right to be naturalised without taking the Anglican sacrament. A vociferous public reaction ensued in which both anti-Semitism and High-Church Toryism played important roles, whipped up by the prospect of the coming parliamentary election of 1754. The Act was repealed in 20 December 1753. See David Katz, *The Jews in the History of England, 1485–1850* (Oxford, Clarendon Press, 1994), pp. 240–53.

p. 225, l. 36: Bulls *and* Bears: specialised language of the stock market. A bull is one who endeavours by speculative purchase to raise the price of stocks; a bear is one who speculates for a fall in the price of stocks (that is, one who sells stock for delivery at a future date in the expectation that the price will fall, and he will be able to buy in at a lower rate what he has contracted to deliver at a higher: also known as short-selling) (*OED*).

p. 225, ll. 37–8: *an Act of Parliament against that ... Sir* John Barnard's Act *they call it*: in 1734, Parliament passed Sir John Barnard's Act (7 Geo. II, c. 8), entitled 'An act to prevent the infamous practice of stock jobbing', which was intended to reduce speculation by banning options, futures and short sales of stock. It didn't work.

p. 226, l. 44: *the KING'S ARMS*: a tavern in Cornhill with an entrance also in Exchange Alley, known as the Swan before the fire in 1747.

p. 226, l. 45: *the* South-Sea-House: in Threadneedle Street, the place of business of 'The Governor and Company of merchants of Great Britain trading to the South Seas', incorporated in 1711 with a monopoly of a nonexistent trade with Spanish South America.

p. 227, ll. 7–8: Moses *never was in* Westphalia, *or he would not have prohibited* Pork: Westphalia, a part of the Duchy of Saxony in Germany, renowned for its hams smoked with juniper berries and beech-wood (like prosciutto, sliced thinly and eaten without further cooking). Pork is forbidden to Jews according to the kashrut dietary laws established in Leviticus, the third book in the Torah.

p. 227, ll. 23–4: *drink THE OLD CONSTITUTION*: an enduring Tory slogan.

p. 227, l. 34: Register Office: an office in which a register is kept, recording all kinds of commercial intelligence, such as those who want work, or who have something to sell. This usage predates the earliest *OED* reference. In the first essay of *The Gray's Inn Journal*, Murphy stated that Charles Ranger had opened a 'Set of Chambers in Gray's Inn which are to serve the Purposes of a Register Office, where all Articles of Information will be given in, by my Emissaries' (No. 50 [i.e. 1], 29 September 1753, p. 5).

p. 227, l. 43: Pour faire bon bouche: French, 'to make a good impression'.

p. 228, l. 5: *Miss* Nossiter: Maria Isabella Nossiter (1735–59), an actress, probably the illegitimate daughter of the 3rd Earl of Cholmondeley. Aged eighteen, she fell in love with the actor and impresario Spranger Barry (1717–77), and made her debut appearance as Juliet at Covent Garden on 10 October 1753. Murphy, in *The Gray's Inn Journal*, No. 52 [i.e. 3], 13 October 1753, p. [18], lauded her performance.

p. 228, ll. 11–12: *Destroy his Fib ... Pope*: Alexander Pope, *An Epistle from Mr. Pope, to Dr. Arbuthnot* (London, J. Wright for Lawton Gilliver, 1734), p. 5, ll. 89–90.

p. 228, l. 13: *Bedford Coffee-House*: the Bedford Coffee-house (Lillywhite 99), in the north-east corner of Covent Garden, with an entrance under the Piazza (as the colonnaded ambulatory was called). The Bedford was renowned at this time for its nightly gathering of theatrical and literary wits and critics, including Fielding. The first essay of *The Gray's Inn Journal,* stated (ironically) that the Bedford had been chosen for a weekly meeting, on Sunday evening, of the Board of Criticism, comprised of representatives drawn from 'the Number of Critics, within the Liberties of the City', where they would 'take into consideration the State of Criticism for the preceding Week' (No. 50 [i.e. 1], 29 September 1753, p. 6).

p. 228, l. 21: *Drury-Lane Play-House*: one of the two Patent Theatres in London, the Theatre Royal in Drury Lane was entered down a passage on Drury Lane, with further access from Russell Street and Bridges Street.

p. 228, ll. 22–3: *VENICE PRESERVED*: Thomas Otway's *Venice Preserv'd* (1682) was performed at Drury Lane on Monday 29 October 1753, with David Garrick (1717–79) as Jaffier, Henry Mossop (1727–74) as Pierre, and Susannah Cibber (1714–66) as Belvidera (see *London Stage*, part I, p. 387).

p. 228, ll. 29–30: *Foote ... in the Character of* Fondlewife: William Congreve's *The Old Batchelor* (1693) was performed on Wednesday 24 October 1753 at Drury Lane, with Samuel Foote (1720–77) as Fondlewife and Hannah Pritchard (1711–68) as Laetitia.

p. 229, l. 7: Quales Threiciæ cum Flumina ... *VIRG.*: Virgil, *Aeneid*, XI.659–60: 'Such are the Amazons of Thrace, when they tramp over Thermodon's streams and war in blazoned armour' (trans. by H. Rushton Fairchild, rev. by G. P. Gould, Loeb Classical Library (Cambridge, MA, Harvard University Press, 2000), p. 283).

p. 230, l. 25: *throws the Dart like a Tyrant*: George Grenville, Lord Lansdowne, 'The Progress of Beauty' in *A Collection of Poems* (London, 1693), p. 201: 'like a Tyrant throws the dart'. A panegyric to the leading ladies of the Court of William and Mary.

p. 230, ll. 35–6: Cui flavam religas comam?: Horace, *Odes*, I.v.4: 'For whom dost thou tie up thy golden hair?', *Horace: the Odes and Epodes*, trans. by C. E. Bennett, Loeb Classical Library (London, William Heinemann, 1914), p. 18.

p. 230, ll. 49–50: Macklin's *new Scheme*: In September 1753, the actor, Charles Macklin, took a 21-year lease from the Duke of Bedford for the chamber under the arcades of the North Piazza of Covent Garden, rooms formerly occupied by Lord Mornington's gambling club. There he proposed to establish a 'Magnificent Coffee-Room & a School of Oratory' (letter of Thomas Birch to P. Yorke, 15 September 1753, BL Add MS, 35, 398, f. 159). He overspent on renovation and rebuilding works, and opened the coffee-room on 11 March 1754, and an institution called the British Inquisition in the room above on 21 November. Women were admitted to the latter (price one shilling). See William Appleton, *Charles Macklin: an actor's life* (Cambridge, MA, Harvard University Press, 1961), pp. 98–108.

p. 231, ll. 34–5: *Bucks, Bloods, and Rakes*: men adopting forms of rowdy and libertine behaviour: bucks (a gay dashing fellow, full of 'spirit'); bloods (a hot spark, a fast and foppish man, a rake or roisterer); and rakes (a man of loose habits and immoral character) (*OED*).

p. 232, ll. 14–15: Barry *in the dying Scene of* Romeo: Shakespeare's *Romeo and Juliet* was staged at Covent Garden on 10 October 1753, and thereafter regularly through the season, including 18 December 1753 and 5 January 1754. Spranger Barry played Romeo, opposite Maria Isabella Nossiter as Juliet (see above, note to p. 228, l. 5).

p. 232, l. 16: *a Party of* Piquet: a card game for two people fashionable in high society, played with 32 cards, at which very large sums of money could be won or lost.

p. 232, l. 20: Harlequin Fortunatus: Numerous Harlequin burlesques were produced in London in the early 1750s, usually as pantomime afterpieces 'involving mimicry, foolery, machinery, mythology, music and dance' (*London Stage*, part I, p. cxlviii). Henry Woodward's *Harlequin Fortunatus* was performed on Wednesday 26 December 1753 at Drury Lane; and received an ironic endorsement in *The Gray's Inn Journal*, No. 14, 29 December 1753, p. 83.

p. 232, ll. 27–8: an Equal Empire o'er the World: Nicholas Rowe, *The Fair Penitent. A Tragedy* (London, Jacob Tonson, 1714), p. 30 (III.i.50–2), acted at Drury Lane on 31 October 1753, and 4 January 1754.

p. 232, l. 32: Six-pence *at the Bar*: at this price, Murphy's proposed ladies coffee-house would be pitched at the exclusive end of the coffee-house market. To undercut this, Murphy also proposes to admit actresses, who were widely considered to be, or to be little better than, prostitutes.

p. 232, ll. 33–4: Capillaire, Citron-Water, or Ratafia: exotic liqueurs: capillaire, a syrup or infusion of maidenhair fern (*Adiantum capillus Veneris*); citron-water, a liquor made of brandy flavoured with citron- or lemon-peel; ratafia, a liqueur flavoured with almonds or peach-, apricot- or cherry-kernels.

p. 232, l. 45: White's: White's Chocolate House, St James's Street (Lillywhite 1511) was famous for gaming. In 1736, White's incorporated itself as a subscription club, and by 1743 may have excluded all who were not members. See Percy Colson, *White's, 1693–1950* (London, William Heinemann, 1951).

p. 233, l. 10: Talk of Beauties ... they never knew: Rowe, *The Fair Penitent*, II.2, p. 25: 'You talk of Beauties that you never saw, / And fancy Raptures that you never knew'.

p. 233, l. 21: Limbs framed for the tender Offices of Love: Otway, *Venice Preserv'd*, I.1, p. 21.

p. 234, ll. 1–2: his Grace *the* Dutchess of Dorset: Lionel Cranfield Sackville, 1st Duke of Dorset (1688–1765), Lord Lieutenant of Ireland 1730–7 and again 1750–5. His wife was Elizabeth Sackville (1687–1768). Between 1751–4 there was an ongoing conflict between the crown and the Irish parliament about the Irish revenue surplus, in which Dorset and his advisors were mercilessly satirised. Murphy's joke about the sexuality of the Duke reflects the widespread rumours about the homosexuality of his chaplain and private secretary, George Stone (*ODNB*).

p. 234, l. 5: *Wapping. Wind, N.N.W*: hamlet on the river, populated by people connected with the seafaring trades. The fictional report of Foote's arrival in London is delivered in a parody of mariner's argot, reflecting the role of the sailor he intends to play in Congreve's *Love for Love* (1695).

p. 234, l. 6: Samuel Foote: Samuel Foote (1721–77), actor and playwright, who had made a name for himself in the 1740s with a series of satirical reviews, including *A Dish of Chocolate* (1747) and *Tea* (1748).

p. 234, ll. 13–14: *intends to do very shortly in the Part of* BEN *in the Play of* Love for Love: William Congreve's *Love for Love* opened at Drury Lane on Wednesday 16 January 1754, with Foote in the role of Ben, a sailor. Murphy's warm account of the performance was in the *Gray's Inn Journal*, No. 17, 19 January 1754, p. 102.

p. 234, l. 24: Literary Bill of Mortality: a quip against the hack-writing: the bills of mortality were a weekly published official return of the deaths in a certain district, published since 1592 for 109 parishes in and around London (*OED*).

p. 234, l. 25: Cloacina: in the Roman mythology, the goddess of the sewer and cess-pit. Murphy suggests that the pamphlets will be used as toilet paper.

p. 234, ll. 29–30: *Abortive, Five hundred plays, including Tragedies, Comedies, and one* Parody of Five Acts on *Boadicia*: a swipe at the flood of minor satires. Richard Glover's tragedy *Boadicia* was first performed 1 December 1753 at Drury Lane by Garrick, with nine performances. Murphy commented favourably in *The Gray's Inn Journal*, No. 11, 8 December 1753, that it was 'deserving of a Place among the best of our modern Tragedies'

(p. 66). Murphy also regrets that the first performance was marred by a riot against the presence of a party of Jews in the audience. See *London Stage*, part I, pp. 394–5.

George's coffee house. A poem

p. 237, ll. 1–2: *GEORGE'S COFFEE HOUSE*: the coffee-house described here is probably George's at Temple Bar, on the corner of the Strand and Devereux Court (Lillywhite 445). This is a coffee-house with literary associations, known to have maintained a library, and mentioned by the writers Shenstone, Walpole and Armstrong in their correspondence. Stephanus Scriblerus's miscellaneous satire *The Censor. Numb. 1. To be continued occasionally. Containing a variety of curious matters […] with an epistolary dedication to Orator Mack—n* (London, T. Lownds, 1755) is also addressed to the 'Professors of Criticism' at George's Coffee-House. An anecdote dated from the early 1760s concerning Sir James Lowther confirms that it was kept by a widow at this time.

p. 237, l. 5: Arma virumque cano. *VIRG.*: Latin, 'Of war and a man I sing', Virgil, *Aeneid*, I.1.

p. 237, ll. 12–13: *Where may be had the King of Prussia's Letter to his friend MAUPERTIUS*: *The Seventh Epistle attempted in English, from the King of Prussia's Oeuvres du philosophe de Sans Souci. To Maupertius* (London, T. Osborne and W. Owen, 1761). Pierre Louis Moreau de Maupertius (1698–1759) was a French philosopher and mathematician who was invited to the enlightened court of Frederick the Great of Prussia, where he became the president of the Berlin Academy of Sciences.

p. 239, ll. 12–13: *the fumigating Sons of* Mundungus: mundungus, a foul-smelling cheap form of tobacco.

p. 240, ll. 1–2: *no* Preface *at all*: the author's joke about prefaces, and the preface itself, exhibits a kind of learned satire that had recently found popularity in Sterne's *Tristram Shandy* (1759–67). Sterne's notion of the 'hobby-horse' is imitated here by the poet's long-winded equation of his muse with a series of horses in classical mythology.

p. 240, l. 3: *Jade of PARNASSUS*: the poet's muse is liked to a horse (a jade), resident on the Mount Parnassus, the home of the muses of poetry and learning.

p. 240, ll. 6–7: *hackney PEGASUS … limpid spring of HELICON*: Pegasus was a winged horse in Greek mythology: everywhere his hoof struck the ground, an inspiring spring burst forth. Mount Helicon was the location of two springs sacred to the Muses.

p. 240, ll. 16–17: *King CHARLES the Second … ROSCOMMON, BUCKINGHAM and WILMOT*: three aristocratic satirists closely associated with the court of Charles II (1660–85): Wentworth Dillon, Earl of Roscommon (1637–85);

George Villiers, 2nd Duke of Bukingham (1628–87); John Wilmot, 2nd Earl of Rochester (1647–80). Naming these poets as his antecedents suggests the poem will be neo-classical, Horatian and old fashioned, although that is not entirely borne out by the text itself.

p. 240, l. 20: *HELICONIDES*: the Muses.

p. 241, l. 2: *MECCA*: the holiest site of Islam.

p. 241, l. 3: *CASTALIAN spring*: a nymph transformed into a fountain at Delphi, at the base of Mount Parnassus. Those who drank the waters of Castalia were inspired to write poetry.

p. 241, l. 4: *Donquixotly*: the hero of Cervantes's *Don Quixote* (1605–15), whose idealistic and impractical behaviour coined the adjectival construction.

p. 241, l. 6: *INDAMORA*: a conventional name for a heroine in seventeenth-century romance, used by Dryden in *Aureng-Zebe* (1676), and satirised by Pope and the Scriblerians in *The Memoirs of Martinus Scriblerus* (1738), where Indamora is one of the conjoined twins courted by Martinus.

p. 241, l. 9: *CLIO*: the muse of heroic poetry and history.

p. 241, l. 11: *Buck of the Turf the pedigree of her PALFREY*: a buck of the turf is a follower of horse-racing; a palfrey is a type of horse, characterised by its smooth gait

p. 241, l. 14: *ORONTOPHITUS*: untraced. The name was used by several race-horses in the 1770s: see Thomas Fawconer, *The Sporting Calendar*, 8 vols (London, 1777), vol. VIII, p. 151.

p. 241, l. 17: *PANSOPHIA*: universal knowledge or a scheme or work attempting to embrace all knowledge (*OED*).

p. 241, l. 17: Veni, vidi, vici *Mare of Julius Cæsar's*: In 47 BC, Julius Caesar announced to the Senate his victory over Pharnaces II, King of Pontus, with the words 'I came, I saw, I conquered'.

p. 241, ll. 18–19: *Sire BUCEPHALUS*: the horse of Alexander the Great (356–23 BC), who won the animal in 344 BC, when it was supposedly wild and unridable.

p. 241, ll. 21–2: *the City* Bucephela, *near Hydaspes*: Buecphalus died in 326 BC after being fatally wounded at the battle of Hydaspes. Alexander founded a city in honour of the horse called Bucephela, on the west bank of the Hydaspes river.

p. 242, l. 1: *LAIS*: a courtesan of Corinth who earned huge sums for her sexual favours.

p. 242, ll. 2–3: *BELLEROPHONTISIBUS*: Bellerophon was a hero who rode the winged horse Pegasus in his quest to kill the Chimaera, a monster half lion, half goat.

p. 242, ll. 4–5: *SEMIRAMIS ... the* Persian Cyrus *on the plains of Persepolis*: Semiramis (*c.* 800 BC) was a legendary Assyrian warrior princess, Cyrus was the king of Persia, and Persepolis was the capital of the Persian empire.

p. 242, l. 7: *BOSPORUS* ... Via Lactis: In Greek mythology, the river maiden Io became the lover of Zeus (Jupiter), and was turned into an ox or heifer. The Via Lactis is the Milky Way of the night sky.

p. 242, l. 11: *ACTÆON's stables*: Actaeon was a son of Aristaeus and Autonoe in Boeotia. Out hunting, he encountered Diana bathing naked, and was turned into a stag by her, so that he would be hunted by his own hounds.

p. 242, l. 13: *PHAETON's car*: Phaeton in Greek mythology is the son of Helois, the sun god.

p. 242, ll. 14–15: Priam *of* Troy: Priam, king of Troy during the Trojan War.

p. 242, ll. 16–17: *PEGASUS VOLATUS ... MEDUSA*: Pegasus, the winged horse, was born of the earth as Medusa's blood spilled onto it when Perseus beheaded her. Pegasus was later turned into a constellation.

p. 242, l. 19: *PEGASUS* æthere summo veloces agitat pinnas, & sidere gaudet: Claudius Caesar Germanicus, *Aratea*, ll. 222–3.

p. 243, ll. 4–10: "*Great are his perils ... C. CHURCHILL*: Charles Churchill, 'The Apology, Addressed to the Critical Reviewers', ll. 15–20, in *Poetical Works*, ed. by George Gilfillan (London, Cassell, 1880). Charles Churchill (1732–1764) was a poet, whose enormously successful mock-epic *The Rosciad* – a satire on the theatre and actors – was published in March 1761, running to eight editions within two years.

p. 244, l. 11: *From my moving Villa of SANS SOUCI*: not traced. Possibly a reference to Frederick the Great (1712–1786) of Prussia, who built a palace at Potsdam called Sans Souci, which became the centre of his 'enlightened' court.

p. 245, l. 4: *pay their teasters*: a slang term for a sixpence, from the name of a teston, a depreciated and debased coin issued by Henry VIII (*OED*).

p. 246, l. 12: *witty CHURCHILL to the SCOTCH PORTMANTEAU*: for Charles Churchill, see above, note to p. 243, ll. 4–10. *The Scotch Portmanteau opened at York* (London, 1761) was a satire on the influence of Lord Bute.

p. 246, l. 14: *TRUTH in RHYME ... the MINOR – Wilkinson'd*: David Mallet's *Truth, in Rhyme* (London, 1761); William Balfour Madden, *Bellisle, a poem* (London, 1761); and Samuel Foote's *The Minor*, a satire on the Methodists first acted in London at the Haymarket Theatre on 28 July 1760, published as *The Minor. A comedy* (London, 1760). Tate Wilkinson (1739–1803) was an actor renowned for his impersonations and mimicry: in Foote's *The Minor* he parodied Foote and Garrick.

p. 246, l. 16: *th' ANTI-ROSCIAD*: *The Anti-Rosciad* (London, 1761), a satirical reply to Churchill's *The Rosciad* (1761), sometimes attributed to Thomas Morrell.

p. 246, l. 17: *VIC—s history*: untraced.

p. 246, ll. 23–4: *ROBSON's Psalms, There TARRATARIA frights*: John Robson, *The first book of the Psalms of David, translated into heroic measure* (London,

1761), and *Tarrataria: or, Don Quixote the second. A romantic, poetic medley* (London, 1761).

p. 246, l. 26: *the pedantick, monthly mean REVIEW*: the *Monthly Review*, founded in 1749 by Ralph Griffiths, the first periodical to systematically review works of entertainment as well as of learning.

p. 246, l. 30: *poor Miss BELL*: probably a reference to the then notorious case of Miss Anne Bell, a gentleman's daughter turned prostitute who was murdered by the rake Captain Holland in a bagnio, seemingly in the course of some sexual encounter. The case was described in detail in numerous accounts, including *A Most Cicumstantial [sic] account of that unfortunate young lady Miss Bell, otherwise Sharpe, who died at marybone on Saturday October 4* (London, 1760).

p. 247, ll. 1–2: *HYMN to HOPE, / There ELOISA's letters – not by POPE*: John Langhorne, *A Hymn to Hope* (London, R. Griffiths, 1761), Jean-Jacques Rousseau, *Eloisa: or a series of original letters* (London, R. Griffiths, 1761).

p. 247, l. 3: *Mr. OAKLEY in the JEALOUS WIFE*: Charles Oakley, the hero of George Colman's *The Jealous Wife* (1761), a comedy based on Fielding's *Tom Jones*.

p. 247, l. 5: *MACKLIN*: Charles Macklin (1699–1797), actor, playwright and theatre impresario.

p. 247, l. 8: *a translation from the SANS SOUCI*: *The Seventh Epistle attempted in English, from the King of Prussia's Oeuvres du philosophe de Sans Souci. To Maupertius* (London, T. Osborne and W. Owen, 1761).

p. 247, l. 12: *CHURCHILLIAD*: *The Churchiliad: or, a few modest questions proposed to the Reverend author of The Rosciad* (London, J. Williams and T. Lewis, 1761), a reply to Churchill's mock heroic satire on actors, *The Rosciad*.

p. 247, l. 17: *FIZGIG*: Thaddeus Fitzpatrick, known as Fizgig, an instigator of the theatrical riots of March 1763, who first came to public notice in 1753 when his squabble with Woodward spilled over into the periodicals.

p. 247, l. 21: *RICHARDI NASH*: Richard Nash (1674–1761), master of ceremonies at Bath, died on 8 February 1761 in Bath, and was buried in Bath Abbey.

p. 247, l. 22: *pious PENTECOST – Parnassian trash*: unclear, perhaps a reference to Robert Lloyd's *The Tears and Triumphs of Parnassus* (London, P. Vaillant, 1760).

p. 247, ll. 23–4: *Jackadandy, / The yawning frontispiece of TRISTRAM SHANDY*: Volumes 3 and 4 of Laurence Sterne's *Tristram Shandy* were published in 1761 by R. and J. Dodsley, with an illustrated frontispiece by Hogarth. A 'Jackadandy' is a little conceited fellow (*OED*)

p. 247, l. 26: *CHARLES at Charing-Cross*: the bronze equestrian statue to Charles I by Hubert Le Sueur at Charing Cross (*LE*).

p. 248, l. 1: *JONATHAN's*: Jonathan's Coffee-house, Exchange Alley (Lillywhite 656), the principal coffee-house for the market in stocks and bonds, and hence very sensitive to changes in the fortunes of the government in the conduct of the war.

p. 248, ll. 6–8: *Lord B—TE ... BUSSY's arriv'd – HANS STANLEY*: events associated with the attempt to negotiate a peace in July 1761 (during the Seven Years' War, 1757–63). John Stuart, 3rd Earl of Bute (1713–92), was the leading figure of the 'peace party', having been sworn in as Secretary of State on 25 March 1761, the first sign of his rapid elevation under George III, leading to Pitt's resignation on 5 October 1761. Abbé François de Bussy was the French emissary to London, bringing with him an offer of a negotiated peace from the Duc de Choiseul. Hans Stanley (1721–80), politician, left for France on 24 May 1761 to negotiate a peace, remaining there until 20 September, when it became clear the mission had failed. See Julian Corbett, *The Seven Years' War*, ed. by Jeremy Black (1907; repr. London, Folio Society, 2001), pp. 405–10.

p. 248, l. 12: *GIDEON*: Samson Gideon (1699–1762), Jewish financier.

p. 248, l. 13: *LOYD's*: Lloyd's Coffee-house (Lillywhite 736), the principal coffee-house for marine insurance, sensitive to shipping losses as a result of military campaigns.

p. 248, l. 18: *From BELLISLE, HODGSON is repuls'd*: A naval invasion of Belleisle, an island in Quiberon Bay, was launched in April 1761, in order to relieve pressure on British forces in Germany. Led by Admiral Keppel and Major General Studholme Hodgson, the British were initially repulsed on 13 April, but on 22 April captured most of the island except for the principal town, Palais, which capitulated on 8 June 1761. See Corbett, *The Seven Years' War*, pp. 465–87.

p. 249, l. 3: *JERUSALEM*: The Jerusalem Coffee-house (Lillywhite 626), the principal coffee-house for merchants and traders with business in or for the East India Company.

p. 249, l. 4: *NABOB CLIVE*: Robert Clive (1725–74), army officer, returned from India in July 1760 with a fortune amounting to £300,000, derived from his role in securing the transfer of power in Bengal to nawab Mir Jafar after the battle of Plassey (23 June 1757) (*ODNB*).

p. 249, ll. 8–14: thro' CHANGE ALLEY ... SOMERSET: the poet's muse travels west from Change Alley in the City, over Temple Bar, adorned with the decollated heads of Jacobite rebels of the 1745 rebellion, past St Clement Danes in the Strand, to Somerset House, the run-down palace built originally in 1547, and demolished in 1775.

p. 249, l. 21: *busby Bobs*: a busby is a kind of large bushy wig (*OED*).

p. 249, l. 22: *ruralizing ...* Stepney, Chelsea, Red Caps *or the* Hill*: ruralising, or sojourning in the country (*OED*), in villages close to London: Stepney in the east on the river; Chelsea to the west on the river; Mother Red Caps, a public house in the countryside between Hampstead and Kentish Town; and the hill-top villages of Hampstead and Highgate.

p. 249, l. 27: *EDMONDS*: untraced.

p. 250, l. 2: *TOM'S*: Tom's Coffee-house, Russell Street, Covent Garden (Lillywhite 1366). Having been the home of critics in the late seventeenth century, Tom's had gained a reputation as a place for gambling in the eighteenth.

p. 250, l. 3: *Bett on the BARON*: unclear, possibly a description of gambling on the outcome of a card-game.

p. 250, ll. 10–11: *"Ye Gods! such hair ... some Italick strain*: untraced.

p. 250, l. 21: *the BEDFORD*: the Bedford Coffee House (Lillywhite 99), in the Piazza, Covent Garden.

p. 250, l. 27: *Whitfieldites*: followers of George Whitefield (1714–70), Methodist leader who preached a sermon against theatre-going in 1759.

p. 250, l. 28: *O'NEALES, M'DUGGLIS and the BURKS*: untraced. On p. 262, an erratum corrects the spelling of Macdugglis to McDuggle's.

p. 251, l. 5: *HOGARTH*: William Hogarth (1697–1764), painter and engraver.

p. 251, l. 6: *COLEMAN*: George Colman (1732–94), playwright and theatre manager, author of *The Jealous Wife*, which appeared at Drury Lane on 12 February 1761.

p. 251, ll. 7–8: *JACKSON ... the LIBERTINE*: untraced.

p. 251, l. 10: *ROSCIADS, NAIADS, 'POLOGIES*: satires on the critical community in London: Charles Churchill's *The Rosciad* (London, W. Flexney, 1761) and *The Apology. Addressed to the Critical Reviewers* (London, W. Flexney, 1761); Arthur Murphy's *Ode to the Naiads of Fleet Ditch* (London, M. Cooper, 1761).

p. 251, l. 12: *the young VOLTAIRE*: François-Marie Arouet, known as Voltaire (1694–1778), French writer and philosopher.

p. 251, l. 16: *RUSSEL-STREET*: the principal street leading from Covent Garden to Drury Lane, the location of many renowned coffee-houses and taverns.

p. 251, l. 17: *the PIAZZA hall / (By MACKLIN first intended for a ball)*: Macklin's Piazza Coffee-house (Lillywhite 774). In March 1754, the actor Charles Macklin opened a combined coffee-house and theatre of oratory in the North Piazza of Covent Garden. He spent large sums on the renovations, and went into bankruptcy in late 1755. The coffee-house reopened as the Piazza Coffee-house (Lillywhite 994), with the grand upper room used for a variety of entertainments.

p. 251, ll. 20–1: *the ST. GILES's race, / In bob-wigs some, and some in MONMOUTH lace*: St Giles, a poor slum to the north of St Giles's Broad Street, whose inhabitants were a by-word for poverty. Bob-wigs had the bottom locks turned up into bobs (*OED*), unfashionable in 1761, while Monmouth Street was famed for the sale of second-hand clothes and rags (*LE*).

p. 251, l. 23: *She left their GUILDHALL*: the guildhall or courtroom of the 'apish' crowd of vulgar people assembling at Macklin's Piazza Coffee-house.

p. 251, l. 23: *the Widow's den*: the widow is the coffee-woman of George's Coffee-house (untraced).

p. 252, l. 4: *WALGRAVE*: untraced.

p. 253, l. 13: *ISPAHAN*: perhaps a reference to George Lyttelton (1707–73), author of *Letters from a Persian in England to his friend in Ispahan* (London, J. Millan, 1735).

p. 253, l. 15: Much less than Woman, in the shape of Man: an effeminate or cowardly man. John Dryden, *The Indian Emperor, or, The Conquest of Mexico* (London, H. Herringman, 1670), II.ii, p. 21: 'Thou less than Woman in the shape of Man'.

p. 253, l. 19: *in his plad struts in a HIGHLAND blade*: a Scottish Highlander wearing plaid or tartan twill woollen cloth.

p. 253, l. 23: *metoposcopy*: the art of judging character or telling a person's fortune from the forehead or face (*OED*).

p. 253, l. 24: *WILL!*: the name of the coffee-boy.

p. 254, l. 4: *"An IRISH GAMBOLER*: a gamboller is one who performs antics (*OED*), but here the reference seems to be to an Irish gentleman awaiting his remittance.

p. 254, l. 7: *a Smart*: one who affects smartness in dress, manners, or talk (common in the eighteenth century, now rare) (*OED*).

p. 254, l. 22: *ON—W, want GR—LE, HOL—SE, wan't B—TE*: two 'stagers' (veterans) – possibly Arthur Onslow (1691–1768) and Robert D'Arcy, Earl of Holdernesse (1718–78), who both left high office in March 1761 – argue in the coffee-room in support of competing political factions led by George Grenville (1712–70) and Bute, who clashed over the concessions to be made to the French in the peace negotiations of 1761.

p. 256, l. 8: *does the PRINCE the MARSHAL yet engage*: Ferdinand, Prince of Brunswick-Wolfenbüttel, commander of the Hanoverian forces in Germany; Maréchal Victor François, Duc de Broglie, commander of the French forces in Germany. See Corbett, *The Seven Years' War*.

p. 256, l. 10: *BROGLIO*: see above, note to p. 256, l. 8.

p. 257, l. 2: *HODGSON's victorious, PALLAIS, PALLAIS's fell*: see above, note to p. 248, l. 18.

p. 257, l. 13: *a gay Aid de Camp*: an aide-de-camp is an officer who assists a general in his military duties (*OED*) – in this sense, supposedly close to the freshest intelligence.

p. 257, l. 16: *the Gazette, thro' PITT*: William Pitt (1708–78), prime minister in the summer of 1761, was opposed to a peace treaty with France, until forced to resign on 5 October 1761. The *London Gazette* published official news and ministerial versions of news stories: here, the news story of the capture of Palais.

p. 257, l. 21: Lynch: untraced, possibly the printer Daniel Lynch, who published Churchill's *Poems* in 1769.

p. 258, l. 7: *The nut-brown NAIADS of the sable flood*: Arthur Murphy's *Ode to the Naiads of Fleet Ditch* (London, M. Cooper, 1761), l. 1.

p. 258, l. 10: *CLOACINA*: in Roman mythology, the goddess of the sewer and cess-pit.

p. 258, l. 13: *A fair angelick Sister of the NINE*: that is, Cloacina.

p. 258, l. 14: *thy SEWER ODE*: Murphy's *Ode to the Naiads of Fleet Ditch*.

p. 258, ll. 19–22: *fair* Leda *and her Swan ... the Naked Boy*': unclear, possibly printers ornaments on titlepages.

p. 259, l. 5: *MEDICI*: a Florentine family of legendary power, wealth and influence from the thirteenth to the seventeenth century.

p. 259, l. 7: *a fring'd Curtain in theatrick taste*: a corner of the room which can be separated by a curtain, used by the coffee-woman when she dines, or by any lovesick 'Romeo' who seeks seclusion from the crowd.

p. 259, l. 17: *Lord DOWNE*: Henry Pleydell Dawnay, 3rd Viscount Downe in Ireland, saw distinguished service in command of a regiment at the battle of Minden; he was wounded three times at the battle of Campen, 16 October 1760, and died 9 December 1760.

p. 259, l. 24: *MINDEN*: The Battle of Minden was fought on 1 August 1759, resulting in the defeat of the French army under Broglie by an inferior force of Prussian-Hanoverians under Prince Ferdinand of Brunswick.

p. 260, l. 1: *MUCIUS, CORDUS*: in Roman mythology, Mucius was a soldier who attacked Lars Porsena, the leader of an invading Etruscan army, and proved his bravery by plunging his hand into a fire (Livy, *Ab Urbe Condite*, II.xii–xiii). Aulus Crematius Cordus (d. AD 25) was a Roman historian of the civil wars who was forced to commit suicide by Sejanus.

p. 260, l. 3: *the CLUSIAN Chief*: untraced.

p. 260, l. 7: *the THEBAN [EPAMINONDAS]*: Epaminondas was the commander of the Theban army at the Battle of Mantinea in 362 BC. Thebes defeated the allied Athenian-Spartan army, but in the course of battle Epaminondas was killed.

p. 260, l. 10: *WOLF*: General James Wolfe (1727–59), commander-in-chief of the British forces in the Canadian campaign of 1759, in which he attacked Quebec and was killed on 13 September. The French capitulated five days later on 18 September. News of the victory, which reached London a few days after Wolfe's own despondent account of how difficult the situation was, created considerable excitement.

p. 260, l. 13: *QUEBEC's Hero*: Wolfe (see note above).

p. 261, l. 2: *If from the* Cross CHARLES *o'er the* Bridge *should trot*: the poet imagines the equestrian statue of Charles I at Charing Cross coming to life and crossing the river at Westminster Bridge.

p. 261, l. 12: *A* Cow *on* 'CHANGE *an* Earthquake *may appear*: an obscure joke on irrational volatility in the financial markets (the 'Change), where a bull market may shake the confidence like an earthquake.

p. 261, l. 15: *like* SPARTAN *Virgins*: Sparta was a city-state in ancient Greece whose people were renowned for their austere way of life and lengthy military training. Spartan unmarried women were called virgins.

p. 262, l. 17: *BL—K—EY*: Baron William Blakeney (1671–1761), a popular army officer who was lieutenant-governor of the island of Minorca in the Mediterranean from 1747 to 1756, when the island was attacked by a French expedition.

p. 262, l. 20: *GEORGE and* GEORGES: King George III and George's Coffee-house.

Memoirs of the Bedford Coffee-House

p. 267, ll. 1–2: *To the* MOST *Impudent* MAN *alive*: The phrase 'The most impudent man alive' was strongly associated with William Warburton (1698–1779), who was described thus by Bolingbroke (or Mallet, as his hired pen), who had attacked Pope and raised Warburton's ire. Warburton wrote *A letter to the Lord Viscount B—ke. Occasion'd by his treatment of a deceased friend* (London, A. Moore, 1749). In reply, Henry St John, Viscount Bolingbroke (1678–1751), wrote *A familiar epistle to the most impudent man living* (London, 1749), addressed to William Warburton, reprinted 1751 (with the instructions that it 'may be bound with the new edition of Pope's works' i.e. Warburton's edition). In reply, Warburton wrote *A view of Lord Bolingbroke's philosophy; in four letters to a friend* (London, 1754). Burney told Johnson that Mallet wrote a pamphlet addressed to 'The Most Impudent Man Alive', and that Warburton had answered it. Mallet and Warburton were the respective leaders of contending parties in a controversy between the friends of Pope and Bolingbroke. See *Life of Johnson*, 2 vols (London, C. Dilly, 1791), 8 March 1758. To complicate matters further, *Joe Miller's Jests*, 12th edn (London, *c.* 1755), refers to 'the most impudent man living, Mr Henley', meaning John 'Orator' Henley (1692–1756).

p. 271, l. 4: *noxious effluvia of St Bride's*: a disgusting odour from St Bride's, an area near Fleet Ditch off Fleet Street, around St Bride's church (*LE*).

p. 271, ll. 5–6: *Eau de Luce from Pallmall*: smelling salts (a medicinal preparation of alcohol, ammonia and oil of amber (*OED*)) from Pall Mall, a fashionable street in St James's (*LE*).

p. 271, l.7: *ambergrise*: ambergris, a wax-like substance secreted by the sperm whale, used in perfumery (*OED*).

p. 271, ll. 8–9: *wholesome tar of Thames-street*: tar (a thick black inflammable liquid obtained by the distillation of wood or coal (*OED*)) of Thames Street, a busy commercial street that ran parallel to the wharves along the Thames in the City of London (*LE*).

p. 272, l. 4: *King of Prussia*: Frederick II, king of Prussia (1712–86).

p. 272, l. 6: *F—te*: see above, note to p. 234, l. 6.

p. 272, ll. 10–12: *a battle in Saxony, or a rout in Westphalia*: news of engagements and battles from the European theatre of the Seven Years' War (1757–63).

p. 272, l. 17: *a cue-wig*: a long roll or plait of hair worn hanging down behind from a wig like a tail (*OED*).

p. 273, ll. 11–12: *the* little man *still remains at the* helm: David Garrick (1717–79), actor and playwright, who purchased the patent of the Theatre Royal Drury Lane in 1747 with James Lacy, and went on to manage the theatre with Lacy until 1774 (attribution in MS in BL, 12330.bb.33).

p. 273, l. 13: *Mr. P——*: Thomas Pelham-Holles (1693–1768), created Duke of Newcastle in 1715 (attribution to 'Pelham' in MS in BL, 12330.bb.33). Pelham had been prime minister 1754–56, and Pitt's minister of finances from 1756, when on 26 May 1762 he was forced to resign the Treasury by Bute, and later that year, in December, purged the government of almost all his followers (*ODNB*).

p. 274, l. 10: *the Bedford*: the Bedford Coffee-house (Lillywhite 99), in the north-east corner of Covent Garden, with an entrance under the Piazza. The Bedford was renowned at this time for its nightly gathering of theatrical and literary wits and critics, including Fielding.

p. 274, l. 21: *Mr. Hobster*: William Hobster, proprietor of the Bedford Coffee-house.

p. 275, ll. 13–15: *Dr. H— commenced a new paper under the title of* Inspector: Dr John Hill (1714–75) began 'The Inspector' as a column in *The London Daily Advertiser and Literary Gazette* on 5 March 1751, continuing until 1753 (attribution in MS in BL, 12330.bb.33). Hill was prolific writer on a wide range of scientific topics, including medicine, botany and gardening, and received a Swedish knighthood for this work. His literary productions included drama, satire and occasional essays. He was endlessly provocative to his enemies.

p. 275, l. 17: *Mr. Grey's elegy in a country church-yard*: Thomas Gray's (1716–71) *Elegy, Wrote in a Country Church-Yard* was published in February 1751 by Dodsley. John Hill, 'The Inspector Numb. 1', *The Inspector*, 2 vols (London, R. Griffiths, J. Whiston, B. White et al., 1753), vol. I, pp. 1–5.

p. 276, ll. 10–11: *A duel at the Braund's head in Bond-street*: Braund's Head, New Bond Street. Old and New Bond Street run between Piccadilly and Oxford Street, and were built-up by the end of the 1720s.

p. 277, ll. 1–2: *Mr. B—, an Irish merchant*: 'Mr Broom' (attribution in MS in BL, 12330.bb.33).

p. 277, l. 21: *Ranelagh*: Ranelagh Gardens, a pleasure garden in Chelsea (*LE*).

p. 278, l. 4: *Diogenes*: Diogenes (412–323 BC), Cynic philosopher who avoided all earthly pleasures, and lived in a tub belonging to the temple of Cybele.

p. 278, l. 19: *Mr. Fielding, who then wrote the Covent-Garden Journal*: Henry Fielding (1707–54), author and magistrate, launched *The Covent Garden Journal* in January 1752, ending it on 25 November 1752, after continual abuse by Hill and others (*ODNB*).

p. 279, ll. 8–9: *the Lion from Button's, which proved so serviceable to* Steele: In *The Guardian*, No. 71 (June 1713), Addison announced that he had erected a dead letterbox in Button's Coffee-house, for the receipt of news, intelligence, correspondence and contributions to his periodical. The letterbox itself took the shape of a large lion's head, with the letters received though an aperture in its mouth. After the eclipse of Button's, the lion's head moved to the Shakespeare's Head Tavern, in Covent Garden Piazza (proprietor Packington Tomkyns), and thereafter, for a time, to the Bedford Coffee-house. See Charles Richardson, *Notices and Extracts relating to the Lion's Head, which was erected at Button's Coffee-house in the year 1713* (London, Saunders and Otley, 1827), and *The Inspector*, vol. II, pp. 78, 117, 154, 164.

p. 279, ll. 19–20: *Mr. Woodward, who performed Harlequin*: Henry Woodward (1714–77), actor and pantomimist. In 1752 he was acting with Garrick at Drury Lane, and both were made the subject of satire by Samuel Foote at Drury Lane, who was championed by Arthur Murphy (known as Charles Ranger). On 6 November, Woodward acted an afterpiece at Drury Lane called *Harlequin Ranger*, satirising Foote for having lowered Covent Garden to the standard of a fairground attraction (on 2 November 1752, Covent Garden had an afterpiece called the Fair, which consisted of a rope-dancer and some exotic animals).

p. 280, ll. 1–2: *a person, who threw an apple from one of the boxes*: Thaddeus Fitzpatrick (attribution in MS in BL, 12330.bb.33). During the performance of *Harlequin Ranger* on 6 November, a gentleman in one of the boxes, Thaddeus Fitzpatrick, who belonged to Foote's clique, threw an apple at Woodward. In response, Woodward claimed to have said 'I thank you', but by Fitzgerald's account, his words 'implied a challenge' (*Gentleman's Magazine*, November 1752, p. 535). Hill's *Inspector* supported Fitzgerald; Fielding's *Covent Garden Journal*, Woodward. See *London Stage*, part I, p. 331.

p. 280, ll. 3–4: *in a letter to the Doctor*: *A Letter from Henry Woodward, comedian, the meanest of all the characters; (see Inspector, No. 524) to Dr John Hill*,

Inspector-General of Great-Britain, the greatest of all characters ([London], M. Cooper, 1752).

p. 280, l. 15: Errato: 'Beaumont' (attribution in MS in BL, 12330.bb.33). See also below, note to p. 281, l. 21.

p. 281, ll. 13–15: *Dennis's axiom, that "he who would pun, would pick a pocket"*: Alexander Pope, *The Dunciad, variorum* (London, A. Dob, 1729): 'A great Critick formerly held these Clenches in such abhorrence that he declared, "He that would Pun, would Pick a Pocket". Yet Mr *Dennis's* works afford notable examples of this kind', Book 1, p. 6n. (l. 61). Dennis said 'A man who would make so vile a pun would not scruple to pick a pocket'. Benjamin Victor, *An Epistle to Richard Steele, on his Play, call'd, The Conscious Lovers* (London, W. Chetwood, 1722).

p. 281, ll. 21–3: *a letter … written by* Errato *to Mr. L— the singer, all in puns*: Thomas Lowe (1719–83), singer and actor (attribution in MS in BL, 12330. bb.33), who appeared at Covent Garden 1748–59. The letter in puns was published in *The Inspector*, 'No. 90', vol. II, p. 58, signed 'W. B—'.

p. 282, ll. 3–4: *the* punning apothecary: In the British Library copy of the first edition (12314.ee.11), marginalia identify this figure as 'Dr Hill', yet the sense here plainly identifies Errato (that is, W. Beaumont) as the 'punning apothecary'.

p. 282, l. 5: *Mr.* Town: identified as 'Chitty' in MS in BL, 12330.bb.33, but more likely George Colman (1732–94), critic and playwright. Mr Town was the pseudonym of George Colman in *The Connoisseur*, an essay periodical that he began with Bonnell Thornton in January 1754 (*ODNB*).

p. 283, l. 16: Philocleus: M. Morgan (attribution in MS in BL, 12330.bb.33). Macnamara Morgan (1720–62), Irish actor and playwright, who trained as a lawyer at the Middle Temple. He wrote a tragedy called *Philoclea* (1754), which ran for nine nights at Covent Garden in January 1754 (*ODNB*).

p. 284, l. 1: *the tall actor*: Spranger Barry (1717–77), actor (attribution in MS in BL, 12330.bb.33).

p. 284, l. 5: *Miss Nossiter*: see above, note to p. 228, l. 5. Morgan published *A Letter to Miss Nossiter* (London, W. Owen, 1753) in October 1753, which praised Nossiter and made disparaging remarks about Mrs Cibber and Arthur Murphy. On Thursday 1 November 1753, Morgan and Murphy exchanged 'high words … at ye Bedford Coff. H. … & 'tis thought a Duel will be ye consequence', Richard Cross, 'MS. Diary', in *London Stage*, part, I, p. 389.

p. 284, l. 9: *Mr. M—y*: Arthur Murphy, (1727–1805), critic, actor and play-wright (attribution in MS in BL, 12330.bb.33)

p. 284, ll. 19–21: Prosopopœia … *Demosthenis, Cicero*: prosopopoeia is a rhetori-cal figure by which an imaginary or absent person is represented as speaking or acting (*OED*). Demosthenes (384–22 BC) and Marcus Tullius Cicero

(106–43 BC) were regarded as the greatest orators of ancient Greece and Rome.

p. 285, l. 2: *Glassiopoeia*: a nonce word that sounds like a rhetorical term, but means having a glass of some beverage thrown in one's face (in this case, capillaire, a syrup flavoured with maiden-hair fern or orange-flower water).

p. 285, ll. 17–20: *Mr. Sheridan ... these two new figures*: Thomas Sheridan (1719–88), actor and elocutionist, published a series of works on oratory and education between 1759 and 1762, including *A course of lectures on elocution: together with two dissertations on language* (London, 1762).

p. 286, l. 10: *Ranger*: the pseudonym of Arthur Murphy in the *The Gray's Inn Journal* (attribution in MS in BL, 12330.bb.33).

p. 286, l. 17: *the Republic of Letters*: the collective body of those engaged in literary pursuits (*OED*), a term first used pejoratively in the late seventeenth century. See Anne Goldgar, *Impolite Learning: conduct and community in the Republic of Letters* (New Haven, CN, Yale University Press, 1995).

p. 287, l. 2: *Mr. B—y*: Spranger Barry (attribution in MS, in BL 12330.bb.33).

p. 287, l. 9: *Mr. M—y first wrote in the* Craftsman: Murphy (attribution in MS in BL, 12330.bb.33). Arthur Murphy's *The Gray's Inn Journal* began as a column in *The Craftsman*, before beginning a separate life under its own title. See headnote above, p. 221–2.

p. 287, ll. 12–13: *Bolingbroke, Pultney, and the rest of the anti-league*: the leaders of the opposition to Sir Robert Walpole's administration (1721–42): Henry St John, Viscount Bolingbroke (1678–1751), Tory politician; and William Pultney, Earl of Bath (1684–1764), Whig politician. Bolingbroke and Pultney launched *The Country Journal; or The Craftsman* in December 1726 as a vehicle for their opposition to Walpole, edited by Nicholas Amherst in the guise of Caleb D'Anvers. *The Craftsman* finally ceased publication in 1750, although the title was immediately taken up by others (under the fictional editor Joseph D'Anvers).

p. 288, l. 3: *true intelligence*: Murphy's periodical *The Gray's Inn Journal* included a section entitled 'True Intelligence', which was a miscellany of short pieces including satirical anecdotes, literary reviews and theatrical notices.

p. 288, ll. 7–8: *news for a hundred years*: an article in the 'Gray's Inn Journal' column in *The Craftsman*, 'a very fine stroke upon the Jew Bill'. Murphy wrote several essays against the Jewish Naturalisation Act (see above, note to p. 224, ll. 11–12). Murphy's essays claimed to admire the principles of tolerance expressed in the Act, but dramatised the consequences in alarmist and anti-Semitic terms (see 'Numb. 35: On the Jew Bill' (16 June 1753), *The Gray's Inn Journal*, 2 vols (London, W. Faden for A. Vaillant, 1756), vol. I, pp. 222–5). 'Numb. 39: News for one hundred Years hence' (14 July 1753) imagines a Britain in which a Jewish commercial, political and religious elite has usurped the Christian one extant in his own time (vol. I, pp. 246–52).

p. 289, l. 3: Specio: untraced, identified as 'H. Chitty' (attribution in MS in BL, 12330.bb.33). 'Mr Henry Chitty of Ormond Street' appears on several subscription lists in the period 1739–61.

p. 290, ll. 7–8: *a bumper extraordinary … the powers of a Valetudinarian*: a cup or glass of wine filled to the brim. A 'Valetudinarian' is a person in weak health who is constantly concerned with his own ailments.

p. 290, l. 11: *an Adonis*: a beautiful or handsome young man.

p. 290, l. 15: Mopsy: an untraced dissipated fop, identified as 'Tracey' in MS in BL, 12330.bb.33.

p. 292, l. 15: Harmonicus: Dr Arne (attribution in MS in BL, 12330.bb.33). Thomas Arne (1710–78), composer and musical performer, was the son of an upholsterer, also Thomas Arne (1682–1736). Arne was one of the premier composers of opera and theatrical music in London from the 1730s to his death. He married the singer Cecelia Young in 1737.

p. 292, l. 19: *Handel*: George Frideric Handel (1685–1759), composer. Born in Halle, in Germany, Handel came to London in 1710. Arne was a founder member, with Handel, Boyce and Pepusch, of the Royal Society of Musicians in 1738.

p. 294, l. 5: *the bawdy-box*: the box at the Bedford Coffee-house in which these men met, notorious for its indecent and 'bawdy' conversation and punning, as the ensuing dialogue demonstrates.

p. 295, l. 1: *the Porte*: the Sublime Porte, the Ottoman court at Constantinople.

p. 295, l. 12: estate in tail: a bawdy pun on entailed estates (the settlement of the succession of a landed estate, so that it cannot be bequeathed at the will of any one possessor): Errato suggests that all a Mahometan inherits is his procreative ability.

p. 295, ll. 14–15: *Janissary … Petersburgh*: a janissary is a kind of Turkish soldier whose corps constitute the Sultan's life guard and the main part of the standing army. St Petersburg, Russia, was the location of the court of Catherine II (1729–96). She was notorious for taking a large number of lovers from among her military elite.

p. 297, ll. 13–15: *so few ten thousanders, and so many Xantippes, without my being the least of a Socrates*: a ten thousander is one whose annual income exceeds ten thousand pounds; a Xantippe is named after the wife of Socrates, renowned as a shrew or scold.

p. 298, ll. 11–13: *Mrs. Diamond … Mrs. H—*: unidentified prostitutes.

p. 299, ll. 3–9: *Mrs. A— … Mr. Lovell … Mr. C—y*: Mrs A— is an unidentified prostitute, Mr C— is also unidentified. Mr Lovell refers to John Hill's lost novel, *The History of Mr. Lovell*, 'in which he had endeavoured to persuade the world he had given the detail of his own life' (see David Erskine Baker, *Biographia dramatica, or a companion to the Playhouse* (London, Mssrs Rivington, T. Payne et al., 1782).

p. 300, l. 14: *Sabine-like brutality of lust*: a reference to the rape of the Sabine women, an event in the legendary history of the founding of Rome, in which the women of the Sabine region were forcibly resettled by Romulus.

p. 301, ll. 12–18: *public stews ... Venice*: brothels or stews operated under license from the public authorities. Bernard Mandeville's *The Fable of the Bees: or, Private Vices, Publick Benefits* (London, J. Roberts, 1714) advocated this policy, which he explained with reference to the regulation of brothels in Venice and Naples (p. 69).

p. 302, l. 13: *bagnio-bills*: a bill for services and commodities consumed in a bagnio or brothel during the course of one night, not including the fee of the prostitute, quoted on p. 303.

p. 303, ll. 3–4: *Soals and dressing ... Scotch collops*: dressed soles, a common flat fish (*Solea vulgaris*); Scotch collops, a savoury dish 'made of slic'd veal, bacon, forc'd meat and several other ingredients' (Nathan Bailey, *Dictionarium Britannicum*, (London, 1736)) (*OED*).

p. 304, ll. 6–12: *chair-hire ... any magistrate, even though he lived in Bow-street*: the fees for hiring sedan chairs were set by the magistrates. The brothel's chair has been charged at six shillings, a higher rate than the distance of a mile from Covent Garden would allow, as any magistrate who lived in Bow Street (in Covent Garden) would know.

p. 304, ll. 17–18: *Mrs. D—g—s, Mrs. G—d, nor Mrs. B—t*: Douglas, Gould, Best (attribution in MS in BL, 12330.bb.33; 'Douglas' confirmed in MS 12314.ee.11). Prostitutes active in London in the 1750s.

p. 305, l. 1: birch to light your fire with; *"To rouse the Venus lurking in your veins," (As* Armstrong *has it)*: John Armstrong, *The Œconomy of Love: a poetical essay. A new edition* (London, M. Cooper, 1747): of flagellation, he says 'To rouse the Venus loitering in his Veins!', l. 531.

p. 305, l. 10: *Pharmatic wit*: medicinal or drug-related wit, pharmaceutical (not in *OED*). Jellies were commonly used after coitus to restore spirits.

p. 305, ll. 10–11: *his prime minister, Jack H—rr—s*: Tracey's servant, Jack Harris, the notorious pimp and Grub-Street hack. Harris started work as a waiter at the Shakespeare's Head Tavern, next door to the Bedford Coffee-house in Covent Garden. He was the author of *Harris's List of Covent Garden Ladies: or, New Atlantis for the Year 1761. To which is annexed, The ghost of Moll King; or a night at Derry's* (London, H. Ranger, 1761), a guide to the prostitutes of London first published in 1761, with many subsequent editions. See Hallie Reubenhold, *The Covent Garden Ladies: Pimp General Jack and the Extraordinary Story of Harris's List* (London, Tempus, 2005), pp. 52–72.

p. 306, l. 6: Pertinacio: untraced.

p. 307, l. 7: *his barber Mr. B—*: Mr Brown (attribution in MS in BL, 12330. bb.33).

p. 308, l. 11: *M—ss—p*: Mossop (attribution in MS in BL, 12330.bb.33). Henry Mossop (1727–74), actor and theatre manager, who made his name at Sheridan's Smock Alley theatre in Dublin before coming to London in 1751, making his debut at Garrick's Drury Lane on 26 September. His distinctive stage mannerisms were widely satirised (for example by Churchill in *The Rosciad*) (*ODNB*).

p. 309, ll. 11–12: *the* Englishman in Paris: Samuel Foote's farce *The Englishman in Paris* was performed at Covent Garden on 24 March 1753, with Charles Macklin as Buck, but the play was not deemed a success, and was acted only twice. In the 1753–4 season, Foote acted in it at Drury Lane (20 October 1753), where it was a great success. Although comprising only two acts like a farce, Foote made the claim that it was in fact a comedy. See *London Stage*, part I, pp. 360, 385–6.

p. 312, l. 6: Spintilo ... *Cheapside*: untraced. Spintilo is *nouveau riche*, having begun life as a haberdasher in Cheapside, a prosperous shopping street in the City.

p. 313, ll. 19–20: *Hyde-park*: Hyde Park, a royal park west of St James's, was one of the favoured places for making assignations.

p. 314, l. 13: *Cræsus*: Croesus, king of Lydia (560–47 BC), legendary for his wealth. The West India sugar colonies were renowned as the source of extreme prosperity.

p. 315, ll. 5–7: *a party to Ranelagh; a jaunt to Richmond; a journey to Scarborough*: Spintilo proposes trips to a pleasure garden, a rural retreat close to London and a distant seaside spa town, suggesting a rapidly escalating infatuation.

p. 317, ll. 16–17: *Dryden's translation of* Ovid's art of love: Ovid (see above, note to p. 53, l. 14), author of the *Ars Amatoria*, a didactic poem on getting and keeping a lover. Dryden published his translation of Book I of 'Ovid's *Art of Love*' in 1700 (see *Poems of John Dryden, Volume 5: 1697–1700*, ed. by Paul Hammond and D. Hopkins (London, Pearson, 2005).

p. 318, ll. 10–11: *seat of pleasure, which might an anchorite have warmed*: an anchorite is one who has withdrawn themselves from the world, a recluse, a hermit (*OED*).

p. 318, l. 17: *enamorata*: an inamorata, a female lover, sweetheart or mistress (*OED*).

p. 318, l. 21: *— his —*: coital misadventure through premature ejaculation or impotence.

p. 319, l. 20: *Dorimont*: untraced. The name was widely used as a cognonym for a rake, derived from Dorimant, a character in George Etherege's *The Man of Mode: or, Sir Fopling Flutter* (1676), a courtier and libertine.

p. 322, ll. 8–10: *ignominious chastisement ... to the seat of honour*: the seat of honour is the posterior. Samuel Butler, *Hudibras in three parts*, ed. by Zachary

Grey, 2 vols (Cambridge, J. Bettenham 1744), vol. II, p. 95 (II.iii.1066): 'the Breech ... the Place where Honour's lodg'd'.

p. 322, l. 14: *toad-eater and* sycophant: one who eats toads, originally the attendant of a charlatan, employed to eat toads, or pretend to, so that the master could exhibit his skill in expelling the poison they were held to contain (*OED*).

p. 322, l. 16: *Punctilius*: untraced.

p. 323, ll. 16–18: *Q—n had lately given the salutary advice of* soaping his nose to Poltronius: James Quin (1693–1766), an actor who retired at the end of the 1751 season, famous for his gourmandising, his enormous girth and his obsequious attention to the nobility at Bath. A poltroon was a sluggard, or lazy coward.

p. 324, l. 16: *honest Teague*: Irish, 'wise poet'; although born in Covent Garden, Quin came from an Anglo-Irish family, and was raised and educated in Dublin.

p. 325, l. 8: Didlius: untraced fop.

p. 326, ll. 3–4: *the message-book, which may be stiled the Bedford Coffee-house Journal*: a book for recording messages left for the regulars of the coffee-house, with a title that parodies those of the essay periodicals of the day.

p. 327, ll. 3–4: nem. con.: shortened form of Latin *nemine contradicente*, a legal term for a motion passed without anyone speaking or voting against it (*OED*).

The British coffee-house. A poem

p. 331, ll. 6–11: *To that rare Soil ... STUARTS without end*: Charles Churchill, *The Prophecy of Famine. A Scots Pastoral* (London, for the author by G. Kearsly, 1763), p. 6. The lines punningly connect James Stuart, Earl of Bute, with the Stuart pretender.

p. 333, l. 3: *Colloden*: the Battle of Culloden on 16 April 1746 was the last major conflict of the Jacobite rebellion of 1745.

p. 333, l. 4: *Charley*: Charles Edward Stuart (1720–88), the 'Young Pretender' to the thrones of Scotland, England and Ireland.

p. 333, l. 8: *Jenny's* *: Jean 'Jenny' Cameron of Glendessary (*c.* 1700–90), Jacobite activist, known as the 'Pretender's Diana', who raised a force of 300 soldiers and led them to the raising of the Jacobite standard at Glenfinnan on 19 August 1745. See Maggie Craig, *'Damn Rebel Bitches': women of the '45* (Edinburgh, Mainstream, 1997).

p. 333, l. 11: *WILLIAM*: Prince William Augustus, Duke of Cumberland (1721–65), appointed to command the British forces in England on 21 November 1745, defeating the Jacobites at Clifton in England, and then decisively at

Culloden. Both the battle, and the subsequent British reprisals, were notoriously brutal, giving Cumberland the soubriquet of 'the Butcher'.

p. 334, ll. 1–2: *northern Loon ... the* Stuarts ... *the chair of* Scoon: derived from Scots, a loon is a worthless person, a rogue, scamp or idler (*OED*). The 'chair of Scoon', or Stone of Scone, was an ancient monument made of marble, thought to be a 'stone of destiny'. It was brought to London by King Edward I in 1296 as a sign of his rule in Scotland, and was incorporated into the coronation chair in Westminster Abbey.

p. 334, l. 9: *ambitious SAWNEY*: a colloquial and derisive name for a Scotsman (*OED*).

p. 335, l. 8: Chield: a representation of a Scottish pronunciation of child.

p. 336, ll. 11–14: *Mc Donald ... Mc Duggle ... Campbell*: Scottish names, representing three Highland clans. McDuggle is now more commonly spelled MacDougal.

p. 337, l. 4: *CHARON will deny to cross the Styx*: in Greek mythology, Charon was the ferryman over the river Styx in Hades.

p. 337, l. 5: *BERWICK*: Berwick-upon-Tweed, the northernmost town in England.

p. 337, l. 20: *the Thane*: in Scottish history, a person ranking with the son of an earl, holding lands of the king, the chief of a clan (*OED*).

p. 337, l. 22: *th' Earl of Bute*: John Stuart (see above, note to p. 248, ll. 6–8).

p. 338, l. 11: *Cyrus*: in the Old Testament, Cyrus the Great (559–29 BC), king of Persia, is the patron and deliverer of the Jews.

p. 338, l. 16: *St Paul's ... from Highgate's lofty top*: St Paul's Cathedral, at 365 feet, by far the highest structure in London in the eighteenth century, was first seen from Highgate Hill by travellers from the north (*LE*).

p. 339, l. 5: *HOLYROOD*: the Palace of Holyroodhouse, the principal residence of the Kings and Queens of Scotland since the fifteenth century.

p. 339, l. 7: *chair which FERGUS caw'd his own, / Was dragg'd to London from it's state of SCONE*: see above note to p. 334, ll. 1–2. Fergus I of Dalriada, also known as Fergus Mor Mac Earca, was king of Dalriada *c.* AD 500. He is often considered the first king of Scotland, and according to some narratives was crowned on the Stone of Scone.

p. 339, l. 14: *Holborn-Hill*: the Holborne was a stream flowing into the Fleet, paved over to make a steeply-inclined street (*LE*).

p. 339, l. 16: *Aldgate ... Temple Bar*: gates to the City of London, Aldgate on the east, and Temple Bar on the west.

p. 339, l. 19: *LUCRETIUS*: Titus Lucretius Carus (99–55 BC), a Roman poet and philosopher, whose poem *De Rerum Naturae* was a systematic account of nature and ethics.

p. 339, l. 22: *C**: the Royal Court.

p. 340, l. 11: *A LARGE sash'd room at th' end of Cecil-street*: a court or alley off St Martin's Lane. This club or coffee-house is not identified, although St Martin's Lane was home to some celebrated coffee-houses, including Slaughter's Coffee-house (Lillywhite 903), noted for its clientele of 'extravagant young men' (William Hickey, *Memoirs*, ed. by Alfred Spencer (London, Hurst and Blacket, 1913)), much like the horse-racing 'Yorkshire bucks' noted here.

p. 341, l. 3: *Meretricious Catherine-street*: Catherine Street ran between Drury Lane and the Strand, and was notorious for street prostitution. Several taverns and coffee-houses stood on the street.

p. 341, l. 4: *A Turk's head*: The Turk's Head Coffee-house (Lillywhite 1436) stood on the Strand opposite Catherine Street. Boswell records visiting with Johnson on 22 July 1763, noting 'a good civil woman and wants business' (*London Journal 1762–3*, ed. by Frederick Pottle (London, Heinemann, 1950)).

p. 342, l. 8: *Whig's go to plough, and Tories rule the sphere*: After the accession of George III to the throne in 1760, it was expected that the Tories would be asked to form a government, but in fact they had to wait until Pitt resigned on 5 October 1761. John Stuart, Earl of Bute, formed a Tory ministry (the first since 1714). He resigned 8 April 1763.

p. 342, l. 10: *WILKS imprison'd*: John Wilkes (1725–97), MP for Aylesbury 1757–64, siding with Pitt. On 23 April 1763 he published a famous essay in a periodical *The North Briton* (No. 45), denouncing the government's actions in making the King, in the King's Speech, support the peace treaty signed with France. The ministry prosecuted Wilkes for seditious libel, and briefly held him under arrest. When he was released on 6 May 1763, crowds of people vented their anger against the ministry with shouts of 'Wilkes and Liberty'. Controversy and riot followed (*ODNB*).

p. 342, l. 12: *F—x and D—d*: the 'Patriot' opposition in Parliament were Whigs disaffected with the ruling ministry, claiming to defend the national interest from ministerial incompetence. One such was Henry Fox, 1st Baron Holland (1705–74).

p. 342, l. 13: *Pitt retir'd, that G—le took his place*: Bute resigned as prime minister on 8 April 1763, and as Pitt no longer sought the job, George III turned to George Grenville.

p. 342, l. 14: *T—b—t appear'd ... Bt—e said grace*: William Talbot, 1st Baron Talbot of Hensol (1710–82), lord steward of his majesty's household; 'Bt—e' is presumably Bute.

p. 342, l. 16: *E—g—t*: John Perceval, 2nd Earl of Egmont (1711–70), politician, appointed first lord of the Admiralty on 10 September 1763 (*ODNB*), a post he held until 1766.

p. 343, l. 16: *GRANBY*: John Manners, marquess of Granby (1721–70), a hero of the Seven Years' War, where he commanded the army in Europe 1759–63 (*ODNB*).

p. 343, l. 18: *Hungerford, where Tars repair*: the Hungerford Market at Charing Cross was built as a rival to the fruit and vegetable market at Covent Garden. The building was demolished to make way for Charing Cross railway station in 1862.

p. 344, l. 13: *Will's ... where Saunders stood aloof*: at least six coffee-houses of this name operated in London in the mid-eighteenth century. Will's Coffee-house, under Scotland Yard Gate (Lillywhite 1545), was well known as a place of resort of 'Neptune's Gentlemen' (l. 18), or officers of the navy (see *An Oration Spoke at Will's Coffee-House in Scotland-Yard, Whitehall. Containing, reflections on the British Marine* (London, J. Robinson, 1744).

p. 345, l. 14: *that Fabric, where, in naval state / Neptune's Vicegerents reign*: Admiralty House, built in 1723–6 by Sir Thomas Ripley, where the Admiralty commission was responsible for command of the Royal Navy.

p. 345, l. 19: *ANSON*: George Anson, Baron Anson (1697–1762), naval officer and first lord of the Admiralty 1751–8, where he introduced many reforms in naval career structure and ship design. In 1758 he returned to sea as the commander of the western squadron, and played a key role in a series of British naval victories in the Seven Years' War, including Quiberon Bay (*ODNB*).

p. 346, l. 19: *KINDRED G—— next appears, / G——*: George Grenville (1712–70), treasurer of the navy in 1761, known as 'the Gentle Shepherd' after Pitt mocked him as such in March 1763, prime minister 1763–5, after the fall of Bute.

p. 347, l. 9: *Cinque port*: the Cinque Ports are five ports in Kent and Sussex granted special commercial privileges by Edward I in return for men and ships in time of war. The reference here is probably to August Hervey (see below, note to p. 349, l. 18).

p. 348, l. 8: *the Orlean * Maid*: Joan of Arc, the Maid of Orleans (Pucelle D'Orleans), the national heroine of France.

p. 348, l. 19: *E—g—t's*: John Perceval (see above, note to p. 342, l. 16).

p. 349, l. 10: *the Gaskets ***: the Casket or Gasket Rocks, two high rocks at the western end of Alderney, in the English Channel, the scene of many ship-wrecks.

p. 349, l. 12: *Hawke*: Edward Hawke, 1st Baron Hawke (1705–81), naval officer, popular admiral of the western squadron during the Seven Years' War and a close associate of Anson (*ODNB*).

p. 349, l. 18: *HERVEY*: Augustus Hervey, 3rd Earl of Bristol (1724–79), naval officer associated with Anson who saw action during the Seven Years' War and turned to politics in the early 1760s. He was a renowned libertine, duly celebrated in his *Journal* (*ODNB*). *Augustus Hervey's Journal, being the intimate account of the life of a Captain in the Royal Navy ashore and afloat, 1746–59* (London, W. Kimber, 1953).

p. 349, l. 20: *the BRITISH door*: The British Coffee-house (Lillywhite 179), opposite Suffolk Street over against the King's mews in Charing Cross. This coffee-house was in operation as early as 1709, and was known as a favourite resort of Scots in London from 1720.

p. 350, l. 6: *the Berwick Oath*: perhaps a reference to the Jacobite oath of allegiance.

p. 350, l. 13: *HOGARTH's grin*: William Hogarth (1697–1764) caricatured John Wilkes with a savage squint and holding the cap of liberty (see below), in a popular print called *John Wilkes Esquire*, published on 16 May 1763.

p. 351, l. 6: *WILKES*: John Wilkes, see above, note to p. 342, l. 10.

p. 351, l. 13: *TARTUB come forth, — thou Falstaff of thy age*: Lord Talbot, lord steward of the Royal Household (akin to Falstaff in Shakespeare's *Henry IV*), who fought a pistol duel with Wilkes on 6 October 1762.

p. 351, l. 16: *FORBES the Sancho Panza of thy train*: John Forbes of Skellater (1732–1808), a Scottish Jacobite who served in the French army's Scottish regiment. In August 1763 he challenged Wilkes to a duel when Wilkes visited Paris, on account of Wilkes's abuse of Bute and Scottish political influence in the *North Briton*.

p. 353, l. 13: *Mrs. D—s*: presumably the coffee-woman of the British Coffee-house, not otherwise recorded.

p. 355, l. 4: *GRANT **: Sir James Grant of Grant, 8th Baronet (1738–1811), only son of Sir Ludovick Grant (1707–73), landowner. Educated at Westminster School and Christ's College, Cambridge (1756–8), he completed a Grand Tour in 1758–60, and married in 1763. In later life, after the poem was published, he gained fame as an agricultural improver and politician.

p. 356, l. 18: *CHERROKEES*: a Cherokee embassy visited England in 1762 following the Anglo-Cherokee War (1759–62), meeting George III despite being denied official recognition. The embassy was led by Cunne Shote or Cumnacatogue (Stalking Turkey), and escorted by Thomas Sumter and Henry Timberlake.

A Sunday Ramble; or, Modern Sabbath-Day Journey

p. 360, ll. 6–7: *coffee-houses near the Royal-Exchange*: the Royal Exchange was the principal bourse or mercantile exchange in London, with offices for Lloyd's insurance market in the upper floor. The coffee-houses in nearby alleys were the resort of merchants and brokers: especially Jonathan's and Garraway's in Exchange Alley.

p. 360, l. 9: frizeurs: a friseur or hairdresser, from the French, often contemptuous (*OED*).

p. 360, ll. 22–3: *schemes for paying the national debt* without any taxes at all: The cost of the Seven Years' War had led to a significant increase in the National Debt. There were many tracts analysing the debt, and many schemes promoted to reduce it without resorting to new or increased taxes, such as lotteries.

p. 360, l. 24: *humble the Americans*: taxation on tea (and coffee) in the British North American colonies paid for the colonial administration: the 1773 Tea Act levied the tax at 3*d.* in the pound of tea. The Act was very unpopular, and was used as a rallying point by American patriot rebels, who launched a series of spectacular demonstrations against the tea tax, including dumping imported tea into Boston harbour on 16 December 1773. In response to the 'Boston Tea Party', as the event became known, the ministry in London decided to take coercive measures against the resistance.

p. 361, l. 8: *a Caledonian*: a native of ancient Caledonia, humorously, a Scotsman.

p. 361, l.12: *the letters T. S.*: Tom Scribble (see below, p. 363, l. 7). The name recalls the Scriblerian tradition of learned dunces.

p. 362, ll. 20–1: *shopman, boarding-school usher, clerk, and out-rider*: low trades requiring literacy and a modicum of education: respectively, an assistant in a shop; a teaching assistant or under-master; a writer of accounts or commercial secretary; and a tradesman's travelling agent.

p. 363, l. 13: *Pope – "A little learning is a dangerous thing"*: Alexander Pope, *Essay on Criticism* (London, W. Lewis, 1711), Part II, l. 14.

p. 363, ll. 27–8: *St. Mary Axe*: a street in the City between Leadenhall Street and Camomile Street, that takes its name from the church which once stood there. In the eighteenth century it was largely residential, and was associated with the marine insurance trades. The Spanish and Portuguese synagogue at Bevis Marks is located in an alley off the street, which accounts for this Jewish merchant ('a son of Israel').

p. 365, l. 23: *the Quebeck-Bill*: Quebec was a large colony in Canada previously controlled by France, granted to Britain under the terms of the Treaty of Paris (1763). The Quebec Bill was introduced into the House of Lords on 2 May 1774, and received the Royal Assent on 22 June, despite considerable opposition in the Commons and City of London. The Act gave the citizens of Quebec the liberty to enjoy their language, religion and legal system.

p. 366, l. 25: *worth upwards of a* plum: a plum is a slang term for the sum of £100,000, or one possessed of that amount.

Johann Wilhelm von Archenholz, *A Picture of England*

p. 371, l. 9: *The English*: The English gentleman, that is.

p. 372, l. 9: *Lloyd's*: Lloyd's Coffee-house (Lillywhite 736) was established by Edward Lloyd in or about 1691 in Lombard Street and quickly became the centre of the London trade in marine insurance, establishing an extensive correspondence network concerning shipping movements, and publishing a range of shipping newspapers. In 1769 the clientele incorporated themselves by subscription as a members-only coffee-house and removed to New Lloyd's Coffee-house, first in Pope's Head Alley and then in the upper floor of the Royal Exchange itself.

p. 372, ll. 12–13: *who in 1778 amounted to six hundred*: see Charles Wright and Ernest Fayle, *A History of Lloyd's from the founding of Lloyd's Coffee House to the present day* (London, Macmillan, 1907), pp. 64–125; and D. E. W. Gibb, *Lloyd's of London: a study in individualism* (London, Corporation of Lloyd's, 1957), pp. 1–57.

p. 372, l. 14: *subscribe ten guineas*: the substantial subscription and limited number of members (names) at Lloyd's was designed to exclude speculators and gamblers in life insurance from the coffee-house, and to monopolise the news and correspondence networks operated by the business.

p. 373, l. 26: *billiards nor backgammon tables*: billiards, a game played with small ivory balls on a rectangular table with a smooth cloth-covered surface; backgammon, a board game with draughtsmen whose moves are determined by throws of the dice. Both were the occasion of much gambling in German kaffeehauser and French cafés.

p. 374, l. 4: *PAPERS*: Trapp's translation (London, 1797) adds the following to the account of newspapers in coffee-houses: 'The best frequented coffee houses take in ten or twelve copies of the same paper not to make persons wait, together with the best periodical publications. The papers are bound up in large folios at the end of the year, and carefully kept, as they always find readers. It is customary for each individual to chuse the coffee house he thinks most convenient for him; though he sometimes visits others, it is always his duty to give the preference to his own as there are often great advantages to be derived from it. He is treated there as if he belonged to the house, he may use the same freedom as if he were at home; people are appointed to meet him there, and letters addressed to him' (p. 315).

p. 374, l. 20: *Ragouts, sauces, and* made dishes: dishes prepared in the French manner: a ragout consisted of meat cut in small pieces stewed with vegetables and highly seasoned; and a 'made dish' was a fancy dish composed of several ingredients depending for its success on the cook's skill (*OED*).

p. 376, l. 26: *Sillabub*: syllabub, a concoction of milk or cream curdled by the admixture of wine, cider or liqueur, sweetened and spiced.

p. 377, l. 3: *warm * beer [Purl]*: purl was formerly a liquor made by infusing wormwood or other bitter herbs in ale or beer; later, a mixture of hot beer with gin, also called dog's nose.

p. 377, ll. 16–18: *eight thousand ale-houses in the metropolis and its neighbour-hood*: probably not an exaggeration. According to his survey of 1739, Maitland estimated there were 207 inns, 447 taverns and 5,975 alehouses in London and surrounding districts (William Maitland, *The History of London, from its Foundation by the Romans, to the Present Time* (London, Samuel Richardson, 1739), Book II, pp. 519–20).

p. 377, l. 21: *Swift and Sterne*: English satirists and clergymen, Jonathan Swift (1667–1745) and Laurence Sterne (1713–68). Although neither was espe-cially known for their tavern-going habits, the fact they went to taverns at all perhaps surprised some when it is considered they were clergymen.

p. 378, l. 3: *drunk very weak*: Archenholz argues that the high duty on coffee (7*d*. per pound) forced down the quality of the coffee sold in coffee-houses. See Simon Smith, 'Accounting for Taste: British coffee consumption in historical perpsective', *Journal of Interdisciplinary History*, 27:2 (1996), pp. 183–214.